Being German, Becoming Muslim

PRINCETON STUDIES IN MUSLIM POLITICS

Dale F. Eickelman and August Richard Norton, series editors

A list of titles in this series can be found at the back of the book

Being German, Becoming Muslim

Race, Religion, and Conversion in the New Europe

Esra Özyürek

PRINCETON UNIVERSITY PRESS

Princeton and Oxford

Copyright © 2015 by Princeton University Press

Published by Princeton University Press, 41 William Street, Princeton, New Jersey 08540

In the United Kingdom: Princeton University Press, 6 Oxford Street, Woodstock, Oxfordshire OX20 1TW

press.princeton.edu

Cover photograph © Lia Darjes

Library of Congress Cataloging-in-Publication Data

Özyürek, Esra.
Being German, becoming Muslim : race, religion, and conversion in the new Europe / Esra Ozyurek.
    pages cm.—(Princeton studies in Muslim politics)
Includes bibliographical references and index.
ISBN 978–0–691–16278–2 (hardcover : alk. paper)—ISBN 978–0–691–16279–9 (pbk. : alk. paper)
    1. Muslim converts—Germany. 2. Islam—Gemany. 3. Conversion—Islam. I. Title.
BP170.5.A1O99 2015
297.5'740943—dc23
2014003822

British Library Cataloging-in-Publication Data is available

This book has been composed in Stempel Garamond LT Std

Printed on acid-free paper. ∞

Printed in the United States of America

1 3 5 7 9 10 8 6 4 2

In loving of memory of Dicle Koğacıoğlu

Contents

Acknowledgments

I was able to write this book only because so many people, institutions, and organizations helped me so generously at every turn. I especially benefited from the generosity of a few extraordinarily smart and supportive women. I am so lucky to have met Katrin Simon shortly after my arrival in Berlin. She held me by the hand, took me to all the major German-speaking mosques, and introduced me to a number of insightful German converts to Islam. Riem Spielhaus and Yasemin Shooman helped me understand the dynamics of German society and academia, and showed me how one can combine political iconoclasm with scholarly excellence. Last but not least, Nina Mühe inspired me to write the book, challenged my ideas at every point, and gave me the gift of sisterhood.

Through this project I got to know some remarkable scholars, who deeply influenced my thinking. Matti Bunzl and Paul Silverstein are my role models for asking questions that reveal central tensions in "Europe" as an idea and project. My work follows the trail they blazed earlier. Damani Partridge, Fatima El-Tayeb, Schirin Amir-Moazami, Werner Schiffauer, Kader Konuk, Yasemin Yildiz, and Ruth Mandel continue to be major sources of influence on me in figuring out what Islam and Muslims represent in Germany.

The research for the project was generously funded by residential fellowships and research grants from the American Academy in Berlin, Alexander von Humboldt Foundation, Fulbright Foundation, German Academic Exchange Service, and University of California at San Diego. My academic hosts in Berlin, Gudrun Kraemer at the Free University and Rolf Scheider and Gökçe Yurdakul at the Humboldt University, made my life as easy as possible. I am thankful for my colleagues at the University of California for supporting my extensive research leaves. I also am grateful to Craig Calhoun, who made it possible for me to take a leave before I started my new position at the London School of Economics so that I could devote a year to finishing up this book.

I have presented parts of this research in countless contexts in the United States, Europe, and Turkey. I am grateful to these audiences as well as Marc Baer, Keith McNeal, Gökçe Yurdakul, Nina Mühe, Silvia Horsch, Joel Robbins, Lara Deeb, Rachel Harrell-Bilici, Ellen Moodie, David Gramling, and Barbara Kosta for engaging my ideas and reading versions of this manuscript. I am especially thankful for Andrew Shryock, who intervened in a crucial moment of intellectual confusion and convinced me to write this book rather than be distracted by another project. Parts of chapter 2 appeared in "Converted German Muslims and Their Ambivalent Relations with Born Immigrant Muslims," in *Islamophobia/Islamophilia: Beyond the Politics of Enemy and Friend*, ed. Andrew Shryock (Bloomington: Indiana University Press, 2010), and a short section of the conclusion appeared in "Convert Alert: Turkish Christians and German Muslims as Threats to National Security in the New Europe," *Comparative Studies in Society and History* 51, no. 1 (2009): 91–116.

Needless to say, my deepest gratitude goes to the German Muslims who welcomed me into their communities, homes, and lives. My respect for their strength in facing challenges in order to pursue their spiritual calling kept growing in every phase of my research.

I was able to write this book with twin toddlers only because my loving parents, Sünter and Mustafa Özyürek, supported me once again. They came to Berlin for long stretches of time so I could do the research. Once when I went to San Diego to write, they came along to help me out so that I could concentrate. My greatest hope is that I have learned something from their flawless, unending parenting, and will be able to pass some of it on to my children.

During the past ten years of my life, Keith McNeal has held my hand at every step, and made my mind, heart, and life expand in ways I could not even imagine. The loving friendship and thoughtful insights of Gökçe Yurdakul are present in every page of my life and this book. Dicle Koğacıoğlu, one of my biggest intellectual and spiritual inspirations, left this world too early. I never have envisioned that I would write a book that she would not be able to read. I miss her painfully and dedicate this book to her memory.

I think through the past and present as well as share my life across three continents with Marc David Baer. At this point it is impossible to tell who learned what from who, but I know that the best of the ideas presented in this book are more his than mine. The most wonderful experience we share is having Azize and Firuze in our lives. I am grateful to my two angels, who are teaching me the most important lesson: how to brace oneself for life in the face of its fragility.

BEING GERMAN, BECOMING MUSLIM

INTRODUCTION

Germanizing Islam and Racializing Muslims

"I would never have become a Muslim if I had met Muslims before I met Islam." During my three and a half years of research among German converts to Islam, I heard this repeatedly. Contradictorily, a fifty-year-old man who had converted to Islam in the 1980s after meeting Iranian revolutionaries, a German imam who had converted while trying to convert Arabs and Turks to Christianity, and a twenty-five-year-old former East German woman converted through her Muslim Bosnian boyfriend were all among those who said it. Murad Hofmann (1998, 135), also a German convert to Islam, writes that toward the end of his long life, the renowned German Jewish convert Muhammad Asad told him that he doubted that he would again find his way to Islam, as he had done in 1926, if he were a young man in today's Muslim world. "With some bitterness he shared the frequently heard opinion that one could find lots of Muslims in the Orient, but precious little Islam these days, whereas the Occident had very few Muslims, but now much Islam."[1]

Although almost all German converts I met during my research embraced Islam following intimate relations with born Muslims, since their conversion many nonetheless distance themselves from immigrant Muslims. Converted Germans love Islam, and in most cases they had fallen in love with a Muslim, but they do not always find it easy to love born Muslims in Germany or elsewhere.

Contemporary German converts embrace Islam in a country where Muslims and especially Islam are seen as unfitting. When then president Christian Wulf said on the day of German unification, October 3, 2010, "Islam too has now also become part of German history," his statement was considered a scandal.[2] That week the popular magazine *Stern* published photoshopped images of Wulf with an ostensibly Muslim beard and fez.[3] Conservative political leaders quickly contested Wulf's claim and insisted that it is absolutely wrong to say that Islam can be considered "part of

Germany." Wolfgang Bosbach of the Christian Democratic Union (CDU) said that "while Islam is a part of daily reality in Germany, ours is a Judeo-Christian tradition." Interior Minister Thomas de Maizière added, "If you now ask: will Islam be put on the same level as the Judeo-Christian understanding of religion and culture that we have, then my answer is: not in the foreseeable future."[4] The prominent CDU politician Volker Kauder declared, "Islam is not part of tradition and identity in Germany and so does not belong in Germany."[5] When Germans embrace Islam the same politicians accuse them of being traitors, enemies within, and even potential terrorists who may attack their own nationals (Schmidt 2007; Özyürek 2009).

In a political climate that sees no place for their religion and is antagonistic toward their conversion, some German converts try to open up a legitimate space for Islam by disassociating it from Turks and Arabs. Some promote the view that Islam can be experienced as a German religion; others call for a totally postnational Islam. Both groups argue that being German is not only compatible with but also can even lead to a better way of being Muslim, and some advance the idea that becoming Muslim can be an especially proper way of being German. In doing so, German converts to Islam simultaneously challenge and reproduce biological and cultural racisms as well as a homogeneous understanding of a German and European culture.

Being German, Becoming Muslim focuses on such contradictions and challenges in the lives of converts to Islam, and aims to understand what it means to embrace Islam in a society that increasingly marginalizes and racializes Muslims. It explores different ways in which converted German Muslims—who now number in the tens of thousands—accommodate Islam to German identity and carve out legitimate space for Germans in the *Ummah*, the global community of Muslims.[6] In other words, this book examines the socially transformative consequences of the seemingly individualistic and politically unmotivated acts of converts for the German society and Muslim community. It inquires into how today's German converts come to terms with their admiration for Islam alongside the widespread marginalization of Muslims. How and why can one love Islam, yet find it so difficult to love immigrant Muslims or their Islamic practices? What does it mean to be a "white" Muslim when Islam is increasingly racialized? How do German Muslims relate to immigrant Muslims once they convert? How do previously Christian or atheist German Muslims shape debates about the relationship between race, religion, and belonging in Germany?

By focusing on the experiences of indigenous Europeans who have embraced a religion that is seen as external to Europe, this book also seeks to understand the complex set of prejudices and exclusionary practices that

are called Islamophobia. The reactions of both mainstream German society and born Muslims to converted Muslims, and the latter's responses
to born Muslims, shed light on the intersection of biological with cultural
racism. Muslim identity is something that is scripted on the bodies of immigrant Muslims, but Islam can also be chosen by indigenous Europeans.
Can we call converted Muslim criticism of born Muslims and their traditions
Islamophobia? What are we to make of the abhorrence that converted
Muslims generate in mainstream society? Or to put it another way, where
do belief and individual choice fit in the racialized and religiously defined
exclusion of Muslims in Europe?

I explore these questions in the context of social and political developments that shape German society at large, paying special attention to the
political consequences of conversions. The arrival of millions of Muslim
workers to rebuild the war-torn country was one of the most significant
post–World War II developments. It transformed, and continues to transform, Germany. These workers and their families brought an unexpected
challenge to the mostly homogeneous post-Holocaust German society,
and forced it to come to terms with difference again. One result of this
development was the construction of racial dichotomies between Turks and
Germans as well as between Muslims and Christians/Europeans/secular
subjects. Another related, perhaps inevitable outcome was cultural inter-
penetration and boundary crossing between these dichotomies. Hundreds
of thousands of Muslim immigrants and their children took citizenship
after changes in the German citizenship law in 2000, while a small but increasing number of formerly Christian or atheist Germans converted to
Islam. Such border crossings have a profound effect on transforming these
categories because they challenge how we define Germans and Muslims.

Mainstream society marginalizes German converts to Islam, and questions their Germanness and Europeanness, based on the belief that one
cannot be a German or European and a Muslim at the same time.[7] Converts
to Islam are accused of being traitors to European culture, internal enemies
that need to be watched, and potential terrorists (Özyürek 2009). Having
become new Muslims in a context where Islam is seen as everything that
is not European, ethnic German converts disassociate themselves from
Muslim migrants (chapter 2), and promote a supposedly denationalized
and de-traditionalized Islam that is not tainted by migrant Muslims and
their national traditions but instead goes beyond them, Some German
Muslims along with some other European-born ethnic Muslims promote
the idea that once cleansed of these oppressive accretions, the pure Islam
that is revealed fits in perfectly well with German values and lifestyles
(chapter 1). Some even argue that practicing Islam in Germany builds on'
the older but now-lost values of the German Enlightenment (Aufklärung),
including curiosity about and tolerance of difference. For East German

Muslims who converted after the fall of the Berlin Wall, becoming Muslim was a way of escaping their East German identity (chapter 3). Born Muslims who grew up in Germany increasingly adopt these discourses and promote de-culturalization of Islam as a way for Muslims to integrate into German society without giving up their religious beliefs (chapter 4). At the same time, a newer and even more popular trend of Islamic conversion bypasses the questions of national tradition and identity altogether by ostensibly going back to the earliest roots of Islam, with converts isolating themselves not only from non-Muslim society but also from other Muslims (chapter 5).

Religious converts throughout the world have different ideas regarding the relationship of their new religion and indigenous culture. Converts to evangelical Christianity in Papua New Guinea (Robbins 2007) and Ghana (Meyer 1998) believe that their conversion involves a complete transformation, and that they have not only left their old religion but also their old culture behind. In other places, such as Turkey (Özyürek 2009) and India (Roberts 2012), converts to evangelical Christianity believe that they have changed only their religious beliefs and what they have embraced is totally compatible with local culture. At the same time, revivalist religious movements often aim at "purifying" their creeds of antithetical cultural practices. Muslim revivalists worldwide fall back on Islam's foundational texts in an attempt to attain a purportedly true Islam freed of cultural accretions (Göle 1997; Mahmood 2004; Hirschkind 2009). In her study of Shi'i Muslims in Lebanon, Lara Deeb (2006, 20) calls this "authenticating Islam," a process "dependent on textual study and historical inquiry as well as on a particular notion of rationality."[8]

Regardless of how clear such a differentiation between culture and religion may look to religious actors, the separation between these two realms is problematic. As Nathaniel Roberts (2012, 20) reminds us that there is "no natural ground from which to answer" questions regarding the nature of either religion or culture. Hence, it is important to understand seemingly parallel efforts to separate or relate culture and religion in their social contexts as well as in terms of their political consequences. Purifying Islam for young Turkish women, for example, might mean breaking with the limiting worldviews of their parents and allowing for increased social freedom (Göle 1997). For Shi'i activists in Lebanon, it might mean self-improvement and accepting modern ways of being Muslims (Deeb 2006). For Moroccan Dutch Muslims, it can be a way to negotiate the dilemma of having to choose between being Moroccan or Dutch, while for the Dutch authorities, attempts at Islamic purification might indicate radicalization (Koning 2008).

One of the main arguments of this book is that the call of many German- and other European-born converts for a purified Islam can be best understood in its context of increasing xenophobia and Islamophobia, where being Muslim is defined as antithetical to being German and European. When confronted with unexpected hostility from mainstream society, converts to Islam take an active role in defending the place of Islam in Germany by disassociating it from the stigmatized traditions of immigrant Muslims. The German Muslim take on a purified Islam is inspired by Islamic revivalism worldwide, but also based on Enlightenment ideals of the rational individual and natural religion.[9] While this call for a culture- and tradition-free Islam that speaks directly to the rational individual seems universalistic, in the contemporary German context it ends up being strictly particularistic or, more precisely, Eurocentric. It assumes that the "European" or "German" mind is truly rational—and hence the "Oriental" mind is not—free of the burden of cultural accretions, and thus uniquely capable of appreciating and directly relating to the real message of Islam in its essential form.

CONVERTING TO RACIALIZED RELIGIONS

Voluntary religious conversion is one of the few acts that grant individuals, regardless of their intention, the power to break through established social, cultural, and political boundaries.[10] In their study of colonialism in southern Africa, Jean and John Comaroff (1991) note how religious conversion to Christianity endowed both the colonizers and colonized with different kinds of power. Europeans utilized Christianization in order to deepen their rule and "colonize the minds" of their subjects. At the same time, the Comaroffs observe, individual converts—especially pious ones—disrupted colonial categories that assumed the white colonizers to be the essential Christians.[11]

In the context of India, Gauri Viswanathan (1998) points to the subversive potential of conversion, especially when it involves adopting a lower-status religion. She sees such conversion as a critical commentary on, or opposition to, mainstream religion and society: "By undoing the concept of fixed, unalterable identities, conversion unsettles the boundaries [by] which selfhood, citizenship, nationhood, and community are defined, exposing these permeable borders" (16). Inasmuch as it takes "religion's importance in community, politics, and morality" (Hefner 1993, 102) seriously, *Being German, Becoming Muslim* emphasizes the social and political power of religious conversion. I show that even when individuals do not convert for political reasons, their conversion has political consequences, because they "cross boundaries while altering these boundaries in the process" (Pelkmans 2009, 12). Such transgressions are politically loaded when former Christians convert to Islam in contemporary Europe.[12] When Christian or atheist Germans convert to Islam, they transform both what it means to be a German and the makeup of Muslim communities in Germany. More significantly, indigenous converts to Islam challenge the post–Cold War European ideology that defines itself through the exclusion of Islam and Muslims (Asad 2003, 164), and bring to light inconsistencies in the myth of a European culture that in other instances defines itself as tolerant of diversity as well as respectful of individual choice.

As opposed to earlier generations of converts, who took Arabic or Turkish names, and hence affiliated with those communities, newer converts proudly keep their German names, prefer to marry other converted Germans, and give birth to and raise German Muslims without any immigrant background. They also challenge immigrant Muslim communities by demanding Islamic activities in the German language. In the process, they form alliances with second-, third-, and fourth-generation young Muslims of Turkish and Arab backgrounds who do not feel at home in their parents' language or mosques. As a result, they help establish multiethnic Islamic communities whose language is German.

A smaller group of converts to Islam take an even more activist stance. It is openly critical of mainstream society, especially its ethnoreligious hierarchy. Some German converts write scholarly books and give academic lectures about the intolerance of German society, which once marginalized and then murdered its Jewish citizens, and is now excluding Muslims from the nation (chapter 1). Other converts use their hip-hop music to criticize the exclusion and criminalization of Muslims (chapter 4). Still others oppose the capitalistic and materialistic orientation of German society, and promote conversion to Islam in order to achieve a just society based on communalist traditions such as *zakat*, or charity (chapter 2). And an even smaller number of German converts has joined jihadist groups in Afghanistan, Pakistan, and Syria, and established terrorist cells in Germany (chapter 5).

I take the German convert's act of not identifying with mainstream society and instead forming a new identification with a minority position as an act of "queering ethnicity" with transformative potential. I borrow this concept from Fatima El-Tayeb (2011), who uses it to explain the nature and effect of unexpected alliances among racialized communities in Europe. Rather than as an adjective or noun, El-Tayeb treats the word queer as a verb, and not necessarily in its sexual meaning. She explains emergent youth culture in Europe as "a practice of identity (de)construction that results in new ways of diasporic consciousness neither grounded in ethnic identifications nor referencing a however mythical homeland." As practiced by feminists of color or hip-hop artists, queering ethnicity has the creative potential to build "a community based on the shared experience of multiple, contradictory positionalities." More important, "the new European minority activism demonstrates a queer practice by insisting that identity is unstable, strategic, shifting, and always performative" (xxxvi).

Here I contend that German conversion to Islam involves parallel processes of identity de- and reconstruction that creates multipositional alternative communities while destabilizing the religio-racial boundaries and hierarchies of social life. German conversion to Islam is increasingly a significant aspect of, although not limited to and much older than, the emergent urban European youth culture that brings together diverse and marginalized urban communities. Both white Germans and Germans of color in this case detach themselves from their identification as Christian, and identify with the racialized community of Muslims. In so doing, they establish uniquely German communities that confute the discourse that dichotomizes Germans who were all born and raised in Germany into the categories of Christian natives and Muslim immigrants.

Conversion to a lower-status religion in a racialized context creates a situation that is reminiscent of African American scholar W.E.B. DuBois's ([1903] 2013, 5) concept of "double-consciousness," which he used to characterize "the strange meaning of black in America" more than a hundred years ago. In an often-quoted passage, written shortly after he finished his studies at Berlin University, DuBois describes the "twoness" he saw as central to the African American experience:

> The Negro is . . . born with a veil, and gifted with a second sight in this American world—a world which yields to him no true self-consciousness, but only lets him see himself through the revelation of the other world. It is a peculiar sensation, this double-consciousness, this sense of always looking at one's self through the eyes of others, of measuring one's soul by the tape of a world that looks on in amused contempt and pity. One ever feels his twoness—an American, a Negro; two souls, two thoughts, two reconciled strivings. . . . He simply wishes to make it possible to be both a Negro and an American, without being cursed and spat on by his fellows, without having the doors of opportunity closed roughly in his face. (10–11)

These observations, made in Berlin over a century ago, still resonate today. The British scholar Nasar Meer (2011) employs this concept of double consciousness to reflect on the peculiar experience of being Muslim in contemporary Europe. Even though it is not a parallel comparison, DuBois's discussion of double consciousness is also exceptionally illuminating for understanding the experiences of German converts to Islam in the city where DuBois formulated these thoughts. The German Muslims I describe are not "born with a veil," as DuBois says of his people. Rather, they choose to don one—not only a metaphoric but also a literal veil in the case of converted women—as adults. Yet this veiling nonetheless affords them "a second sight" within the European world they inhabit. German converts frequently talk about society making them feel the "peculiar sensation" of having irreconcilable identities. Converts therefore strive to be German and become Muslim without being either cursed and spat on by their fellow Germans or excluded by the Ummah.

I concede that this analogy between African Americans in the early twentieth century and converted German Muslims of the early twenty-first century is neither simple nor straightforward. German converts to Islam are not born as Muslims. Many come from the majority group, and most important, they always have the option of either hiding their conversion or leaving it completely behind, along with any stigma associated with it— an option unavailable to racialized groups.[13] As a result of crossing the lines of race and religion, however, converts experience a sudden, unexpected fall in social status that arises from being both German and Muslim. Perhaps because they were not raised with such double consciousness, or because their conversion involves a new and chosen affiliation with the lower strata, many German Muslims try to transcend this twoness, the sense of irreconcilability, by insisting that Islam can have a German face, showing that it fits with German values and can be saved from Turkish and Arab traditions.

The conflicting consciousnesses and identities DuBois talks about are often not only double but in fact multiple as well.[14] Many converts to Islam are not simply Germans but also have marginalized identities as such. For instance, converts may be former East Germans or immigrants with Eastern European, Russian, Latin American, or African backgrounds. Increasingly, too, there are working-class Muslim converts. In chapters 3 and 5, I show how converting to Islam allows some of these "hyphenated" Germans to surmount their sense of being purportedly inferior, second-class citizens of the Federal Republic. Once converted to Islam, they become unquestionably German and also Muslim.

ISLAMOPHOBIA AS SIMILAR TO ANTI-SEMITISM OR HOMOPHOBIA?

In contemporary Germany, there is much evidence that Islam and Muslims are treated unequally. Despite the fact that Islam is one of the most actively practiced religions in the country, regional German governments have resisted granting Islam public recognition even after multiple applications (Fetzer and Soper 2005; Jonker 2002; Özyürek 2009; Yükleyen 2012). Protestants, Catholics, Greek Orthodox Christians, and Jews enjoy the status of a *Körperschaft des Öffentlichen Rechts* (public law corporate body), which enables them to collect church taxes and offer religious classes in public schools. But Islam is not supported by the government or taught in public institutions.[15] Muslims also face obstacles when they want to build new mosques (Jonker 2005), open faith-based Islamic schools, and observe halal rules in slaughtering animals.

In recent major opinion polls, 46 percent of Germans agreed with the statement "there are too many Muslims in Germany" (Zick, Küpper, and Hövermann 2011, 70), 58 percent agreed that "the practice of religion should be severely limited for Muslims" (Decker et al. 2010, 134), and more than half said "they do not like Muslims."[16] In the face of such sentiments, a 2010 study conducted by the Open Society in Berlin found—not surprisingly— that 89 percent of Muslims feel they are not perceived as Germans by others; 79 percent felt racially and 74 percent felt religiously discriminated against at least once in the past year; and young Muslim women feel impeded by the headscarf ban when attempting to secure meaningful employment (Mühe 2010).[17] Indeed, discrimination against Muslims is well documented, especially in the labor and housing markets.[18] Last, but not the least, Germany has witnessed several hate crimes in the past few years. These include the hate crime killing of Marwa El-Sherbini in 2009 as well as nine Turkish or Turkish-looking men by a terror cell of the right-wing National Socialist Union between 2000 and 2006.

This complex interplay of subtle and overt forms of discrimination and violence against Muslims, though, is generally seen as insufficient grounds for considering Islamophobia as a form of racism. Part of the problem arises from the fact that even though the term Islamophobia has been widely used for several decades, there is no agreement about what it means (Shryock 2010). The 1997 report prepared by the Runnymede Trust Commission on British Muslims and Islamophobia, titled *Islamophobia: A Challenge for Us All*, popularized the term in public culture. The European Monitoring Center on Racism and Xenophobia followed this report with others invoking the same notion.[19] The original report defines Islamophobia as "an unfounded hostility towards Islam and therefore fear or dislike of all or most Muslims" (Runnymede Trust Commission 1997, 4). Neither the first report nor its sequels differentiate Islamophobia from other forms of racism involving discrimination against immigrant Muslims (Allen 2010). A number of scholars of racism, such as Robert Miles and Malcolm Brown (2003, 116), also see Islamophobia as a redundant concept because it can easily be incorporated into existing theories of racism and xenophobia. Others, such as Fred Halliday (1999), are critical of the notion because they suggest it "culturalizes" a political reality. French scholars Jocelyne Cesari (2002) and Michael Wieviorka (2002) contend that Islamophobia is too vague to be fruitful.

Despite a lack of consensus on the usefulness of the term Islamophobia, these commentators agree that patterns of exclusion and racism are transforming, especially in Europe, and that immigrants of Muslim heritage are bearing the brunt of those shifts. Whereas pseudoscientific theories of heredity were used to justify exclusionary and oppressive practices during the colonial era, in the postcolonial period, there has been an upsurge in theories that legitimize similar practices based on allegedly irreconcilable cultural differences (Balibar and Wallerstein 1991; Stolcke 1995; Wieviorka 2002). Biological justifications for racism never disappeared, but cultural explanations, which scholars refer to as "new racism" (Barker 1981), "neo-racism" (Balibar 1991), "cultural fundamentalism" (Stolcke 1995), "differentialist racism" (Taguieff 1987), "culture talk" (Mamdani 2004), and even "racism without race" (Rex 1973), have become prevalent.

Throughout Europe and especially in Germany, the most important litmus test for the legitimacy of Islamophobia is whether it is similar to or different from anti-Semitism. The camp that devalues the reality of discrimination against Muslims argues that the comparison is not valid because Islam is a culture or religion that can be taken or left behind at will. The British Islam critic Polly Toynbee defends this stance by saying that "race is something people cannot choose and defines nothing about them as people . . . [whereas] beliefs are what people choose to identify with. . . . The two cannot be blurred into one which is why the word Islamophobia is a nonsense" (quoted in Meer 2013, 12). Necla Kelek, a Turkish German Islam critic who is especially liked by right-wing Germans, also echoes this perspective. In defending Tillo Sarazzin's controversial 2010 book *Deutschland schafft sich ab* (Germany is abolishing itself), which blamed Muslims in Germany for the failure of German immigration policy, she declared that Sarazzin cannot be called a racist because "Islam is not a race but rather it is a culture, a religion" (quoted in Shooman 2011, 59). Such critics frequently point to indigenous Europeans who convert to Islam as well as Turks, Arabs, Iranians, and others who leave Islam behind and themselves become so-called Islam critics.

The other camp that wants Islamophobia to be recognized as a form of racism operative throughout Europe is committed to showing that Islamophobia is not really different from the other fully acknowledged forms of racism, especially anti-Semitism.[20] Rita Chin and colleagues (2009, 14) demonstrate that both biological and cultural elements are equally present in anti-Semitic, anti-immigrant, and anti-Muslim discourse. Meer and Tariq Modood show that the so-called culture-based critique may also be racist. Hence, they suggest that we should see Islamophobia as "not merely a proxy for racism but a form of racism itself" (Meer and Modood 2010, 79). The German scholar Shooman (2011) embraces the phrase anti-Muslim racism rather than Islamophobia because "Muslimness," she argues, "is a racialized state of being from which people marked as Muslim cannot escape."[21]

Bunzl adds a new perspective to the debate inasmuch as he regards Islamophobia as a bigger challenge than anti-Semitism, both in terms of Europe's future and the geopolitical situation at large, while nonetheless asserting that anti-Semitism and Islamophobia are different. "Whereas anti-Semitism was designed to protect the purity of the ethnic nation-state, Islamophobia is marshaled to safeguard the future of European civilization," writes Bunzl (2005, 506). Like Bunzl, I see elements unique to Islamophobia that make it qualitatively distinct from its predecessor. I suggest that what is most distinctive about Islamophobia is that it is based on the premise of a rational individual subject who is responsible for their actions and thus their consequences. Islamophobes maintain that Muslims do not qualify for the legal protection granted to other groups that are systematically discriminated against, such as women or blacks, because belief is not ascribed at birth but instead is willingly chosen or held by Muslims (Bloul 2008). Since they are free to choose or leave their belief behind, so the reasoning goes, they disqualify for any kind of protection against discrimination. This kind of thinking, which holds individual Muslims responsible for any difficult situation they may find themselves in, because they brought it on themselves by making these choices, is reflected in a 2007 Frankfurt court ruling in which the judge refused to grant an easy divorce to the battered wife of a Moroccan husband, arguing that since Islam attributes an inferior position to women and grants husbands the right to beat their wives, the battered woman, who chose to marry a Muslim man, could not be seen as experiencing hardship in her marriage. This idea of holding victims responsible for their own fate fits in well with contemporary neoliberalism, which extends the market mentality to citizenship and holds individuals that it imagines to be making rational choices responsible for their actions (Paley 2001; Özyürek 2007; Ong 1999). In other words, "this racism is a racism of its time," as David Tyrier (2010, 104) puts it.

Another related element of Islamophobia is an emphasis on the ostensible neutrality of the secular public sphere in Europe. The ideal model of the public sphere in Germany is essentially a Habermasian one—a social space that is separate from the state, economy, and family, and where private individuals can gather to deliberate about the common good. In his original formulation, Jürgen Habermas entirely neglected to discuss religion (Calhoun 2011). This was not an unintentional oversight.[22] Charles Taylor (2011, 323) shows us that a fixation on religion as a special kind of reason that needs to be excluded from the public sphere has its roots in the Enlightenment thought that sees only secular reason as genuine rationality, and regards religious thinking as "dubious, and in the end only convincing to people who already accepted the dogmas in question." Religious thought is taken as the most dubious and least fit for the secular public sphere especially when it comes to Islam. Hence, seemingly liberal political actors suggest they are not against the religion but rather only against the public expression of Islam. In 2004, France passed a law that bans wearing conspicuous religious symbols in public schools, on the grounds that it is a violation of republican principles (Bowen 2007). School-girls are asked to adapt to French ways by leaving their headscarves at home. Following the French precedent, the states of Berlin and Branden-burg in Germany passed the Law on Neutrality (Neutralitätgesetz) in 2005 prohibiting not students but instead employees of public schools and the justice system from wearing religious signs, symbols, or garments. Not-withstanding that the three Abrahamic religions are treated equally in this respect in France, the idea of a "neutral" public sphere and "free" private sphere is rendered absurd by the experience of practicing Muslim women, for who headscarves are necessary specifically in the public sphere and not in the private one.

Owing to the idealization of individual choice and the limits of public expression in arguments regarding Islamophobia in Europe, I suggest that it makes as much—or more—sense to compare Islamophobia with con-temporary homophobia as it does to liken it with historical anti-Semitism. Homophobic discourses treat lesbians and gay men as responsible for hav-ing chosen the "lifestyle" in which they find themselves discriminated against, and thus as undeserving of legal protection. Christian homophobic lobbies, which are much stronger in the United States than in Europe, en-courage homosexuals to join the heterosexual mainstream. Less radical homophobes urge homosexuals to limit the expression of their sexual identity to the private sphere, forgoing public recognition and legal protec-tion, as in the "don't ask, don't tell" policy adopted by the US military until 2011. These views resonate with Islamophobic discourses in Europe, which similarly promote the idea of an ostensibly neutral public sphere where no one is identified by markers signifying religious or sexual difference.[23]

Issues of sexuality and freedom, then, are intertwined in the case of Is-lamophobia. Even though the Islamic social outlook is heterosexist, Mus-lims regard sexuality as something that needs to be marked and regulated whenever men and women are present together in public. Europeans, however, consider this a queer, misplaced public emphasis on something that properly belongs in the private sphere. The way that practicing Muslims organize sex and sexuality is deeply unsettling to the French, whose repub-licanism is based on the abstract idea of equal citizenship along with the psychological denial of sexual difference and patriarchy, as Joan Scott argues (2007). French law sees the headscarf not only as "conspicuous" when worn to school by girls, Scott contends, but also as indicative of an excess of sexuality and even perversion. Ironically, this is of course precisely the op-posite of how practicing Muslims perceive it.

The ideological centrality of "choice" in conversations regarding the Muslim experience is revealed most clearly in the experiences of the two groups that take the most active differential positions in their commitment to Islam—namely, cultural Muslims, who are socialized into Islam in their families but not necessarily fully observant, and converted German Muslims. It is not a coincidence that the attention these two groups garner in public discourse is disproportional to their numbers or influence. The different yet parallel kinds of marginalization faced by the two groups shed light on the complex matrix of Islamophobia overall. Central here are the concepts of the individual subject who is free to make choices, but is then responsible for the consequences, and a supposedly neutral public sphere, which in reality rejects alternative modes of expressing oneself.

THE RACIALIZATION OF MUSLIMS AND GERMANIFICATION OF ISLAM

Even though Germany has a long history of racializing religion, especially Judaism, the racialization of Muslims with a clear class dimension is relatively new.[24] The story of Muslims is another example of what Rey Chow (2002) calls the "ethnicization of labor" in late capitalist Western societies. Prior to World War II, there was a small but well-off and socially integrated community of Muslims in Weimar Germany (Motadel 2009). This group of Muslims practically disappeared in the aftermath of World War II, whereas masses of other Muslim workers arrived in Germany. Subsidized by the Marshall Plan, the German government invited in workers from southern Europe, North Africa, and the Middle East, including Tunisia, Morocco, and Turkey. Once Muslims became established proletarians in Germany, "an internal boundary between what is considered proper and valuable on the one hand, and foreign and inferior, on the other," came into being (Adelson 2005, 8).

Sociohistorical processes through which even the children of migrants could not be folded into the German nation are readily apparent. For decades, both German officials and migrant workers assumed that the so-called guest workers would go back to their countries. As a result, no one expended much effort in order to ease the workers' adjustment to German society. The first guest workers to arrive were mostly single men, who slept in factory dormitories segregated by nationality. They were similarly separated during the day inasmuch as they worked among compatriots and received orders in their native language through translators (Chin 2009; Yurdakul 2009). As the workers had multiple shifts in demanding jobs, they had no incentive or opportunity to learn the German language or integrate into mainstream society.

This generation of workers responded unexpectedly to the 1973 ban on foreign worker recruitment owing to the global economic crisis. Instead of returning to their countries when confronted with the diminishing availability of jobs in Germany, they in fact brought their families to join them. They knew that once they returned to their countries of origin, which were also in the grip of the global economic crisis, they would not be allowed to reenter Germany. Migrant populations of single men with limited needs were thus transformed into full-fledged migrant communities, calling for schools and housing that would accommodate families (Chin 2009; Yurdakul 2009). As a result, there was an explosion of child immigrants at a time when Germany no longer wanted immigrants. Indeed, "between 1974 and 1980, the number of Turkish children living in West Germany increased by 129% and after 1980 more than 40% of the Turks in Germany were less than 18 years old" (Ostergaard-Nielsen 2003, 33).

Once Muslim labor migrants became fully aware that they were there to stay, they began to organize as migrants. In the 1980s, they started to organize independently of their home countries for the first time, made demands for increased political rights, and became active interlocutors in domestic debates (Ostergaard-Nielsen 2003; Yurdakul 2009).[25] Despite the realities of migrants' lives, successive German governments have repeatedly based their policies on their supposed return. Helmut Kohl, German chancellor between 1982 and 1998, insisted that Germany was "not a country of immigration."[26] During this period, in order to ease the immigrants' desired reintegration into their native countries, the German government delegated their needs for religious facilities and schooling to their home countries.[27] This move prompted their countries of origin, which were dependent on remittances sent by immigrants, to also take an active role in working against their integration. "Both European governments and Muslim states purposely worked against integration for decades by promoting native language retention and the maintenance of distinct cultural and religious identities that did not mingle with the majority society" (Laurence 2012, 38).

In the 2000s, a new trend toward the "domestication" (Laurence 2012, xix) or "institutionalization of Islam" (Amir-Moazami 2013) swept through Europe. Governments accepted the fact that Muslim migrants were there to stay and switched from treating them as invisible to recognizing them. According to the German scholar Schirin Amir-Moazami, though, such recognition has involved "shaping the habits, sensibilities and life-conduct of Muslims in ways and under constraints defined by a liberal constitutional state" (73). In Germany when the Socialist Party and Green Party coalition changed the immigration law in 2000, making it possible for the children of immigrants born in Germany to have German citizenship, millions of residents shifted from being Turks, Bosnians, or Arabs to being German Muslims. Yet the new law had a catch. Between the ages of eighteen and twenty-three, these children had to give up their parents' citizenship in order to maintain German citizenship—a sacrifice not expected from other dual citizens. Far fewer applied for citizenship than expected. Nonetheless, the new law changed the basis of citizenship from blood to soil, and catalyzed intense discussion and debate about what it means to be German.

In reaction to the new immigration law, Christian Democrats asserted that immigrants threatened Germany's *Leitkultur* (leading culture) (Pautz 2005). This view was first formulated by Bassam Tibi (1998), an Arab German sociologist who believed that a unified Germany should base itself on the European values of democracy, modernity, secularism, enlightenment, human rights, and civil society. Following the 2000 law, the concept was taken up by CDU leaders such as Friedrich Merz and Jörg Schönbohm, who argued against multiculturalism and for the assimilation of existing immigrants (Bernstein 2004). Promoters of the Leitkultur perspective shied away from defining the leading culture in nationalist terms, but instead embraced an anachronistic definition of European culture (Ewing 2008). They maintained that immigrants do not fit German society, not because of their nationality, but rather because of their religious and non-European cultural backgrounds.

Ironically, the anti-Muslim and assimilationist discourses promoted by CDU politicians went hand in hand with recognizing Muslims *as* Muslims for the first time. On September 28, 2006, the Chancellor's Office initiated a new project by inviting Muslim representatives to meet at a German Islam Conference. This effort was part of a larger continental process whereby all European countries with sizable Muslim populations organized parallel Islamic councils that brought state officials together with religious leaders in order to foster a dialogue. Jonathan Laurence (2012) contends that these councils indicate a new stage in the Muslim presence in Europe where the European states now accept Muslims as permanent and attempt to domesticate Muslims by fashioning them as national citizens.

The Islam Conference was a significant moment in German history, not because it brought concrete changes for the everyday Muslim experience, but instead because it signaled government recognition of Muslim leaders. Probably the most important thing that happened during the meeting was that Federal Minister of the Interior Wolfgang Schäuble said, "Islam is a part of Germany and a part of Europe, it is a part of our past and a part of our future. Muslims are welcome in Germany," and went around the room shaking hands with every representative—an act that deeply moved the Muslim representatives I spoke with.[28] The German Ministry of Internal Affairs (2006) Web site defines the aim of the conference as "[Germany recognizing] cultural and religious differences while requiring [from people from different cultures] the complete acceptance of Germany's liberal democracy." The German Islam Conference made it clear that Muslims are recognized based on "a privatized notion of religion and more generally [the] adoption of liberal ideals." Hence, the first working group of the

German Islam Conference was asked to concentrate on "the German social order and values consensus" (Amir-Moazami 2013, 75). By doing so, the conference organizers underscored that while recognizing Muslims, they saw their values as fundamentally different from those of Germans.

Those CDU officials willing to shake hands with Muslims also wanted to know and define who were Muslims in Germany, and the Interior Ministry declared that there were four million of them (Haug, Mussig, and Stichs 2009). Since more than half of Germany's Muslims were born in Germany since the end of the 1990s, and now have the option of applying for German citizenship, the government attempted to distinguish them. This estimate, however, considers Muslims as an ethnoracial racial rather than a religious group. The researchers were concerned only with the number of people who came to Germany from Muslim majority countries, and estimated how many children they might have had. These people were simply taken to be Muslims, even though some of them are Christian and Jewish as well as atheist. The case is most obvious with Iranians. Many of the seventy thousand Iranians in Germany are there because they escaped the oppressive regime of the Islamic Republic of Iran. In the same study, 33 percent of Iranians who live in Germany define themselves as atheists, and 72 percent do not practice religion in any way (ibid., 307). Yet the Interior Ministry counted all Iranians in Germany as Muslims. Moreover, the study did not take German converts to Islam into consideration at all.

As a result of an ethnicized conceptualization of Islam, native German Muslims who blur the boundaries between Germans and Muslims became a matter of serious concern for Christian Democrats. While the Islamic Conference was under way on February 4, 2007, Schäuble gave an interview to the conservative daily *Die Welt* in which he warned the nation against the threat posed by German converts to Islam (Schmid 2007). They therefore took center stage in the national discussion about the place of Islam in Germany. Even though the conference aimed to develop a "German Islam," ethnically German Muslims became the focus of anxiety about the increasingly undeniable incorporation of Muslims into German society along with the mixing of the boundaries between German and Muslim. This new unease about converts as well as the ways in which converts try to navigate between racialized and culturalized definitions of Muslims give us clues to the complex nature of contemporary Islamophobia.

THE ROLE OF CONVERTS FOR A EUROPEAN ISLAM

Over the past decade, scholars have demonstrated how Islamic practice has changed as Muslims have moved to new locations, especially to Europe and the United States.[29] Even though Islam has been a global religion from the beginning, scholars rightly argued that a significant Muslim presence, particularly in secular Europe, has had profound consequences. In his influential study *Transnational Muslim Politics*, Peter Mandeville holds that one of the major outcomes of the Muslim immigration to the West has been the encounter of diaspora Muslims with the plurality of Islamic practice. "In the migratory or global cities, Islam is forced to contend not only with an array of non-Islamic others but also with an enormous diversity of Muslim opinion as to the nature and meaning of Islam. In such spaces Muslims will encounter and be forced to converse with interpretations of their religion which they have either been taught to regard as heretical or which they perhaps did not even know existed" (Mandeville 2001, 107). He also asserts that the result of this unforeseen coexistence of Islamic groups side by side prompts new critical engagement with the plurality of Islamic experience. Mandeville predicts that this set of historical forces coming together for Muslims in the West will "provide fertile venues for the rethinking and reformulation of tradition and the construction of an Islam for generations to come" (115).

Research conducted a decade after Mandeville's work proves some of his predictions about Muslims rethinking aspects of their Islamic practice. Muslims in Europe with immigrant backgrounds are being creative in the ways they adapt to their new home countries. French Muslims navigate through the tension between remaining accountable to the transnational Muslim community and becoming acceptable to the secularist French state by building a pluralistic, pragmatic approach to their practice (Bowen 2010). German and Dutch Muslims reinterpret their Islamic practice according to local conditions as they adapt to their new homelands (Yükleyen 2012; Yurdakul 2009; Schiffauer 2010; Sökefeld 2008; Mandel 2008).

Olivier Roy is one of the few scholars who has focused on converts in Europe, although his interest lies in how conversion is possible and not what converts enable. In *Holy Ignorance*, he argues that new fundamentalisms, including Islamism in Europe, owe their success to their ability to break the link between culture and religion. Roy (2010, 2) contends that secularization pushed religion into a sphere separate from social and cultural aspects of life, where it could be formulated as a "pure religion," while globalization contributed to the standardization of religions in circulation in the world market. It is in this context, he asserts, that Europeans convert to puritanical Islamic movements such as Salafism.

Roy is correct in one sense: movements that emphasize propagating Islam, such as the Salafis and other orthodox groups, endorse an understanding of Islam that is stripped of cultural or traditional interpretation, and promote the idea of returning to the foundational texts. They also claim that the four Islamic legal traditions, which are closely affiliated with national traditions, are not relevant for the correct practice of Islam. In that sense it does not matter if one is a Turk, Arab, Japanese, or German to be a "good" orthodox

Muslim. On the contrary, having been a good Turkish, Bosnian, or Pakistani Muslim can interfere with the practice of true Islam, since people grow up with traditions that are not perceived as properly Islamic.

Hence, Roy's observations are useful for explaining the recent spread of Islam in Europe, but they present only half of the story. His model attributes no agency to converts and converters. I suggest that what guides this de-linking is not only globalization and secularization. The increased racialization and marginalization of Muslims is at least an equally, if not more important dynamic. As a response to the racialization of Muslims, European converts and European-born Muslims make an effort to break the association between being Turkish or Arab and being Muslim mainly because of the increasing Islamophobia that treats Muslims along with their traditions as completely alien and anathema to Europe. In this book, I show that converts promote a universal Islam that is not only open to all. The culture-free Islam that they promote also seems more fitting to European and German values and mentalities than to Middle Eastern or immigrant ways of being. But I first want to underline the fact that even though converts engaged themselves with the idea of a German Islam for a long time, the emergence and specific political consequences of this idea are specific to the contemporary sociopolitical realities of Europe at large and Germany in particular.

GENERATIONS OF GERMAN CONVERTS TO ISLAM

Even though European conversion to Islam is often discussed as a new and surprising phenomenon, it has been going on for more than a hundred years in Germany. Men and women, old and young, rich and poor, gay and straight, religious and atheist, Christian and Jewish, Protestant and Catholic, indigenous or immigrant, Germans have been embracing orthodox and unorthodox interpretations of Islam for quite a while. Different kinds of Germans have encountered different kinds of Muslims at different historical moments. Those involved in Muslim and German encounters at any particular time have largely shaped the vision of Islam that German converts embraced. The following brief history of conversion to Islam is also therefore a history of Islam and Muslims in Germany. A generational perspective challenges the prevailing view of Muslims in Europe as a perpetually new and hence not well-integrated presence.[30]

Although yearbooks of Muslims from the turn of the twentieth century mention a few converts to Islam (Germain 2008), the first real wave of German conversion took place during the Weimar Republic, from 1919 to 1933. A liberal atmosphere open to experimentation in many aspects of life, from art and architecture to political ideas to sexuality, marked this brief but special chapter in German history.[31] Weimar Germany was also home to more than a thousand Muslim students from India, Turkey, Iran, and Arab countries as well as anticolonial activists from India and the Middle East. Like Muslim diplomats and businesspeople, these students were catalysts for conversion. Until the 1920s, however, the number of converts was extremely small.

A real change in the conversion scene happened when the Indian Muslim group known as the Ahmadiyya Society for the Propagation of Islam decided to open European mosques, first in England and then in Berlin.[32] When the Ahmadis came to cosmopolitan and tolerant Berlin in 1921, their aim was to counter Christian missionaries who were proselytizing among Muslims. They aspired to do so by fighting the missionary vision of Islam as a backward religion (Germain 2008). Between 1924 and 1927, the Ahmadis built a beautiful mosque in the bourgeois neighborhood of Wilmersdorf. This still-surviving though poorly maintained mosque is built in the Indian style with references to the Taj Mahal. Soon after its opening, the Ahmadi mosque became a trendy cultural center for open-minded intellectuals and literary types, Muslim and non-Muslim alike. The mosque was also quite effective in its mission of propagating Islam. By the 1930s, about a third of Germany's Muslim population consisted of converts to Islam (ibid.). Some of these encountered Islam in the gatherings of the Ahmadi mosque, and others during their studies of and travels to the Middle East. Regardless, new Muslims now had a place to meet other German-speaking Muslims and talk about issues common to them. Paralleling the Muslim population of Berlin at the time, converts to Islam were a well-educated elite, including Orientalist scholars, aristocrats, and professionals. A number of prominent German converts holding doctorates were present at the opening ceremony of the Ahmadi mosque (Backhausen 2008, 62). In their publications, such as the *Moslemische Revue*, the Ahmadis seem to have been especially pleased with their upper-class converts (Clayer and Germain 2008, 307). The mosque's most renowned convert was a German aristocrat, Baron Omar von Ehrenfels, who converted to Islam in 1927 and went to Lahore to tour India in 1932 (Germain 2008, 107).

German-speaking converts to Islam included Jews who had come into contact with Islam during their travels to Palestine and sometimes through their contact with Muslims in Germany. The most famous German-speaking Jewish converts to Islam include Muhammad Asad—formerly Leopold Weiss—the grandson of a Polish rabbi and later appointed by the Pakistani government to set up the Islamic principles on which the new Islamic state would rest; Essad Bey—formerly Lev Nussimbaum—one of the most prolific German writers, whose books were listed by the Nazi propaganda ministry as "great books for German minds" until it discovered his Jewish roots; and Hamid Hugo Marcus, who edited the first German-language translation of the Qur'an (albeit the Ahmadi version) and remained the leader of the German Muslim society housed at the Ahmadi mosque until the Nazis came to power.[33]

Like all others in Germany, Muslim organizations were greatly affected by the coming to power of the Nazis. Members who would not be approved by the Nazis, such as the Jewish-born Marcus, had to step down. Increasingly more German converts who had close relations with the Nazis or were themselves members of the National Socialist German Workers' Party took the lead. After World War II, Germany was practically empty of Muslims. Ahmadis and other Indian Muslims who had been in Germany as diplomats, businesspeople, or students left during the war, because as British subjects they were considered enemy nationals, and thus liable to imprisonment or worse. They did not return. Their beautiful mosque in Berlin remained with a community of a few German converts, but these people were marginal and insignificant among the Muslims who later came to the city. What changed the Islamic scene in Germany was the invitation of guest workers from Turkey, Yugoslavia, and Italy starting in the early 1960s. As the German economy and institutions improved, in part thanks to the guest workers, students from all around the world, including the Muslim world, began once again to attend German universities.

The number of converts to Islam started to increase again with the arrival of migrant Muslim workers. In the 1960s and 1970s, single men made up the majority of the Muslim population in Germany. Some of these, Muslim students and asylum seekers, in particular, struck up romantic relationships with German women. Asylum seekers, who had to live in apartments designated for them, were especially motivated to establish relations with German women in the hope of marrying them and gaining papers that would allow them to live permanently in Germany.[34] Some of these meaningful encounters initiated conversion, and in this period more women than men converted to Islam. The decreasing cost of tourism also contributed to an increase in German women's contact with Muslims.[35] Once an elite male diversion, travel to exotic, sunny places steadily became popular among Germans of all classes. A number of converted women I met during my research had come into meaningful contact with Muslims for the first time during their trips to places such as Turkey, Egypt, Tunisia, and Morocco.

By the 1990s, the number of German converts to Islam had reached a critical mass, and they began forming German-speaking Muslim groups and developing a new group identity as "German converts to Islam."[36] Since they were especially alienated from their own families and friends, but also could not feel completely at home in the society of native-born Muslims, converted women sought emotional support in groups of German Muslim women.[37]

In the 2000s, the dynamic changed once more. Even though old trends still continue, today there is a new cohort of converts who are young, male, lower class, and often Germans of color. These young men—and some women—convert to Islam through contact with native-born Muslim friends with whom they drink, smoke marijuana, and enjoy graffiti and hip-hop. As Islam becomes further marginalized and criminalized in German society, it becomes attractive for some marginalized non-Muslims. German youths with multiple backgrounds who live in the affordable but relatively undesirable marginal areas of German cities—like Neukölln and Wedding in Berlin, where I did my research—convert to Islam. These neighborhoods are home to many Turks and Arabs, along with lower-class white native Germans and non-Muslim immigrants from Russia, East Europe, Africa, Asia, and Latin America.

The transformation of the convert demographic from twenty-to-thirty-year-old women to teenage males also has something to do with the transformation of what Islam represents in Germany. Until recently, Islam was associated with things female. Even if the headscarf, honor killings, and forced marriage were all problematic issues, they were all nonetheless "women's" issues. In the 2000s, on the other hand, Islam is increasingly presented in masculinist terms. Muslims are depicted as a problem, not only owing to women's issues, but also because Muslim men are seen as terrorists, drug dealers, and machos who beat up their wives and sisters as well as German kids in the schools. Katherine Ewing (2008) shows how the Muslim male is increasingly imagined as something alien to the German nation. It is therefore unsurprising that this oppositional image attracts teenage boys alienated because they are darker skinned and socioeconomically underprivileged. The significant increase in the number of converts during early 2000s went hand in hand with the global rise of Salafism. Unlike other ethnically based mosques in Germany, Salafi ones are eager to attract and accommodate new Muslims, and teach their interpretation of Islam in German. Moreover, a number of Salafi leaders have German wives, and these women have been active in seeing to it that German converts are made welcome in the mosques, where they are able to meet like-minded people and learn more about Islam.

My historicization of conversion to Islam in Germany demonstrates its democratization.[38] One way of reading this history is as an index of Islam's declining value. As the perceived value of Islam decreased in Germany, the socioeconomic background of the converts did too. In other words, the more marginalized Islam became, the more people from more marginal segments of German society found it attractive. Yet a closer look at German conversion trends also leads to another, more positive interpretation. Whereas in the early 1900s there were a handful of converts, today the number is estimated to be in the tens of thousands, and even close to a hundred thousand. Conversion to Islam is almost always a result of a meaningful relationship between a Muslim and non-Muslim, and affects the lived experience of both native Germans and migrant Muslims as well as the definitions of these terms. Hence, the dramatic increase in conversion shows what an inseparable part of German society Muslims are. As Muslims have been transformed through their migration to Germany, they also transform German society—at the very least, increasing the number of individuals who embrace Islam—in fundamental ways. In the process, Islam has become an unquestionably national religion in Germany.

The immense diversity of the types of Germans who have converted to Islam and Islamic traditions they have embraced mean that there is no one type of European conversion to Islam. There is nothing intrinsic to Islam that attracts certain types of people, nor is there any certain type of individual who is attracted to religious traditions with particular characteristics. What the changing trends about who in Germany converts to which type of Islam reveal, however, is the importance of the social, political, and cultural contexts that make only certain kinds of conversions possible at a given time, and the others unlikely.[39]

RESEARCH AMONG CONVERTED MUSLIMS

The research for this book was done over three and a half years (2006–7, 2009–11, and half of 2013). I met local converts to Islam primarily by regularly attending German-language lectures organized for converts along with devotional and social activities organized by a handful of mosques whose operating language is mainly German. There are over one hundred mosques and prayer houses in Berlin (Spielhaus and Farber 2006), but when I began conducting research in 2006, only six of them—eight by the end of my second period of fieldwork in 2011—had activities designed for German-speaking Muslims and especially newcomers to Islam. I attended countless weekly lectures, prayers, Arabic-language classes, picnics, and fund-raising activities organized by the Deutschsprachiger Muslimkreis (German-speaking Muslim circle, or DMK), Interkulturelles Zentrum für Dialog und Bildung (Intercultural Center for Dialogue and Education), and al-Nur mosque. I also attended numerous activities organized by the Muslimische Jugend, Islamische Gemeinde deutschsprachiger Islam und Freunde des Islams Berlin, and Weimar community in Potsdam. I always had my field book with me, and took extensive notes during events and gatherings. I talked about the choice of discussant, event, or the direction that conversations took with others in the mosque whenever I could. I conducted semi-structured interviews with sixty-six converts and fourteen native-born Muslims active in German-speaking Muslim contexts.[40] I completed my interviews over one sitting with some, and spoke with others over three or four sittings. With many of them, I had a chance to revisit some aspects of their lives outside the interview setting over my long research period. Like all ethnographers, however, I gathered the most important insights regarding trends and tensions in this small but more or less tightly connected community of German Muslims through taking part in countless hours of mundane everyday activities and conversations over an extended amount of time. Genuine friendships eventually developed that allowed me to better discern German Muslim lives in their complex integrity and immense diversity.

Spending time among German converts to Islam as a native-born Turkish Muslim researcher who lives in the United States brought a special productive tension to this study. On the one hand, because I am a Muslim, we shared some basic beliefs and dispositions. On the other hand, unlike many converts, I do not organize many aspects of my life according to Islamic principles and do not practice many requirements of my religion. In many ways, I fit the stereotypes that German converts have about what they call "cultural Muslims." My knowledge of Islamic sciences and practices is far from systematic, and based on bits and pieces I learned from my grandparents, or just picked up along the way while growing up in Turkey. My being Muslim eased my presence in Islamic contexts and relationship to the Muslims I worked with. My not being a practicing Muslim and being Turkish brought a variety of tensions to the surface that converted German Muslims often have with other practicing and nonpracticing Turkish Muslims. This particular tension, though, gave me the most insight into the complex relationship that German Muslims have with immigrant Muslims.

Although there are sizable convert communities in every major western German town and city, the position of converted Muslims in Berlin has its specificities. Berlin's history before the fall of the Berlin Wall as an island of West Germany surrounded by East German territory marks communities in Berlin. Berlin is unique in being home to numerous East German converts to Islam who belong to the same German-speaking Muslim communities as West German converts. Native Germans from all parts of Germany as well as immigrants from diverse corners of the world live in Berlin, a liberal, cosmopolitan city. In German-speaking mosques, I thus met not only former indigenous German Catholics, Protestants, atheists, and seekers who came to Islam after trying out a number of different religions but also converts with Latin American, African, or eastern European backgrounds. I attempt in this book to give a good sense of the diversity of contemporary indigenous Sunni Muslims in Germany, while pointing to commonalities in their experiences.[41]

Chapter 1

GIVING ISLAM A GERMAN FACE

Afeefa looked flustered at the weekly breakfast for women at the DMK that meets at the Bilal mosque in Wedding, a poor neighborhood with many immigrant residents.[1] About ten to fifteen women, all converts to Islam, attend these breakfasts every Wednesday at 10:00 a.m., right after they drop their kids off at school and perhaps run a few errands. They say it is a great place to catch up with friends and have a few hours to oneself. It also offers a unique opportunity for converted German Muslim women to be among people like themselves and feel comfortable. Because regulars at this breakfast feel it is important to find German Muslim women when they first convert, they make an effort to ensure that the breakfasts are regularly held to welcome potential newcomers to the group. Women who call up to say they have converted to Islam or are thinking about it, and even sometimes those who are worried about their daughters or sisters converting, are heartily invited to this breakfast so that they can meet indigenous German Muslims. As one of the people responsible for this particular Wednesday breakfast, Afeefa brought along about forty freshly baked white rolls, *schrippe*, and a dozen organic eggs that she planned to soft boil. She took several sticks of butter, a couple of berry jams, Nutella, halal cold cuts and sausages, and tubes of cheesy spreads from the well-stocked fridge, and prepared the double coffee maker with many scoops of coffee.

After we sat down and a few of the women took off their headscarves in the intimate company of their Muslim sisters, Afeefa said that she had had it with her non-Muslim cousin, who had been visiting her family for a week. The entire time the cousin had accused Afeefa of not being a German anymore. She told her, "Look, you dress differently, you eat differently, you say these strange Arabic words to your friends, you have nothing German about you anymore." Afeefa was angry with her. She kept saying, "Of course I am German." She compared herself to another cousin in the family.

"Katarina is vegetarian. She also does not drink alcohol. Somehow she can still be German, but I cannot be because I do not eat pork or drink alcohol!" She was especially annoyed at her cousin for sitting at the breakfast table every morning in low-cut shirts: "Why did my husband have to look at her breasts all morning?"

German scholars—and most of mainstream German society—tend to think of German converts to Islam as people who are fleeing their German identity—something still an embarrassment to many Germans more than sixty years after the end of World War II—and symbolically emigrating elsewhere (Wohlrab-Sahr 2002). My research shows that even though converting to Islam transforms ethnic Germans' lives dramatically, and usually in ways that they did not prepare themselves for, most German Muslims are invested in opening a space for themselves where they can comfortably embrace their Muslim and German identities at the same time. The Swedish scholar Anne Sofie Roald (2006), who is also a convert to Islam, states that since the 2000s, a good number of Scandinavian converts have tried to integrate what they see as Scandinavian values into their understanding of Islam as well. A golden mean that brings German and Muslim identities perfectly together is not always easy to find, and definitely not something shared by all members of the German Muslim community. Most German Muslims, especially those who socialize with other German Muslims in contexts such as the DMK, strongly believe that it is possible to be a good Muslim without sacrificing one's German identity. German Muslims claim that as converts, they can even be better Muslims than immigrant Muslims.[2] They imply that by definition, they live a pure Islam not contaminated by cultural practices and urge native-born Muslims also to purify their Islamic practice of the stigmatized cultural traditions.[3] Furthermore, some suggest, their commitment and contribution to a religiously diverse society makes them more tolerant as well as better connected to the lost ideals of the German Enlightenment, best represented in the writings of Johann Wolfgang von Goethe (1749–1832) and Gotthold Ephraim Lessing (1729–81). Hence, many German Muslims promote the idea that their stance is closer not only to the true nature of Islam but also to the best of German and European ideals.

THE GERMAN-SPEAKING MUSLIM CIRCLE

As one of the first German-speaking Muslim associations in postwar Germany, the DMK, founded in Berlin in the 1990s, has a special role in Muslim Germany. The DMK was originally established not by German converts to Islam but rather by non-Turkish and non-Arab Muslim students who came to Germany to study and could not find a religious community for themselves. These students thought that a German-language Muslim community would be able to bring together Muslims who do not speak the languages that are used in mosques in Germany. Once it was founded as the only German-speaking Islamic context in Berlin, the DMK quickly united the diverse German converts to Islam and brought them together as a community, becoming a popular address. The DMK community consists of a few hundred registered members and an approximately equal number of others who attend the mosque without being members. Of its congregation, about half of the people are German, Russian, French, Argentinean, and Polish converts to Islam, and the other half consists of Muslims with roots in different Muslim-majority countries around the world.

Being able to provide a German-speaking Muslim space where no Islamic tradition is preferred over others, and Muslims of different backgrounds thus feel themselves at home, is crucial. The DMK's Web page emphasizes that it bases itself only on the Qur'an and Hadith, and does not prioritize any Islamic legal school or tradition above others. It states: "We follow Allah's word in Sura 2, verse 256 'There is no compulsion in religion!' and we respect different interpretations and legal schools." It defines itself as a community where "Muslims with different mother tongues and cultures get together under the common banner of Islam and the German language. That is why, when a visitor comes to the DMK we do not ask them to which legal school they belong to. Rather we offer all Muslims the possibility to encounter each other with an equal footing."[4]

In addition to its stress on the German language and commitment to a nonsectarian approach to Islam, the DMK differs from other mosques in Germany in that a high proportion of its members have BAs or even PhDs. Most likely because it was first established by foreign Muslim students who came to study in German universities, the mosque continues to be a gathering place for foreign, native-born Muslims along with converted Muslims pursuing graduate or postgraduate studies. The DMK is also unique in Germany for the high number of women among its membership and also at the Shura, a democratically elected consultation board. Women participate to such an extent that the DMK Shura had to institute a bylaw ensuring that neither gender is represented by more than 60 percent on this board. In 2013, the mosque's *amir* (leader) was a woman. The active involvement of women in this mosque is readily apparent from their presence at any event or discussion that takes place there. In its respect for diversity in Islam, commitment to democracy and women's representation, and emphasis on the German language, the DMK promotes itself as both a model democratic German community and an Islamic community that puts the best possible German face on an Islamic practice that its members see as true to its founding principles.

BECOMING MUSLIM WHILE REMAINING GERMAN

German Muslims who convert to Islam share common experiences with immigrant Muslims when it comes to living their religion in a non-Muslim society that is not accommodating to the Islamic lifestyle. Much of the everyday experience of converts is unique to them, however, in that they do not fit in either the German mainstream or Muslim immigrant communities. Zeyneb, a forty-three-year-old convert who embraced Islam around twenty years ago, told me that the most distinctive feeling she has about being a German Muslim is not fitting in coupled with the consequent loneliness. A sensitive and reflective person, Zeyneb observed,

> I feel that as German Muslims, we are doubly marginalized. First Germans push us aside, and then Turks and Arabs turn their backs on us. That makes one feel very lonely. No one thinks about us when people talk about Muslims in Germany. We are totally invisible. Germans most often think we are crazy. Once a politician even said we are dangerous. Others think we converted because we got taken by a macho man. They call us traitors, people who left their culture behind and took someone else's. This is when they realize that I am a convert. Other times, it does not even occur to them that I might be a German. They treat me like an ignorant immigrant who does not speak German, who cannot be an intellectual, who cannot raise her children properly.

The reaction converts received from born Muslims was not all that different. As Zeyneb recounted:

> And Turks do not accept us either. In my son's class, there are some Turks. They tell him that "your mother is a German so she does not need to cover her hair." It is not possible for them to accept that I am also a Muslim. Older Turkish women tell me that I cannot be a Muslim. They think Islam is only for Turks. It is hard even when people have the best intentions. When I first converted, a Turkish family took me in and treated me like their daughter. But even there I felt very lonely, because I was very different from them. They were very nice but very simple people. I couldn't relate to them at an intellectual level. In the end, I feel as though no one understands who I am. And I always feel in the wrong category.

Many German converts to Islam told me that as time passed, they felt more and more strongly that they did not fit in any category. As the intensity of the conversion experience mellows, converts become aware of the new social role they find themselves in and realize the new walls that surround them. What has been most appalling to converts to Islam, especially women who don the headscarf, has been being taken as a foreigner in the society they grew up in comfortably, and hence losing the feeling that they totally belonged to it. During a conversation with Miriam about her early experiences of becoming a Muslim, the most outrageous thing for her was what she called "becoming a third-class citizen." In the women's section of a mosque cafeteria, Miriam told me that her life changed not when she converted to Islam but instead when she put on the headscarf. "I was outraged," she told me. "Overnight everyone on the street lost all the respect they paid me as a regular German woman, with nothing special about her." No one would make eye contact with her, salespeople were rude, and government officials did not let her talk or listen to her carefully.

According to Miriam, this all happens because they think she is a foreigner. Miriam wears long black or dark brown overcoats, large headscarves, and big brown-tinted glasses. Something about her round face or relatively short, plump body actually does make her look more like a Turkish grandmother than most other converts I met. So when she tells people that she is German, they still do not believe her:

> They think I mean I am an immigrant with a German passport. I have often been told patronizingly that I should not assume I am a German just because I hold a German passport. To them, there is no such thing as a German Muslim. One has to be a foreigner. Then if I feel like continuing the conversation at all, I say, "My grandparents were Prussians. Is that German enough for you?"

When it is revealed that she has a German name, the change of reaction is impossible to miss. "When I am waiting for my turn at the government office, everyone would be ignoring me as usual. But when I hand in my papers with my German name, everyone looks horrified. They look at me as if I am a traitor. I know they are thinking that I converted because a man treated me so well in bed. But I used to notice such things only during the early years of my conversion." She laughed bitterly and confessed that after fifteen years of it, she had become pretty insensitive to such treatment. "I do not expect anything different, and at least I do not get disappointed." She stopped and reflected. "Maybe," she said, "as I become older, I care less about others. Or maybe things have changed in Germany in the past fifteen years. I must say, I no longer come home outraged every time I go out, as I used to."

My conversations with more recent converts tell me that Miriam's speculation about things changing in German society and making German Muslim existence easier is not completely true. It is, I suspect, the increase in the number of German converts that has helped Miriam, especially the creation of German Muslim circles where they can learn about Islam, practice their religion, and most important, socialize with one another. As she became more active in such milieus, Miriam established many meaningful friendships with like-minded people. In the process, she also changed herself, and now that she is closely affiliated with a more or less isolationist Muslim community with tight in-group relations, she does not have to rely on mainstream society—or immigrant Muslims, for that matter—for emotional or intellectual support. Most likely, she has learned not to care about or expect much from her obligatory interactions with non-Muslims. She feels good about herself among her German Muslim friends, where she is a well-known and respected woman.

Consisting as they do almost exclusively of German converts, such growing communities develop a deep sense of German Islamic identity that is distinct from a Turkish or Arab one. In fact, some native German Muslims seek to create a German Islamic practice by stripping away Turkish and Arab cultural influences. Intellectuals among them go further and try to construct an alternative German genealogy that is inclusive of Islam based on the history of the German Enlightenment. Converts find ways to raise their children that are undoubtedly both Islamic and German. These efforts aim to open up legitimate space for Germans who have embraced Islam. At the same time, however, they sometimes end up reproducing anti-immigrant discourses that treat born or immigrant Muslims as not fitting in German society.

FINDING ISLAM IN THE GERMAN ENLIGHTENMENT

One of the most commonly heard arguments in Germany about why Muslims do not belong to Europe is that they never had the Enlightenment, and as a result, never learned to be rational and tolerant. A number of highly intellectual German Muslims have been countering these contentions for more than one hundred years, and stress how Islam played a central role in the thinking of the most prized figures of the German Enlightenment, or Aufklärung, and romanticism, particularly Goethe's thought (Mommsen 2001). The contrast with German Enlightenment figures who were tolerant toward both Jews and Muslims, such as Lessing, valorizes religious tolerance and openness to religious minorities, as against both Nazi anti-Semitism and the Islamophobia of the mainstream German public today. German Muslims reintroduce the most tolerant figures of the German Enlightenment as role models who can remind contemporary Germans that a truly open-hearted engagement with Islam can be an enriching experience and indeed already has a long history in the German tradition.

The central part that Islam played in the German Enlightenment is a topic discussed now and again in the DMK of Berlin. Three of the lectures that the DMK finds important enough to upload on its Web page for public view explain how Islam belongs to Europe by virtue of its long yet overlooked history on the continent and how Islam played a key role in the ideas of the German Enlightenment. The first of these lectures, titled "Islam:

A European Tradition," delivered in 2008 by Silvia Horsch, an ethnic German convert to Islam, DMK council member, and specialist in Islamic theology at the University of Osnabruck, sought to counter an assertion by Gerhard Schroeder (German chancellor from 1998 to 2005). Reflecting the common belief that Islam is external to German and European culture, Schroeder claimed "we [Germans/Europeans] are influenced by three great traditions: Greco-Roman philosophy, Christian-Jewish religion, and the heritage of the Enlightenment."[5] Challenging the historical understanding of Europe as a land free of Muslims and the Enlightenment as the negation of Islamic values, Horsch argued in her lecture that Islam and religious tolerance are in actuality foundational to European history as well as modernity as we understand it today.

Horsch reminded her audience that since 2004, the geographic center of the European Union had shifted to Lithuania. This new EU geography includes areas with long, established histories of Islam. Horsch pointed out that more than fifty-six million Muslims live in the lands between the United Kingdom in the west and the Ural Mountains and the Caucasus in the east, with only six million of them in European Turkey. Contemporary discussions of European Muslims usually restrict themselves to the fifteen million immigrants living in western Europe—certainly newcomers to Europe, but constituting only a minority of European Muslims.

Countering Schroeder's statement regarding the exclusively Judeo-Christian tradition of Germany, Horsch noted that until recently, Judaism had been seen as outside the European tradition, as Orthodox Christianity still is today. Moreover, like Islam, the Judeo-Christian tradition does not have European but rather Oriental roots. There is no logical reason to separate these three Abrahamic religions from one another by calling two of them European and the third non-European. Horsch (2004a, n.p.) asked, "So, the fact that Muslims have lived in Europe for a thousand years is not enough to include Islam among European traditions?"

Horsch also challenged Schroeder's statement in regard to the exclusive role played by Greco-Roman philosophy in what he called "our" intellectual tradition by showing that Muslims were pivotal to this philosophical tradition. Finally, Horsch cited three influential German figures who had intimate relationships with Islam: the thirteenth-century Holy Roman Emperor Friedrich II von Hohenstaufen, who had exceptionally good relations with Muslims; Goethe, who had a deep appreciation of Islam, in which he found values such as charity, submission to God's will, and trust in destiny; and finally, Lessing.[6]

Horsch (2004b), who wrote her PhD dissertation on Lessing, and in 2004 published the book *Rationalität und Toleranz: Lessings Auseinandersetzung mit dem Islam* (Rationality and tolerance: Lessing's analysis of Islam), holds that studying the ideas of an Enlightenment figure such as Lessing resets the terms of the contemporary debate about what being a European entails and what it means to be tolerant in a plural society. Even though everything that Lessing read to learn about Islam was full of prejudice against this religion, she contends, he was able to see beyond all that and develop a deep appreciation of it. What Lessing perceived in Islam was an enlightenment that turned "savage warriors" into "scientists and heroes."[7]

Horsch argues that in Islam, Lessing found an approximation of the natural religion of deism, which emphasizes a belief in God, but not a particular religion or revelation. Such a naturalistic approach to religion came out of the Enlightenment ideas that highlighted the natural and innate qualities of humans. According to deists, natural religion works without revelation because humans, owing to their reason, are able to recognize God and act morally. The recognition of God and moral good action are exactly the aspects that one of Lessing's Muslim characters uses to describe his religion, saying, "We believe in one single God. We believe in punishment and reward in the future . . . after our deeds are measured after death."[8]

After showing how Lessing was able to find central Enlightenment concepts in Islam, such as reason and naturalness, Horsch goes on to a discussion of his unique and radically progressive understanding of tolerance. She maintains that for Lessing, tolerance was not a merely tactical bearing but instead a necessity with epistemological foundations. Lessing believed that humans are not able to grasp absolute truth, rather only an approximation of it. For Lessing, the adherents of another religion possess the potential for truth, and one should be tolerant of them and seriously examine their beliefs. In this regard, Lessing shares Goethe's (2013, 609) approach to tolerance, proclaiming, "Tolerance should really only be a passing attitude: it should lead to appreciation. To tolerate is to offend."[9]

Horsch demonstrates that according to Lessing, serious engagement with another religion was open-ended and could even lead to conversion. In his 1774 essay "Von Adam Neusern; Einige authentische Nachrichten" (Some authentic information about Adam Neuser), Lessing defends an antitrinitarian Protestant clergyman who converted to Islam in the sixteenth century. Because of his conversion and flight to Constantinople, Neuser was seen as a traitor to Christianity, and highly vicious and immoral person. Lessing, on the other hand, reconsiders his position and argues that such a step can be seen as a theological consequence of unitarianism when followed thoroughly. It is no coincidence that Lessing, who is so open to appreciating another religion and especially Islam, serves as a great intellectual role model for today's intellectual German converts to Islam. In contemporary Germany, where Islam is not highly regarded, Horsch finds in Lessing a radically fresh and historically well-grounded approach to members of other religions in general and Islam in particular.

Horsch is far from being alone in looking up to certain German Enlightenment figures in search of an alternative genealogy of German identity open to and even inclusive of Islam. In another DMK lecture, Erich Guist

(2004), another German convert, spoke on "Islam and the Enlightenment." Guist asked whether Islam is an enlightened religion, whether its teachings are rational, if there is enlightenment in Islam, and if there was Islam in the Enlightenment. His affirmative answers to all these questions prove that Islamic teachings are in line with those of the Enlightenment, and that Islam had impressed and influenced a number of European, especially German Enlightenment thinkers.

Like Enlightenment thinkers who valued rationality and a feeling of naturalness when it comes to evaluating a religion, Guist appreciated exactly these qualities in Islam. "When I converted to Islam twenty years ago, I was convinced with the clarity and comprehensibility of this belief," Guist said. "It appeared so rational, so reasonable, so close to the reality that I never had the impression that I was taking on a new belief. Rather, I felt that I was rediscovering my own innate belief, the belief I always carried in me."[10] Guist promotes the idea that Islam not only fits the Enlightenment criteria of reason and naturalness as objective realities. These characteristics also make it a perfect fit with the "innate" European ideals—more so than any other religion, including Christianity.

Like Guist, Abdul Hadi Hoffman, a former CDU politician and German convert to Islam, also found the fundamentals of Islamic teaching in the philosophy of the most celebrated Enlightenment figure, Immanuel Kant. In a lecture on "Islam und Kant" that he delivered in 2004 during the Berlin Muslims' Islamwoche (Islam week), he talks about the Islamic ideals he found in Kant seen from an Islamic standpoint.[11] Hoffman defines his purpose in this lecture as reading Kant as a German Muslim, asking new questions, and encouraging reflection on Kant in relation to Islam. From this perspective, he discovers that elements of Kant's philosophy "that were once part of the European world also play a central role in the thoughts and lives of Muslims." His long list of key common values to Kant's philosophy and Islam include an emphasis on peace; the concept of the independent individual, meaning human freedom to choose to believe in God and his commands; a stress on the Enlightenment and learning; a belief in God; the categorical imperative, or focus on the individual's motivation; and most important, rationality.

A few German converts to Islam directly relate their religion of choice to the Enlightenment, and specifically the German Enlightenment. Embracing the tolerance shown by the giants of the Aufklärung, especially when it comes to Jews, offers an alternative moral genealogy in post-Holocaust Germany. German Muslims who point to Goethe and Lessing as examples assert that a deep tolerance of Islam is part of the German tradition that should be revived now.

I took part in many conversations among converted Muslims where their discussions about the place of Islam and Muslims in German society were inspired by the Enlightenment ideas. They both criticized mainstream German society for not being open and tolerant while taking immigrant Muslims to task for letting their cumbersome traditions get in the way of a pure, rational Islam. Enlightenment ideals, they contended, show one how to be a better German and better Muslim simultaneously.

Many converts shared with me that converting to Islam gave them more information about their society than anything they had done before. The "second sight" they had gained as a result of their conversion allowed them to realize that German society is much less liberal and tolerant than they had thought. Kerstin, for example, told me that the experience of wearing the headscarf in particular had taught her something important not only about German society but also about the entire the world. "Before I used to think that I empathized with all the marginalized people, with everyone who is different. But now I understand that I had no clue. Now I know what a big challenge it is to be marginalized every day and in all aspects of your life." Many other socially engaged converts also reflected on how their transformation had been extremely informative in the way they had come to understand German society differently, and how shocking this realization was to them. Samantha explained to me that she had been an active member of the Green Party before her conversion to Islam. "I used to be in the hippie faction," she said with a smile on her face. "I used to feel very comfortable among them and thought they were my people, that they held similar values to me. Only after I converted did I realize that this is not the case at all and that their tolerance is very limited. I still vote for the Green Party, because I do not know who else to vote for. But I know that there is no place for someone like me in it."

After contemplating this experience, Samantha came to the conclusion that "actually, you really do not understand the dynamics of the society you are a part of until you change and look at it from a different position." Until she converted and married her Arab husband, she had no idea how people with foreign names and accents as well as women with headscarves were treated. Since her marriage, she has handled every bureaucratic issue, rented apartments for her family, and met with teachers at her children's schools. She tried to do as much as possible on the phone, because she knew that when they saw her with her headscarf, everything would be much worse. "When I converted to Islam in 1996, I didn't know what it meant to be a Muslim in German society. I was very surprised by the position I found myself in." Even though she was no longer politically active when I met her, at least in the Green Party, Samantha believed that her existence in her new position is a political act: "In my view, I represent a part of German society that is not recognized by the mainstream. I aspire to promote the idea that one can be a German and a Muslim simultaneously. This is very important to me."

Nicole, who converted to Islam over ten years ago, also recognizes that her conversion allows her to make a political statement that she could not otherwise make. While talking about German history one day, Nicole confessed to me that her grandfather had been a member of the Nazi Party. Although he passed away years ago, this part of her family history weighed heavy on Nicole's socially responsible shoulders. She told me that she sometimes fantasized about standing in front of her grandfather with her headscarf and telling him that Germans do not all have to be the way he imagined. Nicole, who I would define as philo-Semitic in the way many educated liberal Germans of a certain generation are, also frequently noticed not only the extent of Islamophobia but also a deeper anti-Semitism in German society. She noted that since she converted, many non-Muslim Germans would come up to her and make anti-Semitic or anti-Zionist statements, expecting her to share their anti-Semitism since she is a Muslim. She told me that these people would often be surprised and respond apologetically when confronted. Nicole was troubled by her unexpected discovery of this otherwise-latent anti-Semitism. At the same time, she was proud that this gives her a new opportunity to confront it, not only as any German, but especially as a headscarf-wearing one.

Another Enlightenment-inspired discussion that I commonly witnessed among German Muslim circles concerned the desire for a "pure" Islam. If the first topic regarding the need to be more tolerant was a critique of mainstream German society, the issue of purification was a critique of the immigrant Muslim community. German Muslims frequently aspire to an Enlightenment-inspired pure Islam—a notion also popularly embraced by Islamic reformists of the past two centuries. This position suggests that when stripped of accretions, Islam will be truer to its original intent and also speak directly to the rational individual. Yet this position carries the paradox inherent to the Enlightenment ideal. Despite its seeming universalism, this stance when explored in its European context ends up being particularistic and more specifically Eurocentric. As I examine in the next section, in practice, this line of thinking assumes that when stripped of accretions, Islam in its pure form will by definition suit European ways of thinking, being, and believing, which are thought by definition to be tradition free.

EUROPEANIZING ISLAM THROUGH PURIFICATION

What is special about being a German Muslim? I asked Hadi, a German convert and active member of the DMK, when we met over coffee and cookies at the organization's humble main office. What German-speaking Muslims practice is "do-it-yourself Islam," he said. "You try to acquire knowledge from totally different sources. There is no religious body and no full-fledged structure. There are no traditions you feel obliged to follow. As a result, you can decide on your own." Hadi did not think this was a bad thing. Rather, he saw it as an opportunity. "As a result, you can approach Islam more critically than you could in an Islamic country," he explained.

> In general, Germans who embrace Islam have to be more critical. They have to be able to differentiate between Islam and culture. Some people like the culture, the music, the people, the style, and take the religion along with it. But most converts try to differentiate between what is Islamic and what is traditional. Also some rules that are taken for granted in Turkey may not fit in Germany. Then converts raise the question of why I have to do things this way, and see if it really has an Islamic basis. Because converts have no roots in any Islamic tradition, they can practice an Islam that is purified of traditions.

All Muslim residents of Germany or any non-Muslim country for that matter have to struggle with the challenge of adapting Islam—or more precisely, a Muslim lifestyle—to the local living conditions. Converts are, of course, those most invested in this project. The dominant approach, especially among them, is to strip Islam of its cultural baggage so as to make it fit a German/European lifestyle.

A lecture at the DMK by Imam Muhammad Salama of the Wolfsburg Islamic Center titled "Islam in Europe—European Islam?" explored the issue of experiencing Islam in Europe as European Muslims. It was attended by over forty members—mostly German converts. The concerns raised by the lecture were discussed intensely over five hours on the first day of spring, a Sunday, after a long winter.

The lecture began with a look at whether we can talk about a European Islam or not. Salama, whose background is Arab, made his position clear by making extensive references to the Swiss Muslim Tariq Ramadan, who promotes the view that one can be a good Muslim and good European through a rereading of the foundational texts of the Qur'an in their European context. According to Ramadan (1999, 2004), it is the cultural traditions that immigrant Muslims bring to Europe and not Islam that gets in the way of their being engaged European citizens. Like Ramadan, Salama saw the European experience of Islam as an opportunity for Muslims in general to free themselves of detrimental accretions and accept the best aspects of Islam, which lie in its foundations.

A good portion of the participants were favorable to Ramadan's approach, and when Salama asked if they had either read his work or attended his recent talk in Berlin, most raised their hands.[12] In this interactive lecture, most participants shared the opinion that a part of what we commonly call religion is culture, and that we can talk about an Arab, Indonesian, or Chinese Islam. They agreed that this conversation opened the doors for speaking about a European or German Islam—but what exactly that meant was not clear to anyone present. A number of participants raised their hands to warn that the term European Islam is usually used to promote a "liberal" Islam stripped of its essential features. A middle-aged German male listener raised his hand to observe that

> there is a difference between saying Islam in Europe or European Islam. When people promote the second, they usually mean a relaxed approach to religion— for example, one where the headscarf is not necessary. An Islam that is open to prostitution or gambling. That is why when I see the words European Islam, my stomach turns. As for myself, I want to say first I am a Muslim and then I am a German. When I say European Islam, I have the sense that it prioritizes the nationality rather than the religion.

Salama suggested that one could talk about an Islam that is influenced by European traditions. For instance, he said, "Arabs bring their own character traits to Islam. But because Europeans have calmer personalities, that will inevitably influence the way they live Islam. Experiences since the French Revolution will of course have an influence on Islam." He added, "God willing, the Islamic developments here are positive influences. For example, in the Middle East men have a patriarchal culture. But as Middle Eastern immigrants eventually become European Muslims, such traditions that are not part of Islam will be left behind. And we will be able to experience an Islam that is truer to itself."

At this point, the conference took a break for the noon prayer and lunch. During the lunch break, women in smaller groups continued discussing what it means to be a European Muslim. A German Muslim woman said, "We also need to question the concept of a European tradition to begin with. Now there is this big talk about Judeo-Christian tradition, and the Jews approach this discourse skeptically. Maybe there is no one big European tradition we need to adhere to. Maybe it already consists of many different segments. Then Islam is definitely one part of Europe." Another German convert to Islam brought a more concrete illustration to the conversation:

> I don't think our lifestyle as German Muslims is entirely different from all other Germans. My mother, for example, is not a Muslim, but her life is not so different from mine. Once in a while she drinks beer, but I cannot see anything that is really different between her life and my life. It is wrong to think that all Germans are always dancing away at a disco or that they are all gamblers. So maybe we Muslims are not all that different after all.

When the conference reconvened, Salama wanted to talk about the specific everyday challenges Muslims face in Germany and the solutions they can find. The problems that listeners listed consisted of a life that does not always respect the prayer times, employers who do not allow them to wear a headscarf, working situations that might require a man and woman to be alone together in a room, and having to be in social contexts where alcohol is consumed. In terms of finding solutions, the imam recommended that everyone decide for themselves and make a choice that allows them to feel comfortable facing God. "Only the person can decide on their own whether they have exhausted all the possible options or not," he said. "Religion isn't like mathematics; there are no firm answers valid for everyone and every situation."

This individualized solution-finding approach made some of the listeners uncomfortable. An older and much more vocal member of the community, who is sympathetic to the Salafi interpretation and regime in Saudi Arabia, accused the imam of giving a covert fatwa allowing for the removal of the headscarf. Salama objected, asserting that religious leaders have the responsibility to take the lives of people into consideration, and that every single individual can decide what to do on their own. He stated, "Naturally, I see the headscarf as a duty, but also as a freedom. But in the end, women can decide if they want to fulfill this duty or not. No woman should be forced to wear or take off a headscarf."

In addition to an Islam that leaves decision making to the individual, the imam also promoted the idea of tolerance. He noted that people prejudge Islam as intolerant, especially of other religions. To counter such a belief, he said, we need to be particularly careful about which translations of the Qur'an we use. Salama recommended to the audience that they use the German Jewish convert Weiss/Asad's translation, and try to focus on pieces of the text that emphasize tolerance and openness. "In three places in the Qur'an it says that those who believe in God—here meaning Jews and Christians—will also be rewarded after death. But then," the imam remarked, "here we are talking about how to live together in this world. It is another thing to say things will be such and such in the other world. Every religion has its own particular approach to this matter, and we are free to say what we like."

It is not only converted Muslims who promote a European Islam stripped of seemingly patriarchal, intolerant, and undemocratic cultural traditions attributed to immigrant Muslims. There are also a good number of born Muslims who promote the idea of a purified Islam that is both truer to itself and true to the European values of equality, freedom, and democracy. These concepts are not new but instead are inspired by earlier Islamic reformers as well as Enlightenment thinkers. Some of the same ideas that were originally promoted by Asad, a European convert to Islam, are now embraced by a number of Muslims with immigrant backgrounds. Still, indigenous European and converted Muslims are much more invested in stripping Islam of its cultural and national baggage, so as to legitimate and normalize their position, not only in mainstream German society, but also in the Islamic Ummah. This perspective is Eurocentric, however, in its assumption that only "Oriental" Muslims pollute Islam with their irrational traditions, and the "Occidental" Muslims are by definition closer to a pure and true Islam because they are not burdened by cumbersome traditions.

ETHNIC-GERMAN MUSLIMS MAKING
SPACE FOR THEMSELVES

Despite their invisibility in the public discourse, German converts to Islam are represented in disproportionate numbers in public functions related to Islam. Leaders of many national Islamic organizations, spokespeople for Muslims in interreligious dialogue, writers of pro-Islamic op-ed pieces in newspapers, and researchers who lead government- or university-funded research projects on Muslims are often German converts to Islam. Even though many born and converted Muslims told me that this trend was a historical necessity when most Muslims in Germany were guest workers, and had insufficient linguistic and social skills, it does not seem to be fading away, and is possibly turning into a tradition.

Several push-pull factors can explain this phenomenon. For one thing, it is quite difficult for ambitious, well-educated, and socially and politically motivated converted Germans to occupy prominent public positions in society, especially when their conversion to Islam is well known. A good example of this is Christian Hadi Hoffmann, who joined the CDU in 1974 and rose through the party ranks to become its spokesperson. After publishing the book *Zwischen allen Stühlen: Ein Deutscher wird Muslim* (Caught in the middle: A German becomes Muslim) in 1995, in which he publicly outed himself as a convert to Islam, Hoffmann was expelled from the party.

His next step was to chair the newly established Muslimische Akademie (Muslim Academy), which aims to be a forum for intellectual discussion furthering openness in German society and reflecting the diversity of Muslim life.[13] The name of the organization makes reference to a major Protestant institution, the Evangelische Akademie (Protestant Academy), the intellectual organization of the Lutheran Evangelical Church, supported by the taxes of twenty-four million members registered with the German state.[14] The Muslim Academy lacks such resources and has no connection to mosque organizations, but it is nevertheless an important organization in that it receives public attention and its representatives are regularly invited to events to represent the Muslim voice. Hoffmann is quite a prolific author; he has written a number of books and many articles regarding the needs and demands of Muslims in Germany.

What is significant about Hoffmann's case is that when a national political party like the CDU excluded him as a convert to Islam, representing

Muslims at a national level became a possibility. Because immigrant Muslim organizations are extremely hierarchical, and based on ethnic or national membership in the community, it is not possible for a German Muslim to rise in them. Instead, a national organization like the Muslim Academy, with no real representative power, seems to be an ideal place for a convert. From such a position, German converts can speak to mainstream German society as well as immigrant Muslims—both of which exclude them.

Inssan is another national, nondenominational, nonrepresentative Islamic organization. It was established and is run mostly by converted Muslims who adhere to a much more orthodox interpretation than the Muslim Academy.[15] It is funded by a group of Muslims seeking to create an umbrella organization for Muslims who organize activities that contribute to cultural, ethnic, and religious diversity in Germany. Inssan organizes interreligious dialogue meetings and a campaign against forced marriages along with activities that contribute to developing neighborly relations between Muslims and others, and also carries out discrimination assessment and prevention training. The founders told me that because the Turkish Islamic organizations were so hierarchical, and they could not find a position for themselves in them, they had decided to establish a new organization. Inssan defines its strength as being open to dialogue with all other religious groups—an aspect that distinguishes it from immigrant Muslim organizations. It has in fact met with some resistance from those organizations, which see it as competing to represent Muslims in Germany, should Islam ever be given the status of a publicly recognized religion.

A good number of individual German converts to Islam with no leadership role or formal institutional affiliation also see themselves as being in a unique position to engage assertively with mainstream German society and publicly present Islam in a way that immigrant Muslims cannot. Iman is one such woman. She converted to Islam about twenty years ago, and is now in her forties, married to a nonobservant Egyptian man, and holds a degree in English literature. Iman feels that as an educated German Muslim who lives in a society where the Muslims are predominantly uneducated and marginalized, she has a responsibility. She is also one of the many ambitious women who, despite their university degrees, cannot achieve their career ambitions owing to their headscarves. Recently, she established the first Islamic publishing house that specializes in Islamic-themed books, especially novels.[16]

Iman believes that she has to represent Muslims and be a voice for them in this society where many Muslims cannot have their voices heard, or say the things they are supposed to. Because she can speak up for herself, for example, Iman maintains that she has to wear a headscarf. "I am not doing this just for myself but for the Ummah," she told me. Iman also thinks it is important for her to appear in public contexts with her headscarf. She regarded going to school and neighborhood meetings as her duty. "If I do not," she commented,

I can be certain that no Muslim voice will be heard, even though there are many immigrant Muslims in my neighborhood. I have to represent the Muslim position on issues such as not serving pork at the school cafeteria, about issues regarding co-ed swimming classes, etc. Sometimes nonobservant Muslims come to these meetings, and their position then represents the "Muslim" voice, which makes life much more difficult for us, practicing Muslims.

But she did not find this role an easy one, mainly because she feels that many people are suspicious of German Muslims. She explained to me that most people put distance between themselves and her, thinking she might be a radical. Despite her enthusiastic efforts at her children's school, it took her a long time to be accepted. She noticed that the teachers were quite at ease with other parents, talking to them comfortably, making jokes. Yet when it came to Iman, they would be distant and stiff. She said at the beginning, the simplest conversation topics with the teachers felt like fights rather than parent–teacher exchanges. Knowing Iman's pleasant, thoughtful, joyous personality, I found this hard to imagine. After several years of being involved with the same teachers, Iman says that they now regard her as a normal parent, if not their favorite one.

Just as Iman feels responsible for informing and educating mainstream society about Islam, she feels a responsibility for educating the traditional Muslim community. She believes as an educated Muslim, she knows what is acceptable in Islam better than many immigrant Muslims. Iman makes a point of showing that Muslim women can take active roles. At Islamic events, for instance, she will be the first to mention patriarchal tendencies that are not Islamic. I heard her repeatedly criticize Muslim men publicly for unnecessarily avoiding Muslim women at mosque events. In 2011, Iman took a role in organizing the International Women's Day celebrations at the DMK mosque. The organizing committee prepared posters depicting the stories of Muslim women through the ages who played an active role in society. In a later conversation, Iman told me that the aim was twofold. The committee wanted both mainstream society and Muslim men to see the vital contributions women were making to the Muslim community. "Many traditional brothers," she contended, "do not understand that this is possible. Many of their beliefs come from patriarchal traditions and not from Islam. And we need to show this to them."

Interfaith dialogue is another area where the responsibility for representing Muslims falls on the shoulders of converted Muslims. The overwhelming majority of Muslims who take active roles in interfaith dialogue are converted ones. Most organizations founded or heavily attended by converted Muslims, such as Inssan, the Muslim Academy, and the Islamic Society of German Muslims and Their Friends, build into their missions the function of engaging in dialogue with other groups.[17] What I found most ironic when

I attended interreligious dialogue meetings was that not only the Christians but also the Jews, Buddhists, and Hindus would all be ethnic Germans, converts to their respective religions. So even though religious plurality is an effect of immigration, in interfaith conversations only ethnic Germans would be represented. "Converts to Islam, especially if they come from a Christian background, are of course better candidates for dialogue," my friend Samantha, who grew up in an observant Christian family, informed me. People who were born Muslims are often quite ignorant about Christianity, she said. Many believe that Christianity is polytheistic, that it has three separate gods. But converts from Christianity are in a good position to lead a serious discussion because they are better informed about Christianity and atheism, and know what mainstream Germans find less or more appealing about the Islamic message. That way, converts become the ones who come face to face with the non-Muslim mainstream society when they want to learn about Islam.

What I observed in Iman and also many other individual German converts to Islam is not only a feeling of deep responsibility but a uniquely assertive stance too. This is most likely so because German Muslims who converted to Islam as adults never internalized the second-class position they are surprised to find themselves in. Consider the following anecdote shared at a DMK breakfast by a relatively new convert. Aadila had just returned from a trip to Switzerland to visit a non-Muslim friend. Her friend took Aadila to an expensive restaurant. When the waiter approached them to take their orders, Aadila asked, "Can you please tell me what is halal on this menu?" When the waiter looked puzzled, her friend tried to save face by inquiring, "How is this guy supposed to know what halal is?" Aadila replied, self-assured, "Well, if he doesn't know what it means, he can very well look it up in the dictionary, can't he?" After disappearing for a good fifteen minutes, the waiter came back and politely said that he recommended the fish dish.

Obviously, Aadila already knew that no other meat item on the menu would be halal. She nonetheless took the opportunity to assert her difference and also educate the waiter at this expensive Swiss restaurant, most likely not usually attended by practicing Muslims. Aadila thought that what she did was funny as well: she was laughing out loud as she relayed the story to other converted women. Everyone found the story amusing, and several others shared similar tales of frustration while eating out and what they felt to be pointless efforts at educating food servers ignorant of halal rules.

I admired Aadila's approach, but also was astounded by her tale and had a strong feeling that no Muslim with an immigrant background would dare to challenge a non-Muslim waiter like that. I shared this story with many immigrant Muslim friends, including those with university degrees and good positions, and asked them if doing something like this would ever occur to them. Most found the story amusing, yet told me that they would never expect a non-Muslim waiter to know about halal food or imagine challenging one in that way. They told me that they would either not go to restaurants where they know the meat will not be halal or just simply order the fish, but never make a fuss like that.

There are many occasions when converted Germans step forward before born Muslims in order to defend Islam and Muslims. Writing letters to newspapers objecting to anti-Islamic statements and sentiments is one such area. If you look closely at the names of the people who submit op-ed pieces that correct misconceptions, indicate the unfair treatment of Muslims, or compare Islam with Christianity, you notice that the writers often have classic Muslim middle names along with German first and last names. Wiebke (Chadijah) Schutt, a typical example with an acquired Muslim middle name, wrote a letter to the daily *Die Welt Kompakt* on March 2, 2007, to complain about the common misinterpretation of the word jihad as a primarily religious war.[18] One can suggest several reasons why converted Muslims are more active in writing letters to the editor than born Muslims. First, converted Muslims follow the mainstream discourses better than born practicing Muslims. Having limited access to education and not feeling part of the mainstream society hinders immigrant Muslims from developing an interest in discussions in the popular editorial pages of newspapers where public commentators explore social issues in depth. Second, because they feel part of mainstream society, converted Muslims are more motivated to intervene in such public conversations and believe that they can play a role in correcting the image of Islam in the country. They take these opportunities to defend Islam and its conformity to the German value system.

Such differences in assertiveness also come up when more is at stake. For example, converted Muslims are more inclined than born Muslims to ask for their legal rights, such as "women-only" pool times and gyms, halal food options in school cafeterias, and the right to work with headscarves. Similarly, in a recent case about a student who was banned from praying in the school outside class time in 2007, it was the converted Muslim father of the student who took the issue to the court versus keeping it quiet.[19]

Immigrant Muslims, and especially practicing ones, resort to such forceful measures less frequently, in my view, because they already feel marginalized and alienated. They expect so little of mainstream society that they usually do not experience injustice as something that can be changed or fixed. The experiences of a team that conducted awareness-raising seminars in mosques attest to this powerfully. During a training against Islamophobia, Anti-Semitism, and Xenophobia presentation, Lydia Nofal, the chair of Inssan and a convert to Islam, described their experiences this way: "When we go to mosques and ask them if they feel discriminated against in society, they often say no, we are not. And then when we tell them how discrimination works, they say, oh, if you mean *that*, of course, it happens to us all the time!" Safter Çınar, the leader of the Turkish Union in Berlin, made similar comments during our discussion regarding his organization's antidiscrimination efforts. He told me that immigrants are extremely afraid of standing up against injustices that happen to them. "When we work with students and parents, they tell us many stories of obvious discrimination. But when we ask these parents to work with us so that we can sue these teachers and schools, they are all afraid. They say we do not want to get ourselves into trouble with the teachers."

Converts are more confident in asking for their rights, not only in mainstream society, but in the Muslim community as well. Converted Muslim women are overall more inclined to go to mosques than born Muslims. And in order to do that, they are ready to challenge some of the common assumptions among born Muslims that the mosque is primarily a male space.[20] Granted, converted Muslims are in greater need of such spaces to learn about Islam and also meet like-minded people. Some Islamic legal schools, such as Hanafism, to which the overwhelming majority of Muslims in Germany subscribe, discourage women from going to the mosque to pray. In most Muslim lands, mosques are more male spaces than female ones. German women Muslims are more assertive than their Muslim-born sisters in contesting the male domination of mosques. Thus, unsurprisingly, the DMK is the only mosque in Germany that has more female lay and board members than male ones, and where most activities attract a larger female than male presence. In a Saturday lecture for women at the DMK, a converted woman encouraged listeners to be creative in finding ways to claim access to mosques. "You may belong to one or another legal school. But it is important to know that the Maliki school encourages women to go to the mosque," she said. "All four legal schools are equally valid, and hence coming to the mosque is our valid right that no one can deny us." "Sometimes," she added, "we need to be more creative and look through different interpretations in order to find out about our rights as Muslim women."

German converts do look for and find textual evidence to support their claim to mosque attendance, and do not hold themselves back from challenging male authorities in order to hold on to their positions. Such debates are common in the Salafi-oriented al-Nur mosque. During one of the lectures for new Muslim women that I attended, a male imam was explaining the significance of and rules regarding daily prayers. He remarked that praying in congregation is regarded as twenty-seven times better than praying alone. After making this point, he added, "But it is better for women to say their prayers at home."

The newly converted women listening to the lectures and taking meticulous notes looked puzzled by his statement. Hannah, who has been active in the mosque for a long time, was quick to comment, asking, "But isn't it a requirement for us to acquire Islamic knowledge? How can we fulfill this duty if we do not come to the mosque?" Before the imam could answer, another young woman jumped in and said, "Besides, you have just told us that it is twenty-seven times better to pray collectively. So why do you say that it is better for us to stay at home and pray alone?" The imam was scratching his beard and smiling affectionately as his students questioned him. When everyone had finished, he replied,

> There are different ways to fulfill Islamic requirements. For example, think about a woman who did everything right, came to the mosque regularly, and said all her prayers collectively, but was not nice to her husband. This is not a good thing. And imagine there was another woman who prayed less, but she had a lot of belief in her heart and was nice to her husband. It is possible that the second one would go to heaven and maybe the first one would not.

He also added that in some mosques, there is no separate place for women to pray. It is better for a woman to pray at home than go to a mosque where there is no designated place for her. "But," he assured his unsettled students, "we do not have such a problem in our mosque. Inshallah, God willing, it is alright for you to come here and perform all of your prayers collectively if you want to."

Many well-educated converted friends underscored the importance of educating oneself in Islamic texts so as not to be subject to patriarchy or other Islamically unfounded practices favored by traditional Muslim communities. My friend Samantha believes that Islam is actually quite flexible on many matters, including gender. If you read the texts closely, she told me, you get a different picture compared to what is often believed. For instance, she said, in the Qur'an men and women are defined as *wali*, meaning friend and companion, to each other. She suggested that it is frequently the view you yourself hold that determines what you get out of a text. "In reality there are many more possibilities available than are reflected in traditional interpretations. So it is important to rely on the text rather than the traditional communities that interpret it." A good number of German Muslims take classes on traditional Islam to learn how to interpret texts and not have to rely on immigrant Muslim leaders who interpret things according to the national traditions they were socialized into.

Despite their conflicts with immigrant Muslims at the mosque, well-educated converts to Islam take an active role in educating the mainstream public about Islam and putting a new face on it. The new face of Islam they strive to present is well educated, well informed about Islamic and German values, and ethnically German, plus speaks flawless German. Converted friends told me that they feel responsible for the way they represent Islam every day. They make an effort to dress respectably, not jaywalk, be polite and helpful, hold jobs, and not receive welfare from the state. Confronted by the challenge of being associated with the most stigmatized groups in the country, new Muslims try to both educate mainstream society about Islam and transform the immigrant community into better Muslims, and hence better Germans.

RAISING CHILDREN AS GERMAN AND MUSLIM

The complexities of being German and Muslim along with the converts' desire to bring these identities together are strongly reflected in how they raise their children. Many German Muslims I met spent most of their emotional and intellectual energy raising their children to feel comfortable as Germans and be good Muslims. They are often frustrated, however, when teachers, neighbors, or other acquaintances accuse them of raising their children with another culture and even language. Sara, a forty-three-year-old convert who is a mother of four children, said: "For me, religion is a way, not a culture. I cannot teach my children a culture I do not know. So I teach them the German culture that I know. They sing German songs, they eat German food. I teach them what I know. Many times people ask me if I speak German to my children. Yes, I speak German because I am a German." Sara gets annoyed when people claim that she cannot raise her son properly because of her beliefs:

> My five-year-old son is a little bit naughty. At his preschool, his teachers told me that because he is being raised by Muslims, he has behavior problems. I was very angry. I told them that I am German, not an Arab, so he is not being raised by people who are different from them. Then they tell me that because his father does not respect women's rights, my son does not learn how to respect me, and that is why he does not listen to me or his other women teachers! I get furious when I hear such accusations. I am an educated woman and I am German. They always think I am a stupid immigrant. That makes me very angry. And what they say is not true at all. My husband always tells my children that they should respect their mother, that they should not make me upset. That is the most important thing, he keeps telling them. Plus, my other children had a very easy time at school. It is just my son's personality; he is a little bit hyperactive. It is not a religious or cultural issue.

The issue of raising German Muslim children is frequently discussed in the DMK. Amina, who gives weekly Saturday lectures to women and works at an Islamic preschool, reminded everyone one Saturday afternoon of the difficulties they face as German Muslim mothers. "Our children are in a different position than children who grow up in Muslim majority countries," she said. "In such places, the fact that God exists and he is all powerful is an unquestioned reality of life. The questions our children ask us here, like if God is really big, where he sits, whether he eats or drinks, are questions asked to us because we live in a non-Muslim country." Amina added: "And that is why we have to be especially clear about the answers we give to our children. More important, we have to be very clear about these answers in our mind before we talk about them, so that we can pass this clarity to our children. We have to be especially good role models if we want to raise them as good Muslims in this non-Muslim society."

All Muslims who live in Germany confront the same challenge of raising their children in a Muslim-minority land. But converts to Islam have other hurdles too. For example, they need to negotiate the ways their non-Muslim parents relate to their children without questioning their beliefs. They also need to invent traditions for their German children in celebrating Muslim holidays. Jolanda, who is accepted as a Muslim by her German family, started to feel some tension building up after she had children. Her parents wanted her to join them along with her other siblings, nieces, and nephews for Christmas. She decided that she did not want to miss the opportunity of being part of a nice family gathering. Her compromise was to go there for Christmas dinner, but not for the service at the church. Jolanda also told her mother that they would not be there when Santa Claus came to bring children gifts. When her son reached the age of four, though, she realized how upset he would be when all the children but him received nice gifts. In the end, she and her mother reached the agreement that for Christmas, Jolanda's son, Ibrahim, would receive a small gift from his grandparents so that he would not feel left out. Jolanda's mother agreed to give him a big gift on Islamic holidays.

As her kids began to grow, Jolanda discovered that negotiating Christmas was not the only problem for a German Muslim mother; she had to figure out how to celebrate the Islamic holidays as well. She told me that she would not mind if her Algerian husband took the initiative and organized an Algerian-style celebration for the family, but he did not seem too invested in that. Jolanda explained that she realized that many of the things they do for holidays in Algeria did not make sense in the German context anyway. During Eid, for instance, Algerian children receive a set of new clothes. "But," she told me, "I felt as though this would be too little for my son. He gets new clothes all the time! So I had to buy him something more significant, something like a train set."

Jolanda then found the solution in bringing what she once did to celebrate German holidays into her Islamic practice. For Ramadan, say, she prepares a calendar for her son just like the advent calendar that is popular among Christian Germans. She told me that she made one herself, with a small gift for every day, so Ibrahim could open it up and find a surprise. She decorated her Ramadan calendar with moons, camels, and minarets, instead of the snowflakes and Santa Clauses that embellish advent calendars. Jolanda does not believe that she has to give up everything. She is a German, and can only celebrate her Islamic holidays in the German way.

It gave Jolanda great comfort to send her son to an Islamic preschool run by converted women and attended mostly by children of converts. These preschools are not openly Islamic. Rather they are registered as bilingual: Arabic and German or Turkish and German. Even though there are many Protestant, Catholic, and even a Jewish preschool in Berlin, Islamic preschools are not allowed, because Islam does not have the status of a publicly recognized religion. Because there are many more converts married to Arabs than to Turks, and because Arabic is the holy language of Islam, converts and their children are commonly found in Arabic German schools and not so much in Turkish German schools. In these preschools, converted German women are active as both parents and teachers.

I visited one such preschool in Wedding several times, and interviewed a converted German teacher about her philosophy in educating children as German and Muslim. Ayat told me that many of their aims are no different from those of other German preschools: they want to have children who can follow the rules, are able to establish social contact, can understand if someone needs help, and so on. In terms of identity, she continued, their aim is for children to recognize themselves as Muslim Berliners regardless of the background of their families. Ayat thinks it is crucial that the children see themselves and their future in Berlin as opposed to being fixated on the background of their parents, be it Arab or German. This sentiment resonates well with a recent survey conducted among Muslims living in the Kreuzberg neighborhood of Berlin (Mühe 2010). Muslim Kreuzbergers did not see themselves as German but instead felt themselves to be Berliners, and were especially emotionally attached to their neighborhood. This survey was quoted in the newspaper as a failure, since most immigrant families did not feel themselves to be German. Along with a few others, I nevertheless saw it as a positive indicator that most people I interviewed felt attached to their city and particularly their neighborhood. This Islamic preschool in Wedding also wanted to foster this sense for a new generation of Muslims without making any reference to the thorny issue of ethnic identity.

As a teacher, Ayat explained, she wanted the children at the school to have an idea about why they do things as Muslims. "For example," she said, "we say a prayer before dinner." She did not find it essential if the children made fun of praying or any other Islamic practice. "Children cannot sin," she told me. "But when I ask them why they think they pray, I want them to have some answer as to why they are praying to God. That is what is important at this stage. As a principle," she told me, "we motivate them positively, and never scare them by saying if you do so and so you will go to hell." What was most critical, in her view, was that the children see people living their religion naturally. "They see that their teacher wears a headscarf and that during the flow of the day she prays. During prayers, the children stay quiet, and older kids take responsibility for that short period of time. They observe Islam as a normal thing, as a part of the flow of the day."

Ayat believes that Islamic preschools fulfill a key function, not only for Muslim children, but also for the mainstream society. It is important to her that they take Muslim children on field trips to visit places such as museums, art exhibits, theaters, concerts, and so forth, as is common with other Berlin preschools. The difference is that the teachers wear headscarves. Ayat mentioned that they get noticed quickly, especially when they are at places that are not usually frequented by Muslims. She thinks it is essential for both mainstream society and the Muslim children to realize that Muslims have a natural place in all parts of the city, that Muslims go everywhere and enjoy art, history, music, and architecture like all other Germans. They realize that Muslims do not need to be confined to certain neighborhoods, certain parks, and their homes. These kinds of gestures seem daring to born Muslims, or most likely never occur to them, because they grow up interiorizing their exclusion from the mainstream society. Converted Muslims, who experience this self-inflicted and externally imposed exclusion at a later stage in their lives, are most invested in changing the landscape and going beyond the segregation of Muslims from mainstream German society.

In my research, I observed that the children of the most active converts turned out to be the most devotedly practicing as well as most active members of German-speaking youth organizations such as the DMK or Muslim Youth. They would participate in activities that are common for mainstream German youths, such as camping trips, sports activities, and outings in the city, but in ways appropriate to orthodox definitions of Islam, such as gender segregation, halal food, and allotted times for prayers. These groups are often ethnically better mixed than most Islamic groups, which frequently cluster around one ethnic group. Children of converts are often ethnically mixed. When I asked teenage children of converted Germans if ethnic background was an issue in their groups, they repeatedly replied that it never comes up. The generation now growing up unambiguously German and Muslim will most likely be able to go beyond the dichotomy of German and Muslim.

CONCLUSION

Many experiences of converted German Muslims are similar to those of immigrant Muslims in Germany. They need to live their lives and fulfill their Islamic obligations in a society not organized for it, and face resistance when they demand the right to do so. Both converted and born Muslims live in a society where Islam and especially headscarves are seen as a symbol of an inherently foreign culture as well as a mark of oppression. Despite these commonalities, many experiences are unique to converted German Muslims. When they convert, they have to deal with a dramatic loss of status in society—something for which they were not prepared. Born Muslims grew up learning the limits that society set for them. Even if they struggle against and challenge them, the marginalization they experience is a routine phenomenon. After being marginalized in the mainstream society to which they once unproblematically belonged, German Muslims face another unwelcome surprise when they realize that they do not fit in or not are welcomed by the existing Muslim communities in Germany, predominantly made up of Turkish and Arab communities that constitute the poorest, least educated segments of German society.

German converts to Islam resist their exclusion from the German national body and their dramatic fall in the symbolic social system by defending an Islam that is culturally compatible with Germanness. Like the African Americans that DuBois discusses, German converts to Islam develop a double consciousness, a peculiar sensation about being Muslim in Europe. In their efforts to easily and simply be both German and Muslim, they find themselves in a position to play a double role in transforming both mainstream German society and the immigrant-majority Muslim community. To Germans, they try to convey the message that there is a place for Islam in Germany, both historically and culturally. They remind them that the most prized intellectuals of Germany history were tolerant of and open-minded about Islam. They try to be model Muslims who do not carry the immigrant Muslims' stigmas and hence put a better face on Islam for German society. Then they turn to Muslim communities to show them what they consider their mistakes as well as encourage them to purify their lives of their un-Islamic and detrimental traditions. German converts to Islam demonstrate that being a German Muslim involves embodying the very best qualities of both German society and the Islamic community.

Many ideas that German Muslims promote to open up legitimate space for Islam in Germany are inspired by Enlightenment ideas of human reason and religion. First, they are based on the notion that fully free, unprejudiced humans (here meaning Germans) will judge for the best and be open-minded about Islam. Second, once stripped of its traditional interpretations, it will be obvious (again to Germans) that Islam is closest to the Enlightenment idea of a "natural religion," which is based on the concept that God simply reveals himself to the rational individual.[21] Needless to say, the particulars of deism are irrelevant for Muslims, yet the repeated emphasis on the naturalness and rationality of Islam are clear references to an understanding of religion seen through the lens of Enlightenment values. In the next chapter, I turn to the flip side of such an understanding to show how despite the stress on a seemingly universal human reason, in practice it has an exclusivist side. In practice, the pure German or European Islam that is being promoted comes across as best suited to the rational European mind, and unsuited to Oriental minds muddled by oppressive cultures and traditions. It thus often ends up being Europeanist and Eurocentrist.

Chapter 2

ESTABLISHING DISTANCE FROM IMMIGRANT MUSLIMS

One evening, Aarika and her mother invited me to dinner at the house they share in Potsdam, a town just outside Berlin, in what used to be East Germany. Aarika is an independent, successful, attractive woman in her forties. No one who saw her would be surprised to hear that she was a fashion model in East Berlin in her twenties. Currently she is the manager of the Berlin branch of an expensive Italian fashion store. After having grown up in a typically atheist East German family, she learned about Islam a few years ago during a trip to Egypt. She also met her current husband, Hasan, on that trip; he was working as a DJ in the hotel where Aarika was staying. Even though Hasan does not practice Islam, knowing him and other people in Egypt was an opportunity for Aarika to learn about the religion. She told me that what startled her the most about Egyptians was how generous and content they were, even though they had so little compared to her. After reading about Islam for a year or so on her own, she slowly adopted Islamic practices such as not eating pork, not drinking alcohol, fasting, and praying. Eventually she converted in a little mosque in Berlin. Her husband learned about Aarika's conversion when she wanted to have an Islamic marriage with him, and he was quite shocked. Because Aarika does not want to lose her well-paying position, she continues to live in Berlin and visits her husband four times a year in Egypt. When she does, she rents an apartment for them to stay in, since her husband shares a room with several other coworkers in the hotel where he is employed. Her husband is not interested in coming to Berlin, she explained to me. So Aarika continues to live in the same building as her mother, but in a separate apartment. Aarika defends her independent position as perfectly Islamic.

At the dinner, the conversation quickly came around to the topic of Muslims. I could see that although Aarika's mother was tolerant of her daughter's new religion, as long Aarika did not cover her hair, she was not particularly fond of Muslims. She especially did not want to have anything to do with Turks, who she had learned about since the fall of the Berlin Wall. When she discovered that I was from Turkey, Aarika's mother started to tell me story after story about how horrible Turks are. She complained that Turkish women always walk behind their husbands, never talk to Germans even when they ask for directions or the time, have too many children, and use their sharp elbows to push you out of the way in the subway or a store. When I turned to Aarika for help with the difficult situation I found myself in as a guest, I was surprised to see my friend nodding enthusiastically and not defending Turks. Then she said to me, "I always tell her that these are traditions, and if these people were to educate themselves better as Muslims, they would know that they shouldn't behave like that. If, for example, they had read the traditions of the Prophet Muhammad, they would know that it is their duty to smile at everyone, even at those who are strangers, and that they should be nice to them." Like the many other Muslim converts (chapter 1), or born Muslims who are part of Islamic reform movements in Europe and elsewhere (chapter 4), Aarika believes that many Muslim practices have little to do with Islam, but are products of local cultures and need to be left behind.

For more than a century, Muslims around the world have eagerly engaged in reform movements that aspire to a true Islam uncontaminated by cultural accretions. They interact with Islamic texts to purge their beliefs and practices of cultural distortions, and "authenticate" them (Deeb 2006).

A close look at the way in which converted German Muslims participate in this discourse shows, however, that even though they are similar to Muslims around the world in their focus on a "true" Islam, the political implications of this move differ dramatically between Muslims in Muslim-majority countries and Muslims in Europe. And the difference is even greater when it comes to converted Muslims of indigenous European background. In most Muslim-majority countries, practicing allegedly true or authenticated Islam differentiates Islamic revivalists from their parents along with what they see as their traditional practices (Göle 1997; Mahmood 2004; Deeb 2006). In Europe, the same practice differentiates Muslims with immigrant backgrounds from their ancestral countries. Europeanist Muslims such as Ramadan see the practice of turning to the true sources of Islam as a way to connect immigrant Muslims to Europe. He argues that just as Muslims in different parts of the world, such as Indonesia, Africa, or India, adopted Islam and molded it to their own cultures, European Muslims need to do the same. According to him, the end result will be the creation of a "European and American Islamic culture [that is] both respectful of the universal principles [of Islam] and sustained by the history, traditions, tastes, and styles of various Western countries" (Ramadan 2004, 216).

When converted German Muslims seek to practice a so-called true Islam stripped of cultural accretions, it has significantly different political implications. In its indigenous German Muslim context, an Islam free of culture means an Islam that has been purged of its often-stigmatized Arab and Turkish cultural practices. Once rectified like this, the reasoning goes, Islam will be more in line not only with its original spirit but also with European ideals of democracy, freedom, and tolerance. In that way, a purified Islam, in the German context, becomes an effort to connect German converts to their parents rather than differentiate them. This process sets apart immigrant Muslims, who are delineated by their traditional and hence by definition "wrong" Islamic practices. This kind of packaging of Islam might open up a space for ethnically German Muslims in the German national body, yet it confirms the suspicions of mainstream society that Islam immigrant Muslims live according to their national or ethnic traditions.

CHOOSING NON-MUSLIM NEIGHBORHOODS

One determining factor in a convert's decision to affiliate or disaffiliate with immigrant Muslims is the location of one's residence. Although many German Muslims choose to live in immigrant Muslim neighborhoods, especially if they are married to an immigrant Muslim, others make a clear decision to live outside these neighborhoods. Berlin houses a large number of people with immigrant backgrounds, around two hundred thousand of them from Muslim-majority countries, and is an ethnically segregated city. Areas such as Neukölln, Wedding, and Kreuzberg have significant Muslim populations. Other parts of the city, particularly those located on what used to be the other side of the Berlin Wall, like Pankow, did not receive guest workers from Turkey in the 1970s and are still occupied mainly by ethnic Germans.[1] "White" postsocialist immigrants from eastern Europe and Russia prefer these areas. Both for historical reasons and because many of these areas are strongholds of neo-Nazi groups, few immigrant Muslims choose to live in these neighborhoods.[2]

As a former resident of East Germany, my German Muslim friend Ada continued living in Pankow after she converted. Pankow is one of the least immigrant-friendly neighborhoods, boasting a vociferous "citizen" campaign to block the construction of an Ahmadi mosque, and with established no-go zones declared and controlled by neo-Nazis. It is not uncommon for darker-skinned people to be beaten up and harassed in these areas. Ada told me that she chose this neighborhood because it is quiet, safe, and clean, and has big green parks where she can take her four-year-old son. When she moved into her current apartment building as a single mother, she was already a Muslim, but was not wearing a headscarf. She found her neighbors quite nice and polite, keeping a friendly distance. After she began wearing a headscarf, which she wrapped tightly around her head, Ada's neighbors became distinctly unfriendly to her. During a Muslim feast, she participated in a project organized by Inssan, the Muslim organization that aims at improving dialogue between Muslims and non-Muslims. She baked cookies and left them at each neighbor's door with a note saying, "Your Muslim neighbor offers greetings on the Muslim Sacrifice Feast." The idea behind the gesture was that this would be a good opportunity for Muslims to meet their non-Muslim neighbors and teach them about their practices. In her apartment building not a single neighbor said a word of thanks to Ada, although they happily took the cookies left at their doors.

The worst incident that happened to Ada in her neighborhood was the morning she woke up to find that her car had been torched. The police never apprehended the perpetrators. Ada herself did not conclude that maybe this happened because of her Muslim lifestyle and appearance. When I asked her more questions about the incident, though, she reported that all the other cars on the street were untouched and she had never seen such a thing in her neighborhood before. When I told her what I suspected, given the high rate of neo-Nazi hate crimes in the neighborhood, she seemed a little surprised, yet admitted that it was possible.

After Ada complained to me so much about Pankow and her neighbors, I asked her why she did not move to another neighborhood, such as Neu-kölln or Kreuzberg, where it would be quite acceptable, even ordinary, to wear a headscarf, since so many Muslims reside there. She looked at me with a flash of astonishment in her eyes, given that I myself at that time was living in the chic former East Berlin neighborhood of Mitte, and replied, "Oh, I cannot live in Neukölln. That is such a dirty neighborhood! Besides, I do not want my son to grow up among immigrants."

Needless to say, Ada has real concerns. Neukölln is an immigrant ghetto occupied mainly by Turks and Arabs. It is the poorest neighborhood in Berlin, with the highest unemployment, crime, and school dropout rates in the city, which is really saying something, as Berlin is worse in these respects than most other German cities. Some Germans, who like the lively multicultural life of such neighborhoods, not to mention the low rents, and others who cannot afford to live elsewhere, choose to reside in such places when they are in their twenties. But when they have children and their children reach school age, they move to another neighborhood, causing the schools in these areas to be segregated. Actually, as soon as they can afford it, many upwardly mobile immigrant families also move out of these neigh-borhoods in order to send their children to schools with German children, so that they can have a better education and keep out of trouble. For Ada, it is important not to identify and mix with immigrant Muslims, especially poor and marginalized ones. She aspires to be an educated, upwardly mobile Muslim, notwithstanding that she finds it difficult to attain this status as a single mother.

Some ethnic Germans, particularly those whose spouses were born Muslim, choose to live in immigrant-majority, low-income neighborhoods. Some feel at home in these neighborhoods, while others do not enjoy the experience. Miles, who converted to Shiʻi Islam thirty years ago when he was nineteen, is one such person. He and his Turkish German wife had moved to Neukölln. When I met him, his wife had taken him to divorce court and was suing for custody of their only child. No doubt this turn of events contributed to his bitterness toward immigrant Muslims living in the area. He told me about his experience in the neighborhood in the following words:

> At first I thought Turkish parents educated their children in an Islamic way. But after living here, I wonder which trash can they come out of. They are dirty, ugly, and disgusting. I said this to my wife, but she wanted a big flat, so we moved to Neukölln. I asked her, "Look, who is urinating on our door? Not the German junkies but Turks." They recently put a girl in a trash can and set it on fire. Jahiliya [pre-Islamic ignorance] is the biggest enemy of Muslims living here. They only care about their own bellies.

Like other converts, Miles sees Muslim ignorance of their own religion as the main cause of their current lower status in society.

Sufi-oriented German Muslims mostly socialize with other native German Muslims and keep their distance from immigrant Muslims. The Weimar Community in Potsdam was the one Muslim group I met during my research that made the most explicit effort to distinguish itself from immigrant Muslims in Berlin. It is made up of Murabituns, a sect first established in Morocco in the late 1960s, which then spread through its converts to Christian-majority countries, including the United Kingdom, the United States, Spain, Denmark, Germany, South Africa, and South American nations. The group lives communally and emphasizes a social welfare system, including collection and redistribution of the Islamic tax, zakat. By choosing to locate in Potsdam, a charming, practically immigrant-free tourist town of Prussian palaces, the community was also deciding to isolate itself from immigrant Muslims by picking this eastern German location.[3] I participated in several events at the group's beautiful meetinghouse on Sunday mornings. These meetings were advertised in the German-only newspaper published by the group, *Islamische Zeitung* (Islamic Journal), inviting people to meet German Muslims. I noticed that the only foreigners were from Spain, the United Kingdom, and the United States, where there are branches of Murabituns.

The group organizes quarterly art fairs, partly as a way to proselytize. At first sight, members of the group look like hippies. The women wear long, loose, colorful skirts coupled with colorful headscarves wrapped in a way that leaves their ears and necks exposed—quite unlike immigrant Muslim women in Germany. At their art fairs, the group also has stands displaying batik clothes. Its members play Indian music. For non-Muslim Germans with stereotypical views of how Muslims look, these Muslims probably appear more like members of an Indian-inspired new age movement than like Muslims from the Middle East. The Murabituns I talked to explained to me that because they are Germans, it is much easier for them to reach out to non-Muslim Germans and tell them about Islam.

It became clear to me that Murabituns find it quite important to differentiate themselves from immigrant Muslims. While describing the effectiveness of the quarterly market they organized, a member of the group told me how they try to teach people about true Islam at the fair. "For example," he said, "we do not charge artists for the stalls. . . . The Prophet Muhammad said the giving hand is always stronger than the receiving hand. We should learn to practice this as Muslims. . . . We are not like those immigrant Muslims here who are always begging from the state without contributing anything to this society—always saying, 'Gimme! Gimme! Gimme!'" I was astounded that an openly anticapitalist Muslim would have such a negative view of his impoverished religious brothers. I inquired, "But these are the poorest and most marginalized people in society. What can they give?" He replied, "Well, if they do not have money, they can at least give you a smile, and they will not even do that." To my initial surprise, this Maribitun Muslim's perspective on immigrant Muslims was not much different from those of my friend Aarika's mother, who also lived in Potsdam. Later I would see that such negative views of immigrant Muslims, specifically Turkish immigrant Muslims, are not uncommon among German Muslims.

NOT LOOKING LIKE A TURKISH WOMAN

Many German convert women I met were more concerned about not looking like or being taken for a Turkish woman than about living in the same neighborhood with them. Some time after converting to Islam, many women develop the desire and inner strength to wear a headscarf. I was told over and over that when they did so, they were most afraid of and annoyed by being mistaken for Turkish women. As such, many came up with solutions that would prevent them from looking Turkish. One simple solution is to adopt the head-covering style of Arab women, who are much higher in the ethnic hierarchy in Berlin because of the different conditions under which Turks and Arabs came to Germany. Whereas the majority of Turkish immigrants arrived as uneducated guest workers in the 1960s, a high proportion of Arabs from more privileged backgrounds come to Germany for a university education. Turkish women in Turkey and Berlin wear shiny, colorful headscarves wrapped tightly around the head, and the part above the forehead is raised. Although this way of wrapping the head-scarf has been quite a fashion and political statement in Turkey for the past two decades, demonstrating that one can be Muslim and modern (Göle 1997), converts to Islam in Germany find this style unacceptable. Most new German Muslims preferred the Arab style of wearing a bonnet inside and wrapping their headscarf freely around it in a way that reveals the bonnet on the forehead. I noticed that young Turkish women who socialize in German-speaking Islamic settings also adopt this style as opposed to that of their mothers. Needless to say, this subtle difference was not discernible to the uneducated eyes of the non-Muslim Germans but rather was more of a code to be read by stylish Muslim women.

One style of head covering that is desirable to many Germans is the African one, where the scarf is wrapped around the head so as to leave the neck and sometimes part of the ears exposed. The Murabitun women, as mentioned, cover their hair in this manner. For my friend Ulrike, changing from the Arab style of head covering to the African style was what made her conversion to Islam acceptable to her parents. Ulrike converted to Islam at seventeen after she met the Moroccan-born man who would become her husband. But it took her ten years to subscribe to the headscarf. She described to me how she had come to embrace the African style as a result of conflict with her parents:

> After I started wearing the hijab, I went to my parents' house. I had told my mother about this change, but my father didn't know. Outraged, he said: "What's this? You look like a Turkish woman." And I said in despair, "No, I don't look like a Turkish woman. This is the Arab style!" We argued for weeks. He even accused me of belonging to Al-Qaeda. A few weeks later I went to my parents' home again for my father's birthday, with my hijab, of course. He said to his friends, "This lady sitting on the sofa is my daughter, although she doesn't look like it. She looks more like a Turk than a German." Later my aunt walked up to me and said, "Ulrike, did you forget to unwrap this thing from your head?" It was not a pleasant party. A few months later it was my birthday. I was crying in my room at my parents' house. My mom came in and said, "Guests are here, and I don't want another argument. Do you really have to wear this thing?" At that moment I felt a little weak and I told her that I would do it like a turban, and my mom said, "That's great!" When my father saw me, he had a big smile on his face and said, "That's much better." And I decided to do it like that from then on. So now, they have gotten used to it, and it is not a problem anymore.

Now Ulrike wears her headscarf like an African wrap, with another scarf around her neck, since the African style does not hide her neck. She says she also feels comfortable this way; no one recognizes her as Muslim with this style. She enjoys sitting in upscale, all-German cafes, and even goes to the lakes during summer and swims with her entire outfit on, and she says that no one mistakes her for a Turk or treats her like a traitor who converted to Islam.

It is much easier to be a male convert to Islam in Germany today—at least sartorially speaking. Unless they wear the Arab-style long white dress and the prayer cap, no one recognizes male converts as Muslims. One German male convert to Islam said me, laughing, "My sparse blond beard does not give the same impression as the Turkish or Arab brothers' beards." These clothes and beards are not considered religiously necessary for new converts but instead seen as more festive mosque apparel. Nevertheless, when they out themselves as Muslims, converted men also have to defend their positions. They also are frustrated with immigrant Muslims, who, they believe, give Islam a bad name.

NOT SPEAKING LIKE AN IMMIGRANT MUSLIM

Amir is the son of a Lebanese father and German mother. He was raised by his Christian mother as a non-Muslim and converted to Islam several years ago. He is now married to a Polish convert to Islam. When I met them, Amir and his wife were volunteers at a mosque in Berlin run by the Turkish government, giving information about Islam to German-speaking visitors. As we sat down on the lush green carpets and began talking about the situation of Islam in Germany, the issue of reform in Islam came up. When he heard the word reform, Amir straightened his posture, made his voice louder, and told me firmly,

> We don't need reform in Islam. What we need is a reform of Muslims. It is really shameful that these Turks have been here for more than forty years, and so many of them cannot speak German. If they were good Muslims, they certainly would have read the Prophet Muhammad's traditions that say, "If you travel in a foreign country for more than fifteen days, make sure to learn its language so that you can communicate with the people there." So if these people were better Muslims, they would have mastered German and be better integrated in society.

German Muslims sometimes feel more empowered than non-Muslim Germans to criticize immigrant Muslims for the way they practice Islam or participate in German life. Miles, the bitter divorcee who suffered from living in the low-income immigrant neighborhood of Neukölln, also accused immigrant Muslims of giving Islam a bad name and inhibiting Islam's spread in Germany. He told me that before immigrant Muslims came to Germany, Islam used to have a good reputation. But now, he thinks, because immigrant Muslims and especially Turks cut themselves off from society, do not practice Islam, and are simply not good citizens, Germans hate Islam, even though converting to it themselves would benefit them so much. He said to me:

> Turks do not learn German because they do not want to be part of this society. I always tell them, "I am telling you this as a Muslim. You should learn German." There is a Turkish Shi'i mosque here, but everything is in Turkish. Leaders there tell me that lack of integration is their fault and they should give at least half of the sermons in German, but in the end they never do. And Islam never becomes accessible to Germans.

Miles's complaints about the Turkish presence in Germany are not limited to their lack of commitment to spreading Islam in the German language. He longs for a time when there were no immigrants in Germany. His critique of their presence in Germany is no different from that of right-wing racists.

> When I walk on this street, I hear Turkish, I hear Arabic. This is unfamiliar to me. I remember a time when everyone spoke German, so that is familiar to me. Now I have become a foreigner in my own country. Imagine this, if you, as someone from Turkey, went to a Turkish village and everyone spoke German, how would that feel to you? Or imagine you went to Istanbul. You are alone. You hear only German. Suddenly somebody shouts something, and you do not understand a word. You may imagine that they said something bad. If it was in Turkish, you would feel safe. I am a young person, so I know that here they also say good things. You learn to read people from their eyes. I learned this from Oriental people. Old people are not accustomed to strange sounds, smells, voices.

Miles's xenophobia even has a pseudoscientific dimension. He observes that

> foreign culture should be maximum 8 percent, meaning "foreigners" should be limited to less than 10 percent of the population. When it goes beyond that, it becomes dangerous for the identity. Here it is at a dangerous level, because there are too many foreigners living here. Streets are like in Istanbul. If you know Turkish, it is nice. My son says *abuu*. That's a gangster word. People in Zehlendorf [a well-off, predominantly ethnic German neighborhood] cannot understand this language. Once a little Arab or Turkish boy passed by my friend and said, "I fuck your mother." I grew up in Germany. A German child would never use that expression. This is typical Arab or Turkish. This is what they bring to this society.

"IMMIGRANT MUSLIMS SHOULD NOT LIVE HERE"

During my research, I met some converted Muslims who suggested that immigrant Muslims who are far from being perfect Muslims do not deserve to live in Germany. I encountered this perspective most strongly at a lecture on the subject of Muslim immigration to Germany and Austria that I attended in the Bilal mosque in Berlin. The instructors were a converted Austrian Muslim woman and Arab German Muslim man.

After introducing the difficulties that Muslims face in Austria and Germany, the converted woman began criticizing the immigrants for not learning the German language, going on welfare despite earning money doing illegal jobs, and living far from Islamic ideals. She believes that

> Muslims need to ask themselves why they live here. A Muslim should not live among non-Muslims unless he or she is there to proselytize. Muslim immigrants who do not proselytize, especially Turks, and others who give Islam a bad name, should go back to their countries. Even though I am Austrian, I also need to ask myself why I live here, and if I do not have a good answer, I should consider leaving Austria.

The Arab German copresenter of the course enthusiastically agreed, saying,

> It is not advisable for Muslims to live in a non-Muslim land. If you are here and do not proselytize, and on top of it, if you are giving Islam a bad name, it is a sin to live here. The main problem we have here in Germany is that people who receive welfare money from the state lie. They actually do not need the money. They make money on the side, and they give Islam a bad name.

When I looked around to see if anyone was getting as upset as I was, I saw that the mostly converted participants were nodding in affirmation.

Energized by the approval, the Austrian instructor added, "We can proselytize here only if we integrate ourselves into this society. And that is possible only by learning the German language well, by having a job, by being economically independent, and by having a good character. Maybe then we can begin impressing people, and they may convert to Islam." The man was eager to give an example about the hopeless situation of immigrant-background Muslims in Germany:

> We came here late last night, and we were looking for the mosque. We saw many young Arab men on the street with beer bottles in their hands. And I heard them say, "Salam aleikum" [Peace be with you] to each other. This is a sin brothers and sisters! Muslims are required to use this phrase to greet each other. And how

can we proselytize with such people around? How can we tell people about the beauty of Islam when the streets are full of drunk so-called Muslims?

When the lecture came to an end, I expected some of the critical-minded German Muslims I know well in that mosque to question this biased discourse. Many hands indeed rose. But to my surprise, almost everyone in the audience was agreeing with the presenters. The only criticism voiced was that it was pointless to have such discussions in the presence of people who all shared the same views. Most participants were German Muslims, who were, of course, fluent in German, hence fitting the first criterion of being good Muslim proselytizers listed by the converted Muslim woman. A converted woman among the listeners said, "As usual we are preaching to the choir here. Muslims in this room are well educated, they are good Muslims, and they would not lie to get on welfare. So how do we carry this message outside, to the uneducated Muslim groups in Germany?"

At this point, I could not contain myself any longer and raised my hand. I said, "But what you are saying sounds so similar to what the right-wing politicians say. They list exactly the same reasons for why immigrant Muslims should not live here. I doubt that if every single Muslim was to work and not go on welfare and not drink alcohol, they would be liked better." The presenter looked completely unconvinced as I was trying to make my argument. Even before I finished, he began drawing a big circle on the board and explained that

> proselytizing [da'wa] is like this. This circle is the community of nonbelievers. As the representatives of Allah in this world, our mission is to call people from this circle one by one to Islam and save them from the fire of hell. This will be complete when one by one, all of them become Muslim. When Muslims here do well, they may influence a few people, and we shall be closer to our goal.

He then likened their position to the first Muslims who had to call people one by one to Islam. "But our job is easier because there are so many more of us. Every Muslim could call one thousand non-Muslims to Islam." That only would be possible, according to him, when Muslims acted like deserving German citizens.

BLAMING THE TURKS

As mentioned above, one powerful dimension of blaming immigrant Muslims for the devaluation of Islam in Germany is pointing the finger not at all Muslim immigrants but instead at Turks, regarded as the really bad

Muslims, who also just happen to constitute the majority of immigrant Muslims. Promoters of this discourse sometimes compare them with Arabs, who they see as good examples. Turks become a stand-in for uneducated working-class immigrants in general.

A typical illustration of this kind of attitude was voiced by Gerhard Abdulqadir Schabel, a fifty-three-year-old German who converted to Islam thirty years ago at the opening speech of the 2011 Islam Week organized by German-speaking Muslim groups in Berlin. Schabel, who plays an active role spreading Islam in Germany, blamed German Turks for the contemporary questioning of the place of Islam in Germany. As he put it, "All Muslims should realize that they belong to their country and that they are responsible for what is happening there. If Turks in Germany were to commit themselves to Germany, and if they were not to send their earnings back to Turkey, then we could more proudly agree with the German president who said, 'Islam belongs to Germany.'"

Similarly, Murad Hofmann, one of the most influential converts to Islam in Germany, also frequently accuses Turks of not making themselves fully part of German society, and hence giving the sense that Islam and Germanness are in conflict with each other. In a 2010 public lecture about Asad, Hofmann indicated that it is the travel patterns of Turks that give the impression to mainstream Germans that Muslims do not belong to this society. "If Turks stopped going back to Turkey every year, not just once but several times," he said, "they could finally be part of this society."

Such charges echo those who blame immigrants for their own marginalization and alienation. Right-wing politicians and some converts believe that what marginalizes immigrants are not German institutions, policies, and everyday racism but rather the immigrants themselves, especially Turks. The victim-blaming narrative voiced by Schabel and Hofmann is outdated, and does not reflect the contemporary reality. In today's Germany, Turkish German immigrants rarely send money to Turkey. It is something the first generation of Turks did, hoping to return to Turkey. Moreover, though many Turks do commonly vacation in Turkey, most often go to holiday villages frequented by Germans, buying their vacation packages from German travel agencies. Such holiday villages use in the German language, and all the meals served consist of German food. Many Turks I met in Germany also go to other destinations popular among non-Muslim Germans, such as Spain or Italy. Another irony of this story is that Hofmann himself lived in Turkey for many years, but did not see this as a challenge to his German identity.

Apart from being quite critical of Turks, many German converts I met are more sympathetic toward Arabs in comparison. Detlev, a thirty-three-year-old man who converted to Islam eight years ago, for instance, perceives himself as an Arab-influenced German Muslim. He distances himself from

Turks. When I inquired about his attitude to immigrant Muslims in Germany, Detlev explained that although he has his problems with Arabs in the sense that they are "too chaotic" for him, he still appreciates everything they do in order to spread Islam in Germany. "Turks, on the other hand, have done next to nothing in Germany to spread their religion," he told me. "Think about it. They have so many mosques, they are so well organized. They could do so much in this country. But what do they do in the name of spreading Islam? Nothing! It is the very few Arabs who do all the work proselytizing." He complained that most people in Turkish mosques do not even speak German. He said, "They are even bad for their own youths. Younger generations cannot understand the Turkish spoken by imams who come from Turkey. And they cannot even learn about their own religion." Detlev commented that he becomes especially angry when Turks expect him to speak Turkish because he had become a Muslim. "I am a totally against this," he told me assertively. "No one can force me to speak Turkish. We are in Germany, and we speak German here."

Throughout my research, I wondered about the roots of such judgmental differentiation between Arabs and Turks—an attitude almost universally shared by the converts. I discussed the issue both with German converts and practicing Muslim German Turks. A number of German Turks also agreed with the German Muslim position. Bülent, a politically active Turkish German Muslim who regularly interacts with Muslims of Turkish, Arab, and German background, also noted that it is the Turkish character that makes it difficult for Turks to be effective proselytizers. Turks like to keep to themselves rather than open up, he contended. Bülent also mentioned that the Hanafi school of Islamic law, to which most Turks subscribe, is rule based, and most Turks learn about these rules through cultural practice.[4] He felt that because they learned these rules through practice, they were ill equipped to explain the reasoning behind each and every ritual to German Muslims, and the latter found this unsatisfying. Bülent shared an example with me of how Turks are bad at proselytizing even when they try:

> The other day I was at the mosque, and a German man came by to ask questions about Islam. I overheard two Turkish men talking to him. They asked him if he had had *ghusl*, the full ablution. He, of course, said, "No. What's that?" And they told him that he had to do it right away or he would go to hell when he died. I went over and told the Turkish guys to take it slowly. The man is not even a Muslim, and you talk to him about the ghusl and hell. Of course, the men left the mosque shortly afterward.

Bülent also complained that Turks are judgmental and critical of any kind of behavior that is different from the Turkish way of practicing Islam.

He informed me that he has a back problem, and because of that, has to open his feet wide while praying. "Every time," Bülent told me, "someone comes over to me and says, you can't pray like that, it's not right. But I notice that Arabs are more relaxed in such matters." Bülent took this opportunity to criticize German Muslims as well, saying,

> There are two tendencies among German Muslims. One group is close to the Salafis, who take the rules too seriously and are very critical of any Muslim who does not practice Islam their way. Another group are too individualistic and do not recognize that Islam is a communal religion. They think they can read the Qur'an and interpret it on their own, decide what is important and what is not important. I call this German stubbornness. For example, they say, I pray just with the word *bismillahirahmanirrahim* [in the name of God, most gracious, most compassionate]. Or they say, the rules about [what is] halal [lawful] and *haram* [unlawful] are too complicated, I don't feel like following them. When you try to tell them that these are important rules, you can't just do what you like and not do what you like, they don't listen to you. But such people often cannot find a place in an Islamic community and practice Islam in isolation.

Furthermore, Bülent, who grew up in Germany and feels more comfortable using German in many aspects of life, felt that when it came to spiritual matters, Turkish expressed emotions much better than the German language. He said, "When I read the German translation of the Qur'an, it feels almost like another book to me." "Of course," he added, "it is only because that is what I got used to." Despite his own personal preference for Turkish in the mosque, Bülent was appreciative of the German Muslims' contribution in publishing books in German. He told me that because there are few intellectuals among practicing Muslim Turks, few write books. He also appreciated German converts' mediation between Arab German and Turkish German Muslims, who are obliged to speak to one another in German, the language they have in common, and because they can function as diplomats between Arab and Turkish Muslims.

Even though it is correct that Turks are not as effective as Arabs in proselytizing, my perception is that such differences have more to do with the history of Turkish and Arab immigration to Germany than with the national character of Turks and Arabs. Turks arrived Germany in quite large numbers and as guest workers. According to most recent surveys, 75 percent of the almost four million Muslims in Germany are of Turkish background (Yükleyen 2012). Arabs, on the other hand, came to Germany mostly as students and also refugees, such as the significant Palestinian population in Berlin. Arab student men found the freedom of meeting and getting romantically involved with German women. They were free of the pressure of their families' arranging marriages for them. Several of my German Muslim friends told me that their Arab husbands kept their relationship hidden from their families abroad for a long time. Free of their families and lacking other connections, in other words, Arabs were more inclined to establish relations with Germans. As a result, some German women converted to Islam. The Turkish community in Germany, on the other hand, is a big one. While plenty of Turks marry Germans, many Turks have the option of finding a Turkish partner in Germany or Turkey.

In addition to this demographic factor, political decisions by both the Turkish and German state isolate Turkish and Turkish Islamic communities in Germany. To this day, 40 percent of mosques in Germany are supported and funded by the Turkish state. Imams come to Germany in rotation from Turkey for periods of five years. They often do not know German, and certainly not well enough to communicate with the majority society. They also do not have any sense of the everyday realities of Turkish Germans. Such Turkish mosques function not only as places of religious prayer but as cultural organizations too, where people expect to meet fellow Turkish-speaking friends. Mosques usually have cafeterias where attendees can gather together for tea and small grocery stores that sell familiar Turkish products. Mosques supported by the Turkish state display a Turkish flag and poster of Mustafa Kemal Atatürk, the founder of the country, and the Friday sermons end with a prayer for the well-being of the Turkish state (Yükleyen 2012).

The Turkish state has benefited from keeping Turkish communities in Germany as Turkish speaking, and sending imams to them as Turkish state employees. Doing so perpetuates the influence of the Turkish government on Turkish subjects, preventing them from being seduced by oppositional political ideologies, and helps ensure that they will keep sending remittances home to Turkey. The German government also favors this situation inasmuch as the secular Turkish state can be relied on not to support radical imams, who can in any case easily be deported back to Turkey, unlike imams who are German citizens.

RELATING TO MUSLIMS IN MUSLIM-MAJORITY SOCIETIES

Parallel to their ambivalent and sometimes-surprisingly antagonistic relationship with immigrant Muslims, many German converts to Islam also have ambiguous feelings about living in Muslim-majority lands. Some of them idealize these populations, strongly desiring to live in their countries, while others feel content about living in Germany and believe they can experience Islam better where they are.

Regardless of whether they want to live in Germany or the Middle East, most converts I met agree that Turks and Arabs living in Turkey as well as the Arab countries are much nicer and simply better people than the ones living in Germany. Often, I heard how especially Turks in Germany have lost their Islamic traditions and even humanity. In after-lecture tea gatherings in the mosques, both immigrant and converted Muslims compared their impressions from visits to Muslim-majority countries, be it trips to an ancestral homeland, a spouse's homeland, or Saudi Arabia for a pilgrimage, or tourist travel to North Africa or the Middle East. Although converted German women would occasionally complain about local men harassing them or people not practicing Islam properly, they would frequently conclude that Middle Eastern and North African Muslims who have not migrated out of their homelands were better than those who had. This kind of evaluation is common among non-Muslim Germans as well, even if the criteria of evaluation are different. My being a professor in the United States, despite the fact that I was born and raised in Turkey, would prompt well-traveled Germans to share their observation that in Istanbul, Ankara, and Izmir, there are many smart, skilled, and sophisticated people like me, unlike the Turks in Germany. Surprised, they would usually tell me, "There, they are not all like the Anatolian peasants who came here for work."[5] Several times I was bluntly told by non-Muslim Germans, "Here we got the bad Turks, not the good ones like you." Whereas non-Muslim Germans typically would admire Turkish artists, intellectuals, and businesspeople for their Western outlook as well as social competency in Western bourgeois ways, converted Germans would admire the non-diasporic Muslims for their commitment to Islam, generosity, and hospitality.

A counterversion of this idealized vision of Muslims in the Middle East exists simultaneously. Sometimes, people would go back and forth between the two images. The same individuals who praised Middle Easterners would later criticize them for not practicing Islam correctly or having been spoiled by Western influences. My friend Ada, the eastern German with the little boy and charred car, shared how this perspective affects the lives of converts, saying that

> German sisters often want to leave Germany for their husbands' countries. I am not sure if this is such a good idea. Of course, there you can hear the call to prayer, go around in your hijab comfortably, eat halal meat, and all. But now Western civilization is everywhere. You can even buy alcohol in Saudi Arabia. I have a friend who recently moved to Jiddah with her husband. She says Jiddah is too Westernized; you can even buy alcohol there. Now they will move to Mecca.

Ada herself wanted to live in Canada or the United States. She claimed never to have liked Germany or the German language. She had lived in the United States for a year as an exchange student, and then in Canada for a year with her Bosnian boyfriend. She liked the easygoing lifestyle in both places, but preferred Canada for its social rights. Ada observed that it would be easy to live as a practicing Muslim in both countries, and she would be able to eat at Taco Bell and Cinnabon, her favorite fast-food restaurants. For her, Canada would be the best place to practice Islam, not the Middle East or Germany.

Other converts had no fantasies about leaving Germany. Verena, who converted at seventeen after she visited a mosque during an open house with a friend, declared to me, "I am proud to be a German. I love this country. I am proud that it has such a great economy and everyone wants to immigrate here. I want to live here as a Muslim." When I asked her if she ever longs to live in a Muslim-majority country, she answered with a big smile on her face: "I of course would love to live in a Muslim-majority country, but I want it to be Germany!"

Another strong tendency I observed was that new German Muslims desired to help and transform Muslim societies, either by alleviating their material suffering or making them better Muslims—and sometimes both at the same time. For example, Irma, a twenty-five-year-old German convert to Islam, expressed a wish to go to Africa and fight against female genital mutilation among Muslims. Irma had been interested in foreign cultures and also human suffering long before she encountered Islam through a Tunisian asylum seeker she met while she was a high school student. She decided to embrace Islam and marry her Tunisian friend, because she had seen how devastating life could be when she lived in a small, economically depressed Moldovan town as an exchange student. She told me that once she graduated from college, she would like to help Muslims around the world. If she could not go to Africa, she wanted to go to Afghanistan to aid women suffering under the Taliban and having to wear the burka. Other converted women I met also expressed a desire to help orphans in Palestine or women traders in Muslim Africa, or work as doctors serving women in Afghanistan. They find themselves in the best position to determine what non-Islamic accretions are being used to exploit women in the name of Islam. Moreover, as Western women, they believe that they are better equipped to eliminate practices that give Islam a bad name, such as honor crimes, domestic violence, fathers not sending their daughters to school, and husbands not allowing their wives to work.

CONCLUSION

Being a converted Muslim is not easy in contemporary Germany. Following their conversion, most indigenous European Muslims find themselves marginalized—a position they never anticipated for themselves. Many German women who had donned the headscarf found themselves suddenly being treated as helpless, oppressed females short on linguistic ability or, worse, intelligence. In other words, overnight, they began to be treated as if they were Turks.

One way in which many converted Germans deal with this unexpected and unpleasant situation is to disassociate themselves from born Muslims, and instead aspire to a genuine Islam untainted by culture and tradition. In trying to attain this pure Islam and save Islam from its negative associations, they reproduce or even further the already-existing racist prejudices against immigrants. The idealized untainted Islam they promote leaves the poor, uneducated immigrant Muslims in Germany, especially Turks, to bear the full brunt of the racialized stigma of Islam.

Chapter 1 showed how many of the ideas behind promoting a pure Islam that is by definition compatible with German culture were based on the Enlightenment concept of the rational individual. Chapter 2 has focused on the flip side of this argument, which sees purified Islam as a perfect fit for the enlightened German mind. Many of the same German Muslims who advocate an idealized Islam compatible with the German culture also condemn immigrant Muslims for being so oppressed by their traditions that they are unable to make their own rational judgments, which would naturally lead them to the truth in Islam. Following the spirit of the Enlightenment, with its clear Eurocentrist emphasis that saw non-Europeans as less than rational, despite its stress on diversity, this line of reasoning contends that if not the only mentality that can easily do so, the European mind is definitely best able to relate to the real message of Islam.[6] A significant number of German Muslims thus believe that especially if one can eliminate immigrant Muslim traditions—if not traditional Muslims themselves, who give Islam a bad name—Germany is the best place to live an Islamic life.

Chapter 3

EAST GERMAN CONVERSIONS TO ISLAM AFTER THE COLLAPSE OF THE BERLIN WALL

Since Berlin has become a unified city, its converted Muslim community brings people with East and West German backgrounds together. These two groups differ from each other in that individuals from the former East Berlin who came of age before 1989 grew up practically without religion and also without contact with Muslims. What is most striking about East German converts to Islam is that a good number of them converted shortly after the fall of the Berlin Wall. They found Islam at a time when their government had collapsed and their society was being taken over by the new Germany, in which they discovered themselves to be second-class citizens. Becoming Muslim first and foremost fulfilled them spiritually. At the same time, it gave them a new way of being German that went beyond the split between the East and West German identities in the unified Germany. These people, who were mostly unaware of the negative stereotypes of Muslims held by West Germans, were caught unprepared when they found themselves marginalized for a second time as Muslims.

This chapter analyzes the conversion and life-story narratives of two East Germans who both grew up during the closed, authoritarian regime of the German Democratic Republic (GDR). When the wall fell, Zehra was a twenty-year-old woman from a family of regime opponents just about to begin her life after graduating from high school. Usman was a thirty-year-old man with an established position as a chemist at an East German state-run factory. The fall of the wall transformed both their lives radically, recasting them as second-class citizens with no foreseeable way out in the united Germany. Both Zehra and Usman converted to Islam shortly after the collapse of the East German Communist regime in 1989.

Their narratives trace the unexpected lives of East Germans who went from being marginalized as *Ossis* in the early 1990s to being marginalized as Muslims in the new Germany. A close analysis of the stories of Zehra and Usman demonstrates how the personal and political lives of German

Muslim converts are tightly intertwined, and how seemingly personal decisions gain new meanings in light of major political transformations. The
dissolution and unification of states create unexpected winners and losers,
and can open up previously unavailable opportunities for individuals to
take control of their lives in the midst of all-encompassing turmoil. First,
let me begin with a brief history of the GDR, its relationship to religion,
and the fate of East Germans in the unified Germany.

THE GDR

The GDR, or East Germany, was established by the Soviet Union in 1949
in the zone that it controlled after Germany lost World War II. The GDR
regime was built on socialist ideals that aimed at scientific advancement,
economic development, and social progress (Pence and Betts 2011). Atheism
was part of this equation, and religion and science were held to be mutually
exclusive (Peperkamp and Rajtar 2007). The country was ruled by a single
party, the Socialist Unity Party, which total control over the economy and
media, and aspired to regulate the work and family life of individuals. A
great number of citizens were not pleased with their living conditions.
During the first twelve years of the GDR, a quarter of the entire population
emigrated to West Germany for economic and political reasons. The Socialist Unity Party made emigration illegal and built walls blocking favorite
escape locations, including the Berlin Wall, which was completed in 1961.
Citizens who tried to escape were shot down.

The GDR regime collapsed in fall 1989, following a months-long peaceful
resistance movement in which a huge segment of East German society
participated. As a result, free elections were held on March 18, 1990, the
first in forty years. In October 3, 1990, the GDR officially acceded to the
Federal Republic, even though East German citizens did not ask for unification with West Germany. The unification process, however, caused frustration among many East Germans. Many East Germans experienced this
process as their organizations, cities, universities, and eventually jobs were
taken over by West Germans. Worse, they found themselves in the position
of second-rate citizens, looked down on, and accused of being "inferior,
backward, and lazy" (Berdahl 1999, 162).

Many observers expected that after the fall of the GDR regime, not only
consumerism, but also religion would become popular in East Germany.
Contrary to these expectations, eastern Germany continues to be the least
faith-based region of the world, with around 50 percent not believing in
God (Frank 2007) and only 25 percent registered as belonging to a church,
compared to 80 percent in western Germany, which had an extremely different relationship to religion in the part of the country occupied by the
United States, United Kingdom, and France after the war. In West Germany,

religion was given an important position in society such that political parties could even be established on the basis of religion. The From 1949 to 1966, the government was run by the CDU, whose platform emphasizes the "Christian understanding of humans and their responsibility toward God," and Angela Merkel, the party's leader, serves as the current chancellor of Germany. Furthermore, the West German government supported and funded certain religions, such as Protestantism, Catholicism, and Judaism. The high rate of atheism now in eastern Germany is attributable to the policies of the Socialist Unity Party. Whereas 38 percent of people born before 1930 in the region comprising the former GDR were reported in 2002 to have declared that they did not believe in God, 70 percent of people born between 1961 and 1974, meaning those socialized during the GDR regime, did so. The ratio of people who reported that they do not believe in God dropped to 57 percent for individuals born after 1975, meaning those who reached adolescence after the fall of the wall (Wohlrab-Sahr 2002).[1]

The two individuals I discuss at length in this chapter, Zehra and Usman, came of age during the GDR regime. Both of them grew up practically without any religion. For them, Islam was a brand-new outlook on life, a new enchanted way of readjusting their orientation in the social rubble that surrounded them after the collapse of the Berlin Wall. I met other East German converts to Islam who came of age well after the fall of the wall, and they did not experience a major shift in their social worlds. But they are similar to Zehra and Usman in the sense that they grew up in families where religion was almost entirely absent. They belong to a new generation in eastern Germany that has a rising interest in religion or transcendence in general.

ZEHRA

I met Zehra at the women's learning group at the DMK. She had just moved to Berlin from a smaller town with her four children and Egyptian husband. I was struck by some of her helpful comments to a newly converted woman about how to handle her relations with her children. She came across as exceptionally articulate, practical, and also empathetic toward a woman she had just met. When I approached her and told her about my project, asking whether she would talk to me about her experiences, she looked excited about it and promised to organize a day when her mother would babysit her children so that she could concentrate on telling me her story.

When she gave me her address, I was not surprised to find out that like other East German converts to Islam, Zehra lives in a formerly East German neighborhood where few Muslims reside. Unlike immigrant Muslims who feel uncomfortable living in the former East Berlin owing to these neighborhoods' known unfriendliness to immigrants and people with darker skin, converted Muslims, especially those who grew up in East Germany, feel more comfortable in these areas. Zehra said she chose this neighborhood because it was close to her mother, there was more green space, and it was quieter than other parts of Berlin. Her apartment was plainly furnished but tidy, despite the fact that she has four children. When I arrived, her mother was getting ready to take Zehra's children to the playground, so that we could talk without interruption. As soon as I took my notebook out, Zehra began talking. It was clear that she had prepared herself well for the interview.

"I grew up as an atheist," she said. "My family was totally materialistic; they believed in only what they could see. God was not a topic of discussion. They were not against God; he was just never mentioned. We went to the church for concerts and also for the Christmas services.[2] But we never went there to pray and we also never prayed at home."

The only religious person in Zehra's family was her grandmother. "But she never wanted to have anything to do with the church," said Zehra. Being engaged with the church was seen as suspicious in East Germany. Still, the woman practiced her religion at home. Zehra remembers that her grandmother would pray before eating and that she learned how to fold her hands to pray from her. "She would always say that she would meet her late husband again in paradise. We would all laugh at her and say, 'Grandma, there is no such thing as paradise!'" Zehra laughed bitterly when she recalled how they used to make fun of her grandmother.

One thing that marked Zehra's life deeply was her family's political orientation. They were opponents of the oppressive regime in East Germany. "My entire family was against the Marxist-Leninist teachings of the East German state. My father was an opponent of the East German regime [*Regimegegner*] and had to escape the country in the early 1960s. I was raised by my mother. My uncle was put in prison for opposing the regime. Like them, I was also very much against the East German state." Although her father and uncle had to pay for their dissidence, Zehra was not afraid to display her political views. For example, she told me how she refused to wear the school uniform as an act of civil disobedience. She had to pay for this too. Notwithstanding her good grades in school, Zehra was not awarded a high school diploma (*Abitur*) that would in turn grant her access to college. She paid a social price as well. Many people around her did not want to be associated with her, and she said she always felt outside society.

Starting in her teenage years, Zehra explained, she had begun looking for groups she could connect with. She joined a number of peace movements in what she experienced as the politically suffocating atmosphere of the East German regime. When she was thirteen, Zehra joined a peace movement that followed Mahatma Gandhi. "We had our meetings at a church. But it was all about organizing opposition against the regime. No one mentioned the name of God even once."

Zehra was part of the rising opposition movement in which the Protestant Church played a role, at least as a place of accommodation. As Daphne Berdahl (1999, 77) notes,

> In the 1980s, with the Protestant Church as a refuge, various peace and environmental movements began to emerge in the GDR. United by their opposition to the international arms race, these groups organized peace seminars, church congresses, prayer vigils, and worship services with contemporary accompaniments. . . . Although their protests were often directed against state policy, their ultimate goal of world peace was not inconsistent with the stated values of the socialist regime.

Zehra remained active in the opposition for political reasons, but at the same time retained some connection to religion through it.

The peaceful resistance that was to culminate in the end of the regime began on September 4, 1989. Organized mass resistance followed a prayer for peace at the Nikolaikirche in Leipzig and was then repeated every Monday. Zehra took part in these protests every week. Peaceful demonstrations grew week by week in Leipzig, a city of 700,000 inhabitants where there were 320,000 protestors. The protests quickly spread to other East German towns and cities. Citizens demanded the right to travel freely and democratically elect their government. The events escalated, and led East German officials to open the doors to Western Germany and then to the fall of the Berlin Wall on November 9, 1989. The Leipzig demonstrations continued until the first democratic elections took place in East Germany in March 1990.

In the middle of all this, an unexpected development took place in Zehra's life. She was granted a visa to visit her father in West Germany for ten days. At the time, the East German regime had relaxed its visa policies. Like many other East Germans encountering West Germany for the first time, she was shocked. "The first thing that attracted my attention was the advertisements everywhere with almost-naked women. I have never seen that before. I was very surprised, and also felt very sad and disappointed. My father immediately understood me and said, 'This is not the Golden West you hear about in East Germany.'"

Zehra's retrospective narrative of her experience of West Germany in early 1989 might be influenced by her contemporary Muslim sensibilities, especially her focus on the use of women's bodies on the billboards. Having grown up in East Germany, Zehra must have been accustomed to nudity such as at public beaches, but most likely not in its commodified form. Nevertheless, she was not the only East German who experienced her first encounter with West Germany as a deeply disappointing shock. John Borneman (1991, 3), who did ethnographic work in divided Berlin during this political upheaval, describes the experiences of East Germans who went to the West for the first time: "Those who returned home usually did so with a feeling of devalued selfhood, of doubt and fear, a bruised sense of having been assaulted by a superior power."

This encounter with West Germany transformed the way Zehra understood what was important to her. "I was quick to understand that this [i.e., the West] was not what I desired. Communism never made us happy. We were always afraid and felt insecure. But I quickly saw that capitalism was not any better." Her father wanted Zehra to stay with him and study there. Zehra wanted to go back, though. "I said to my father, 'I want to be part of the opposition, keep going to Leipzig demonstrations, and be part of the fall of the regime in East Germany.' I wanted to see this happening with my own eyes and I wanted to take part in it. Besides, the West was not for me."

Zehra fondly remembers her time taking part in the autumn revolution that led to the dissolution of East Germany. It was an exciting period. East Germans dissatisfied with the regime felt as though they were finally gaining some control over their lives. At the time, the revolutionaries did not call for the abolition of East Germany or socialism. Rather, they asked for reform, finally a real socialism with democracy. Yet as observers remarked, things took quite an unanticipated turn when the Berlin Wall eventually fell in 1989. As Borneman (1991, viii) succinctly puts it, "[The 1989 revolution] started with the hope of establishing popular control over the government, of restoring meaning to being East Germany. It ended up with West Germany's virtual corporate take over of her sister state."

After a few weeks of euphoria, the dominant feeling that surrounded East Germans was collective depression. Zehra recalls that "when the regime fell, we became sad. We did not want to be all like West Germany. Suddenly everything became expensive. I was twenty years old. And I said, 'Oh, my God, what I wanted happened, but what is happening to this society is not what I wanted.' " What changed things so rapidly from feelings of exhilaration to despair, from triumph to defeat, "was the terrifying feeling of inferiority, the sense that everything they had stood and lived for, their sacrifices and self-satisfactions alike, were worthless in the face of Western prosperity" (Borneman 1991, 33). The new beginning came to a quick end for most East Germans.

Borneman (ibid., 180) explains the situation that an East German friend found himself in:

> The fall of the Wall, the end of the long imprisonment, didn't alleviate Helmut's sense of entrapment. It exacerbated it. He felt a comprehensive and terrifying loss of control over the circumstances of his life. Virtually every certainty in the East Germans' world, from the political structure that laid down the outlines of the citizens' lives to the most elemental aspects of existence—prices, rents, and job security, dissolved into the air.

Like Helmut, Zehra was also at a loss as to what to do with her life. At twenty, when she might have expected to look forward to starting a career, all roads suddenly seemed closed to her.

Shortly after the wall fell, Zehra became quite depressed.

> I began to see everything through dark glasses. It was not possible for me to get a job anywhere as an East German. In East Germany, we did not learn how to use computers. That was a big disadvantage. I had just finished my studies in art history, and now I had to train myself in everything from scratch. They were already firing all East Germans from their jobs and appointing West Germans in their place. There was no GDR, but no alternative, either. Suddenly, we were second-class citizens compared to Westerners. Imagine, suddenly your money is worth nothing, you are poor, no one wants you to work for them, you have no value. Suddenly, you have nothing left. It was very depressing. I had no motivation to pursue anything. I did not see any chance for myself. I became truly ill and could not recover from it. So many people I know got really depressed.

This depressed and depressing moment in her life also opened Zehra's eyes to new realizations about the world: "I was really in a search for something. I felt as though the whole world had opened up in front of my eyes for the first time. If there was no GDR anymore, and if West Germany was not what I wanted, there had to be something else out there. I felt as though the whole world was open to me. I could travel anywhere I liked and I had to see the world." Zehra did not have the money to travel,

> [yet] I always had interest in the Arab lands. In the GDR, we were not allowed to travel freely, but I had fantasies about the Arab lands from reading the books of Karl May.[3] I had never seen a camel or the desert, but I longed to see the Arab lands. I also had never seen a Muslim in my life before. In West Berlin, one of the things that attracted my attention was women in headscarves. I looked at them with great interest. I had a feeling that they had peace. Especially the older women did not look embittered like older German women. I felt as though they were happy in their different worlds.

At the time, Zehra was interested in both different kinds of people and different religions. It was not only Islam that looked enticing to her but also Buddhism. She was curious about everything. Zehra tried to learn more about Buddhism, and even tried to meditate. In her struggle to overcome her depression, she was fascinated by religious people in general. "I wondered where they found the energy to pray. I joined a movement called World Religions for World Peace. We had sit-ins for the Iran-Iraq War [that was] taking place at the time and the Bosnian War. It was for me a religion without confession. The main teaching of the movement was to achieve inner peace in order to attain world peace."

Zehra was not able to travel to an Arab or other Muslim land. Now that the two Germanies were united, however, Muslims came into her life. One day, a Turkish man came to one of their peace meetings and sat next to Zehra.

> He began asking questions about the nature of our movement. I tried to explain it to him, but he looked confused. He asked, "But what do you believe in?" I told him that I believe in one God, but I cannot believe that Jesus Christ bears our sins. That never made any sense to me. It turned out he was teaching a class on Islam at an adult education center [*Volkshochschule*]. He invited me to his class. I went there, and we continued our discussions. One day he told me, "You are already a Muslim. You believe in one God and you believe that all prophets are equal to each other. Go and try it out."

Zehra took the man's recommendation seriously. She went home and started praying to God.

> I felt like a child. I never learned how to pray from anyone. I just began talking to him. I said, "My God, help me. If you are powerful, please show that to me." I really wanted to know if there was a God. I was not interested in being a Muslim. After my prayers, I had certain experiences. It is not possible for me to tell them here to you. They are between me and God. But I saw that we are not alone here in the world. I saw the angels living among us.

This experience of praying and her visions involving angels changed Zehra's life dramatically. "It brought an amazing mental opening to me. I could see that we are not here randomly, but there is a logic and reason to our existence." This was not only an abstract change in thought; it had profound effects on Zehra's everyday experiences.

> Before I would get so upset about injustice in the world. I would say Hitler also lived under the same sun as everyone else; he drank the same water like everyone. I was so angry at that fact. But once I realized that there is a God, this did not bother me anymore. I knew that Hitler would pay for his wrongdoing in the other world. There are criminals who do terrible things, but God will give them their punishment. Knowing this gave me immense peace. Before that I could not read the newspaper or listen to the radio without feeling sick to my stomach. I could not stand the injustice in Bosnia. But then I became able to stand it. "God will take care of all of these [things]," I said. I realized that I am not responsible for what others are doing in the world. I realized that I am only responsible for myself and for my own faults.

Having grown up in an atheist society, the most radical transformation in Zehra's life was not learning about Islam but rather the introduction of the concept of God.

> In my own experience, the most important thing that happened to me through my conversion was to get to know about the existence of God. There are other things that impress people—for example, the discussion of meteorology or the embryo in the Qur'an. Many people get convinced by these. Some people get impressed by the miracle of the Qur'an, the complex numerical system it is based on. I learned about such things accidentally five or ten years later in classes I attended. To me they were not important. What mattered to me was the realization of the existence of God.

Hence, Zehra did not immediately become a Muslim. As she concentrated on God, she also developed an interest in Christianity. She had already studied art history, and she had an interest in Gothic art in churches. Zehra and her mother had rented a house in Brandenburg. She spent a lot of time going around to old churches and taking pictures of Gothic art. At the same time, she began attending theology classes at Humboldt University without registering as a student. After studying the Gothic paintings of Jesus for a long period and thinking about theological issues, she decided that this suffering figure was not her God.

While attending classes at Humboldt University, she met a German convert to Islam in the library. Her brief and unexpected conversation with this man was a transformative moment in her journey toward Islam. He attracted her attention at the library because he looked quite different from everyone she knew. Although she usually would never talk to people she did not know, Zehra felt the urge to sit next to this person and speak to him. They quickly started an intense conversation about religion and God.

> He excused himself by saying, "I never talk to people I do not know, especially women. But I felt like you needed to talk to me." He began asking me my views on God. I told him that I believe in God, but not in the church. I told him about the World Religions for World Peace movement. He told me that there are names such as Allah, Jesus, etc., but they are all the same. I really liked hearing that. When he heard that I was from the GDR, he asked me how I found the West. I told him that here women are being used. I asked him what he was, and he told me that he was a Muslim. He had converted to Islam recently after marrying a Turkish woman. I told him, but that is a religion of the Arabian deserts, how could he be a Muslim in Germany? He told me that God is not an old man who sits in the sky. He is not a being who we can understand. He is beyond our imagination and has nothing to do with the Arabian deserts.

At that point I began crying. I told him that my parents were separated, I had no relations with my siblings, all my relations with men had broken down, I did not have any friends. I couldn't trust anyone. He said, "God loves you. He will welcome you." I told him that I had been born at the wrong time. I should have been born in Germany two hundred years ago. I did not understand why I had fallen to earth at this time, it was not for me. He said, "It is not like that. God sent you to earth for this time, not for the eighteenth century. Now it is the year 1990. The wall fell. Your society has totally broken down. You lost so much you had. You have to accept this." I was deeply moved to hear that.

This West German Muslim's recognition of her suffering as an East German who had lost her country through the unification process made Zehra's heart tender. What he told her made her accept her situation and embrace it, instead of denying it and wishing her life was something else.

I ran back to my apartment. Until then I used to hate my apartment. I always felt bad and lonely there. For the first time in my life, I ran to my apartment. I ran there as if a friend who I loved was waiting for me. I felt as though I would not be by myself this time. I was smiling for the first time in a long time. After this experience, I told myself, you know what, you are beautiful. You are here now. God created you to be here and now. I was laughing all the time. I looked at myself in the mirror with pleasure. I said to myself, my hair is beautiful— before I used to think my hair was too thin. I said, my face is beautiful—I used to think I was ugly. I said, my body is beautiful—I used to think my legs were too skinny, I would wear only long skirts. For the first time, I accepted myself and found myself very beautiful. I accepted having been born in 1969 in East Germany and having experienced the destruction of my society.

Once Zehra accepted who she was, an East German whose society had fallen to pieces, she was ready to embrace both God and Islam fully. But she did not know where to go to learn about Islam. In early 1990s' Berlin, Islamic information in the German language was not easy to come by. "When I converted twenty years ago, there was nowhere to go for information in German. Turks and Arabs would not explain anything. They told me that because I was a woman, I did not need to go to the mosque either. I had no idea where to go to learn about Islam." Now, Zehra reflects, the situation is radically different. "Even if you wanted, you could not attend all the lectures about Islam given in German in Berlin on any given day."

Zehra went back to the Turkish teacher who taught about Islam in the Volkshochschule. "He told me that I should begin praying. He gave me the address of a Turkish family, saying, 'Go there. They will teach you how to pray.' But he told me first lay out a white sheet on the floor, prostrate, and cry, he said. Cry because you have found God and greet him. I did that. I cried for a long time. I remember clearly that he did not tell me to cover my head." The Turkish family that this Turkish man introduced her to practically adopted Zehra. They welcomed her into their home and showed her great hospitality. "I had no job, no family, no friends. This family helped me. They fed me. They gave me everything they could. But they themselves did not know anything. I came from an educated family. I asked many questions, but they could not answer them. In those days, Muslims in West Berlin were very simple people."

At that point, Zehra was getting ready to convert to Islam. Yet she decided that she had to try to see beforehand if it would be possible for her to do everything well as a Muslim. She was especially concerned about fasting. Zehra thought that if she could not fast, then she could not be a Muslim either. When she first attempted it, she found it extremely difficult. She felt weak and sick the whole day. When she shared her experience with the Muslim family that had adopted her, a woman told her to ask for help from God. She directed Zehra to wake up early in the morning and ask God to give her strength for the fast from the depth of her heart. Zehra did as instructed. She was surprised the next day to discover that the fast went much easier. She still felt hunger and weakness, but the experience was radically different. "That day, I understood how it is extremely difficult to fast without belief. But if you believe and if you pray, it makes a huge difference. For me this was a great proof that prayer works. These were all tiny but very meaningful steps for me."

Another issue that she tackled step by step was the headscarf:

At first, I was very much against it. I said to myself, what is this? To me the headscarf and the overcoat looked like the uniforms we had to wear in the GDR. I would not wear a uniform in the GDR, and I suffered for it. So why should I now wear something that looks like a uniform to me? I said to myself, what is important is what I am experiencing in my heart. I do not need the headscarf.

Zehra's attitude toward the headscarf changed during a short visit to Istanbul with a newfound Turkish friend:

We went to the Blue Mosque. I had never seen a real mosque before. I was very moved and I wanted to pray there properly. I went and bought a headscarf for myself at the market by the mosque.

After having gone through all of these [things], I wanted to show my belief publicly, and so I covered my hair. At first, I tied [the scarf] toward the back, like a turban. When I wore it outside, I felt as though all the good energies that would come to me when I performed my prayers would remain with me. You know how children calm down when their mothers caress their hair? Wearing the headscarf felt like that to me. I also felt like no one's gaze would stick to me. All the curious or nasty looks people gave me when I wore a headscarf, just bounced off my headscarf. It shielded me.

After having committed herself to Islam, Zehra went through what she calls "an extreme but not radical" stage:

> At that time I left everything behind. I quit alcohol, I left my friends, I gave all my furniture away. I used to have many pictures of Egyptian gods on my walls, from the museum exhibits where I served as tour guide. I threw all of them away. These were especially important for me to throw away. Art and aesthetics is always about external form. I did not want them. I also used to be so lonely that I used to talk to them. I was not radical but extreme. I did all of this for myself. I would never say everyone needs to do such things. It was the right thing to do for me. I bought only one piece of calligraphy from a Muslim artist. I had one prayer rug, one mattress on the floor. I did not need anything else. I threw away all of my old music. I fasted a lot and prayed a lot. I unfortunately cannot do such things anymore. I fast only during Ramadan and perform my required prayers. It was a very spiritual time for me. I did not miss anything I did not have. I had very deep spiritual experiences at the time.

Not all of Zehra's experiences as a new Muslim were positive. For one thing, her father was quite upset with her decision. Most likely after twenty years in West Germany, he had been socialized into an anti-Islamic attitude.

> My father was very surprised by my conversion. He had always supported my education. He had set up a library for me. He told me that he was really disappointed that I did not continue my career in art history. His wife was especially angry with me. When I prayed, she would stand in front of me and make fun of me. She told me that religions brought only unhappiness and caused trouble. She said, look what is happening in Bosnia; it is because of religion. I told her that it was a power struggle. It had nothing to do with religion. I told them that Hitler or Mao was not religious. Of course, people do things in the name of religion. But it is not because of religion.

Still, it was clear that her father and stepmother were not equally against all religions. They were specifically against Islam. "My stepmother also said, I wish you had become a nun, maybe then we could understand you better. I asked her, what is the difference?"

Things with Zehra's father became much worse ten years after her conversion.

> After 9/11, my father became even angrier and told me that he did not want to talk to me ever again. I tried to tell him that terrorists are people who have left the right path, that the things they do in the name of Islam are not Islamic. The Muslim Council makes statements every time something like that happens. They

say that this has nothing to do with Islam. But everyone misunderstands us. This seems to be our fate!

Following 9/11, her father banned Zehra from seeing his other children. He accused her of proselytizing to them with her headscarf.

Unlike her father's radical reactions to her new religion and life, Zehra's mother, who is a psychotherapist, was much more understanding or at least respectful of the choices she made. Her father's socialization into the anti-Muslim attitude in West Germany during the previous twenty years and her mother's life in an East Germany devoid of Muslims may also have been factors. Zehra and her mother still had a harmonious relationship when I met her.

When I first met my mother with my headscarf, I tried to dress really nicely. I bought a new white headscarf, a pink checkered shirt, and a long blue dress. We went out for a walk. My mother said, "This headscarf you are wearing is very foreign to me." I tried to tell her about my experiences, my spiritual experiences. I told her how I saw angels. Because she is a psychotherapist, my mother said, "You have these visions because you are very lonely. This is a psychological condition." But she said, "Because you are happy, I am happy." Later, too, she said, "I am so happy that you have found happiness and peace," and she told me that she believed I would not have been able to find it without religion.

Zehra does not agree with her mother that her religious experiences are a psychological condition. Nonetheless, she shares her mother's observation that if she had not found Islam, she would be a deeply troubled person. She believes being a Muslim healed her body, allowed her to have a lasting relationship with a man, and gave her the desire to have children.

Islam offered Zehra a new vision that went beyond socialism and capitalism. By embracing it, she was again challenging the norms, as she had done as a dissident in East Germany, rejecting what she saw as false ideals in the name of a deeper freedom. Being a Muslim allowed Zehra to move beyond her depression and disillusionment with West German society—but as a headscarf-wearing woman, she again found herself in a marginalized position.

USMAN

I met Usman in the same mosque where I met Zehra. Born in Dresden in 1959, ten years before Zehra, Usman was a better-adapted East German when the wall fell. Yet Zehra and Usman felt similarly out of place in the new Germany. And Islam was a new vision that became available to them in the new Germany. Their new faith allowed them to see beyond the East and West German categories of socialism and capitalism.

Usman grew up, went to school, and found a job as a chemist in a factory in Dresden—a once-beautiful city left completely destroyed by allied bombing toward the end of World War II. A few years after the wall fell, the state factory where he worked was shut down. Usman was given training to be a store manager. It quickly became clear to him, though, that at a time when younger East Germans could not get jobs, there was no future for him. Receiving sufficient money from the welfare system, Usman suddenly had a lot of time on his hands. He started to read deeply into the topics that attracted his attention. At that time, he wanted to learn more about Islam. "There was a lot of discussion about Islam in the media, and it was all negative," he told me. "I wanted to find out what this religion was really about." Usman mentioned that at the time, he knew no Muslims. He had no one to ask any questions. He went to the public library in his neighborhood and checked out all the books about Islam. Usman was convinced by what he read and decided to become a Muslim in 1998. He met other Muslims for the first time in his life when he moved to Berlin shortly after his decision, precisely because he decided he needed to be around Muslims.

Usman moved to Wedding, an affordable but depressed part of the city occupied by poor ethnic and immigrant Germans. He began attending all the mosques he heard of that offered German-language activities. Usman became attracted to the most puritanical interpretations of Islam. He grew his beard, started wearing a *jalabiyya*, and espoused the view that the only place where Islam was practiced according to its original intentions was Saudi Arabia. Even though he probably would find better company in a Salafi mosque, Usman preferred to attend the more liberal, nondenominational DMK, both because it was the closest mosque to his home and because over the years he felt comfortable there. Usman liked to challenge the more liberal speakers who came to the mosque with his puritanical ideas. The women members of the mosque frequently rolled their eyes when they heard him talk, and his male friends often teased him, saying because he had grown up in East Germany, he liked things strict and orderly. Some joked that Saudi Arabia was his new East Germany.

Because he was usually so vocal, I thought it would be easy to interview Usman. But the idea made him tense. When I approached the current leader of the mosque, David, to ask Usman for an interview, he looked worried. Usman whispered something nervously in David's ear. David, who is also an East German, although a much younger, fun-loving, and trusting man who grew up after the fall of the Berlin Wall, laughed out loud. "No, Usman," he said, "Esra does not work for the German police and neither is she working for the CIA. Look, she herself is a Muslim and she wants to publish a book about us in the United States. You have nothing to hide

Usman, don't be shy." Usman then reluctantly agreed to an interview. It turned out, however, that the mosque office would be without staff at the time we arranged to meet. Usman again became uncomfortable. He turned to David and said, "If there is no one at the mosque, it is not appropriate for her and me to be alone at the mosque." David patiently answered, "Do you remember how we discussed the Islamic rules to observe when a man and a woman are together in a room with the last presenter who came here? If there is an open door through which someone can enter, it is OK for the two of you to meet. Leave the office door open, do not lock it, and it will be acceptable for you to meet." Usman finally agreed, even if he did not look excited about the prospect.

When we met at the mosque office, Usman made sure to leave the door wide open, and we sat at the opposite ends of a quite-large meeting table. I had a headscarf on when I met him at the praying section of the mosque, but I came to the office without a headscarf for the interview. Usman was still a little bit nervous. He asked me to please put on a headscarf, since the office is also part of the mosque. I obliged him. Apart from doing something on the borderline of what is religiously unacceptable by sitting alone in the same room with a woman—even with an open door—he was also nervous about what he saw as meeting with a US woman. The fact that East Germans of a certain generation cannot speak English well is one of the negative stereotypes about them. He came to the meeting prepared with a German–English dictionary. His English was much worse than my German, a pointed mark of distinction between East and West Germans as well as a source of embarrassment for East Germans. He wanted to have our interview in English. When that did not work out, he told me that he actually was quite fluent in Arabic and we could do the interview in Arabic if I wanted. I told him that my Arabic was next to nonexistent, and managed to persuade him that even though I have a strong accent and make mistakes in German, I am pretty good at understanding it, and would make sure to refer to the dictionary he had brought if there was anything I missed.

When we finally began the interview, Usman noted that he was especially nervous because he knew that the German police were suspicious of German converts to Islam. A few years earlier, there had been a big to-do about a couple of German converts to Islam caught collecting explosives that could be used for a terror attack. "You know," Usman informed me, "I used to work as a chemist in a state factory in East Germany. I am afraid that the police will think I am a terrorist. And I was sure you wanted to interview me because of that." I assured him that I had no idea about his past career, and was not interested in either chemistry or terrorism. I told him that I wanted to hear his opinions about Islam, Germany, and his life as a German Muslim.

After telling me briefly about how he encountered Islam, Usman was most interested in talking about the negative image of Islam and the GDR in the new Germany. He told me that both sets of images are politically motivated campaigns and unfair. According to Usman, life in the GDR was much better than in unified Germany in many respects. In addition, he suggested, it was much closer to an Islamic ideal. Usman clearly thought about this issue thoroughly, and provided me with a long list of examples that proved his point. "First of all," he said, "in the GDR there were alcohol and cigarettes, but at least there were no drugs. Because the money was worth nothing, drug dealers would not bother bringing drugs there. Also there was no legal prostitution, no pornography, no advertisements on children's TV. Now TV is a catastrophe. Children watch violence all day long, and nudity is everywhere."

The most important aspect of the GDR regime for Usman was that there was real punishment and hence discipline in society. "Here no one really gets punished for anything." When he came to West Germany, he was astounded to find that Muslims have a disproportionately high incarceration rate. Criminality and criminal Muslim immigrants were two things that they did not have in the GDR, he claimed.

After having told me all about these problems, Usman complained that he could not talk openly:

> Then they accuse you of glorifying the GDR. But this bad image of the GDR is created and supported by the state. How is it possible that everything was bad in the GDR and everything was good in the West? So many things were better than you could ever imagine here. They always talk about the Stasi. Every country has secret police. There is the CIA and there is the secret police here in Germany.

Usman was right that even his good friends at the mosque often made fun of him for being nostalgic about the GDR. Even if they held similar views about the values that make a good society, no one would share his idea that things were better in the GDR.

Like many other disillusioned former East Germans, Usman was "Ostalgic" (a combination of *Ost* [East] and nostalgia) for the GDR. Unlike his contemporaries, however, his feelings were set on defining the GDR regime as more in keeping with Islamic rules. A "host of legal, political, and discursive practices reflected a systematic devaluation of the East German past that challenged some of the very foundations of easterners' identity and personhood," Berdahl (1999, 163) observes. A few years into this postunification feeling of inferiority, some East Germans began to question the idea that everything in the West was better, developing a strong sense of East German consciousness in the process.

After he converted to Islam, Usman conflated the negative Western stereotypes of East Germans and Muslims, since they both personally reflected on him. "People are against us, especially us converts," he said.

"They call us radicals. Is not drinking, not smoking, wearing loose clothes being radical? Everything else is allowed in this country." Usman told me that his biggest fantasy was to live in Saudi Arabia. He said, "Humans are never perfect. Only God is. But the Islamic experience is closer to the teachings of the Qur'an and Sunna in Saudi Arabia." He liked it that Saudi Arabia did not permit alcohol, prostitution, or *fitna*—men and women working together. He noted that in the GDR, he had worked in the same office with women, and to him that was a catastrophe. He thought men and women could work at the same company, provided they are in different offices. Usman had been learning Arabic for a while and thought he would be a great guide for German tourists in Saudi Arabia. But he had no connections, and no idea about how he could go and get a job there.

Usman lived on welfare. He spent his time attending German-language lectures on Islam at the several mosques in Wedding, learning Arabic, fulfilling his religious requirements, and attending to his mother. He had never married. Usman told me that he would love to marry a Saudi woman and go there with her, yet he did not seem to be actively pursuing this goal. Like Zehra, he felt that German unification had taken his ability to be a productive and well-respected member of society away from him, but at the same time, it had unexpectedly given him access to a new religion and worldview that allowed him to see things beyond the East–West dichotomy. Also like Zehra, Usman had experienced a further fall in social status as a convert to Islam, although he also managed to create a wider world for himself, where he could imagine a life outside the debilitating space left for him as a former East German who would never be able to adapt well to the unified Germany.

CONCLUSION

East Germans' conversion to Islam, especially the conversion of those who grew up under the authoritarian regime of the GDR and without contact with the Muslim immigrants who came to rebuild the war-torn West German economy, is a socially specific experience different from that of West Germans' conversion to Islam. For many former East Germans, the disappearance of their state, their fall to second-class status in the united Germany, and their discovery of Muslims and Islam coalesced. Since both East Germans and Muslims ended up being further marginalized following the fall of the Berlin Wall, it unexpectedly brought some of them into close contact with one another.

At first sight, East Germans may appear to be beneficiaries of the unification of the two Germanies, since they were released from an oppressive authoritarian state that controlled its citizens through a regime of fear. In addition, West Germany bore the costs of reunification. The relative deprivation that East Germans experienced as a result of the unequal nature of the reunification nevertheless proved a powerful feeling, particularly for those who had grown up in the GDR, and found themselves unprepared for work and life in a unified Germany run according to West German rules and standards. The other group that experienced a parallel dramatic loss following the collapse of the Berlin Wall consisted of immigrants, refugees, and asylum seekers, many of who are of Muslim background. After the fall of the wall, a number of German politicians publicly declared that there was no longer any need for "foreigners," and they should go back home. Racist nationalism increased dramatically after 1989. Neo-Nazi groups became active and strong, and there was a series of racist attacks, especially against Turks and Africans (Partridge 2012). The worst events included a firebombing in the West German town of Mölln in 1992 that killed three Turkish residents and the arson attack on a Turkish family in Solingen where five people were burned to death in 1993 as well as killings of a number of people of African descent, including the Angolan worker Amadeu Antonio Kiowa in 1990. Neo-Nazi groups often find their most devoted supporters among former East Germans. It is remarkable that while more former East Germans choose to deal with their newly acquired inferiority complex by joining racist groups against Muslim immigrants, others decided to side with the Muslims or even become Muslims.

Scholars and observers concur that what most hurt the East Germans before and after the fall of the Berlin Wall was the material deprivation they felt in relation to West Germans. The working-class Muslims that East Germans met for the first time after unification were an unexpected new group that did not make them feel inferior and opened up new ways of being to them. In cases where this unlikely alliance worked, Ossis could simply be Germans and be welcomed in mosques as such. Among Muslims, it did not matter that they didn't have the right clothes, didn't know how to shop in expensive stores, and didn't speak English—all dead giveaways of their East German identity. The Muslims who they encountered reached out to them and invited them to become Muslim. They may not have fully taken them into the fold of their community, but at least they promised them new meanings that would go beyond the West German capitalist materiality they were deprived of; an orderly flow of time during the day, even if they were unemployed and lived on welfare; a community that could appreciate them at least as Germans, regardless of their East German back-ground; and a future life where the injustices of this world would be re-solved. Becoming Muslim gave a small number of East Germans an op-portunity to get beyond the double consciousness they experienced in unified Germany and simply be German.

Chapter 4

BEING MUSLIM AS A WAY OF
BECOMING GERMAN

"This is the only Islamic youth organization established by Germans, for Germans," says Sümeyye, a friend of Turkish descent born in Germany and an active member of Muslimische Jugend Deutschland (Muslim Youth of Germany, or MJD) from its beginning. Originally established in 1994 by a German convert to Islam, Muhammad Siddiq Borgfeldt, the MJD has been a relatively small but significant organization in promoting a Muslim youth culture based on a strong German identity and lifestyle as well as adherence to Islamic halal practices.

This small organization of not more than twelve hundred registered members promotes Muslim youths of diverse backgrounds coming together to discover ways of becoming active and desirable members of German society. Indeed, young members of the MJD participate in discussions about how to represent Muslims and immigrants in the general elections; arrange trips to Auschwitz in order to shoulder the weight of German history and talk about its meaning for contemporary German society; and organize New Year's evening celebrations along with hip-hop concerts that are Islamically proper.[1] Many born Muslim members confirm that through their participation in the MJD, they start to embrace their German identity in a wholehearted way and define themselves primarily as German rather than Turkish or Arab. Young members of the MJD show that an Islamic lifestyle can be totally suited to life in Germany and a Muslim identity is not in contradiction with a German one. In other words, being Muslim can be a productive way to becoming German—both for born Germans and converted Germans with other immigration backgrounds.

MUSLIM YOUTH GERMANY

Many of the MJD's fundamental principles are based on those that Siddiq established for its mother organization, Haus des Islam (HDI), in 1982.

Siddiq was sixteen when he converted to Islam in 1962. Growing up in postwar Germany as an introverted orphan struggling with the meaning of life, he encountered Islam through some Arab students he met. After converting, he went to Sudan and Saudi Arabia to learn more about his new religion. He established the HDI on his return to Germany with donations from Saudi Arabian friends, who were happy to donate money to support a center dedicated to informing Germans about Islam. Even though the center was at first directed toward German converts, an increasing number of born Muslims began to attend seminars and learn ways to live an Islamic lifestyle compatible with life in Germany. From the outset, Siddiq promoted the idea that Islamic law did not contradict the German way of life. For example, he told a journalist that as a Muslim, he can open an interest-free bank account at any bank in Germany, which usually has lower costs. "[Muslim] belief is universal, but in the past few years a German Islam has sprung up," an HDI participant told the same journalist.[2]

The MJD similarly aims to help young Muslims lead a life that is Islamic and fits the realities of youth culture in Germany. One of its founders told me that at the time, mosques focused on the culture and languages of ethnic Muslim groups. They also provided training about how to recite the Qur'an and taught some of the basic rules, but there was no organization that concentrated on youths and offered Islamic training in German. Muslim Youth in the United Kingdom, an organization run by youths that uses English as its language, impressed the MJD founders. Following a couple of visits to Muslim Youth, the founders established the MJD in Germany. Even though they wanted the MJD to be a German-speaking organization, they did not necessarily define themselves as Germans at the beginning. For MJD members, the idea of a tension between Islamic and German identities surfaced after German unification, and reemerged more intensely again after 9/11. One of the founding members told me: "At first we identified ourselves primarily as Muslims and did not think that much about the national question. But when we began continually to be asked if we were German or something else, the natural answer for us was German. Most of us were born in Germany, spoke German, and felt part of German society. But that was not something we thought that much about beforehand."

Thirty-five people attended the first meeting of the local circle in Berlin in 1994, and two hundred people participated in the first annual country-wide meeting in 1995. The organization grew quickly in the 1990s, spreading to thirty local circles across different cities and towns in Germany; recent annual meetings are estimated at twelve hundred participants. The MJD is the only Islamic youth organization active throughout Germany that is independent of all mosque organizations. On its Web site, the MJD defines itself as a "German-speaking, free, and independent organization and open to all young Muslims between the ages of 13 and 30," and finances itself through membership fees and donations. The MJD aims "to support youth in their self-confidence and their German-Muslim identity, and at the same time to encourage and empower them to constructively take part in social life."[3]

The MJD's primary aspiration is to encourage Muslims in Germany not only to be better Muslims but also to be better Germans. In other words, the MJD seeks to help its membership be proud German Muslims who do not see being both German and Muslim as a contradiction. It is no coincidence that this organization was first envisioned not by a Turkish or Arab Muslim but instead by a German converted to Islam who thought it was important to develop a new space in the ethnically divided field of Islam in Germany where future generations of Muslims could go beyond their ethnic identities and find ways to become German Muslims above all.

In a 2012 interview with the editor of *Islamische Zeitung*, a German-language Islamic newspaper also founded by German converts to Islam, Hischam Abul Ola, the then leader of the MJD, emphasized the German Muslim character of the organization. His interview is revealing of the great stress that the MJD puts on developing a sense of being a German Muslim:

> *IZ*: MJD is a multicultural organization that brings together young people with different backgrounds. What do members have in common?
>
> *HAO*: Our common point is that we speak German, we are German, and that Germany is our homeland. Of course, this is in addition to being Muslims in Germany.
>
> *IZ*: What is your background?
>
> *HAO*: My parents come from Palestine.
>
> *IZ*: Do you feel yourself more German than your parents?
>
> *HAO*: Certainly.
>
> *IZ*: You say that your homeland is Germany. Is it the case for everyone in MJD?
>
> *HAO*: This depends on how long they have been active in MJD. In MJD we try to convey this message very strongly. We tell them, you were born here, you grew up here, you speak German better than any other language. If you think deeply [about it], you will see that you think differently, you act differently than your relatives in Turkey or in Arab countries. We talk about this theme a lot. You first have a responsibility to the society you live in, not to a society that is 2,000 or 3,000 kilometers away. That is the way of thinking we try to inculcate. Active youth in MJD think, "We are German, we live here, and this is a good thing!"[4]

The MJD uses multiple means to try to achieve its goal of developing practices that are Islamically acceptable and compatible with the German way of life. The most important step is emphasizing the German language.

In Germany today, most mosques belong to a particular ethnic or national group (e.g., Turks). Even though now there are increasingly more German-speaking Islamic contexts, they are still a rarity, and were a radical innovation in the early 1990s. Siddiq and his friends were among the first to perceive the need for a German-speaking Islamic context. Since younger generations of Muslims speak German much better than their ancestral ethnic languages, they need German-speaking Muslim situations to learn about their religion. Siddiq also had firsthand knowledge of how German converts like himself as well as Muslims of other backgrounds who do not automatically belong to an existing ethnic mosque are in need of German-language Islamic education.

HOW MIXED MARRIAGES HELP THE UMMAH

The consequences of gathering young Muslims together in a German-speaking context are multiple. First and foremost, it brings together Muslims of varied backgrounds living in Germany whose common language is German. In the context of the MJD, religious Muslims of Turkish, Arab, German, Bosnian, and other backgrounds mix, and from there develop a group identity as German Muslims that goes beyond their ancestral ethnic or national identities. Because the MJD is primarily oriented toward youths, members are at an age when they look for marriage partners. Participants learn to prioritize religious outlook rather than ethnic background, and may end up establishing Turkish Arab, Arab German, or Bosnian Kurdish families, for instance, which ipso facto become German-speaking families in which German Muslim children are raised.

The MJD members I met didn't see mixed marriages as an unintended consequence but rather something they aspired to and worked toward. Many of them believe that establishing families that cut across ethnic communities is a way to counteract nationalism and nurture a stronger feeling for the Ummah among Muslims. Sümeyye told me that it had not been easy for her to accept this standpoint. She vividly remembered attending an MJD meeting in her late teens more than fifteen years earlier. While she was chatting with other female MJD members, the issue of marriage—a favorite subject among female MJD members—came up. Sümeyye found herself saying, "But if I don't marry a Turkish man, I'll feel as though I had betrayed my own people." All the women at the meeting, including Sümeyye herself, were surprised that she would say such a thing. The MJD's entire struggle against nationalism, ethnic identification, and even racism had not really reached her heart, Sümeyye felt. She explained to me why it was difficult for her to come to terms with this:

At [the] MJD, fighting racism was one of our main topics. In lectures, we said that racism came from Satan. Satan said he was better than Adam, because Adam was created out of mud, and he was created out of fire. We saw this as the beginning of racism. We also talked about how the Prophet Muhammad had said, "There is no difference between Arabs and Persians." We continually emphasized that Islam is against racism. In [the] MJD, we talked about how as a vanguard youth movement, we should be the first to fight racism among and within ourselves. I had decided that fighting racism would be my personal jihad, my own personal struggle.

As part of her active engagement with battling racism and nationalism in herself, Sümeyye decided that she should aspire to marry someone who was not Turkish. She ended up marrying a half-German, half-Egyptian man who had been raised by his German mother and converted to Islam. Sümeyye met her husband through the MJD. She told me that she believed marrying her husband was the result of her years-long jihad, her struggle. She believed that her marriage was especially valuable in the eyes of God, because it was a decidedly antiracist decision. Sümeyye knew that it would send a strong message to other young Turkish women in her hometown in western Germany. Up until then, she had never heard of a Turkish woman who had married a convert, and few would marry someone who was not a Turk. "I told them that I was marrying a 'foreigner,' meaning a German," Sümeyye said proudly. "I told them that what was important was that he is a Muslim."

Although MJD members may prefer such marriages, their ethnically homogeneous Muslim families and members of their ethnic group do not always accept them. Furthermore, such couples may find it difficult to establish connections outside the MJD. Sümeyye was fortunate that her family members accepted her marriage. They were quick to embrace her husband because they had socialized at HDI and had similar values to their daughter. As an MJD member of Turkish background who married an Arab man and did not find her married life as easy told the ethnographer Synnøve Bendixsen (2013, 239),

> Many people say that it is good that we have been married and that they respect that and such, but we do not find friends. Like the Turkish men can't talk with him in Turkish, and they do not like to speak German. You know, when I got married, this man who I grew up with and went to school with and had been in the mosque with called me and said that he hoped that I had thought about it all carefully [marrying someone not Turkish,] that they are so and so . . . and that you never know with Egyptians. Can you imagine? I told him that I am 27 years old and can think about these matters fine, yes, thank you.

Because of the unique challenges that ethnically mixed Muslim families face in Germany, the MJD is especially attractive to the children of such families. During my research at the DMK, I realized that the children of most German converts to Islam, who generally had Arab fathers, were active at the MJD. I was told over and over in our conversations that in their MJD circle, ethnic background meant nothing, and they all related to one another as German Muslims. Yasemin, with a fair complexion and strikingly blue eyes, and the sixteen-year-old daughter of a converted German woman, informed me that she is frequently confronted with ethnic stereotypes in her life outside the MJD. She commented on how new teachers assumed that she would speak bad German, and how people she had just met sometimes asked why she wore a headscarf, even though she was a German. But she told me that in the MJD, people do not have such hang-ups, and accept her as a Muslim and a German. Yasemin said that she would like to marry an Arab man who had grown up with Islam in his family. Growing up with her converted German mother, she felt as though they had been compelled to learn everything from scratch. At this point in our conversation, Yasemin's mother, who was also sitting with us, felt the need to intervene. Speaking as a German woman who had married and divorced an Arab man from Morocco, she told her daughter, "My dear, you should marry someone who grew up here. It might be very difficult for you to find common ground with someone who grew up in an Arab country. There are plenty Arab men who grew up in Germany."

ACTIVELY ENGAGING IN SOCIETY AT LARGE THROUGH THE MJD

The MJD encourages its members to take part in the larger German society beyond their ethnic identities. In the words of Chaban Salih, one of the MJD's earlier representatives, "We call on our members to vote, to get involved in organizations. We want them to be model citizens and good believers. We want this in opposition to [the idea of] a parallel society" (Gerlach 2006, 142). Such involvement happens easily when Turkish German youths who come from working-class parents who were not educated in Germany become MJD members. This was made clear to me through the experiences of Hasan, who grew up in a small town in western Germany and is the son of Turkish immigrants from central Anatolia.[5] The MJD expanded Hasan's social networks and horizons. Through his engagement with the MJD, he learned to experience himself foremost as a German Muslim.

Despite the fact that I had known Hasan for a long time, I had never had a chance to have a long conversation with him. When I contacted him to talk about his experiences at the MJD, he told me that the most convenient place for us to meet would be at the Jewish Museum, where he worked as one of the few tour guides specializing in comparing Islam and Judaism.

Hasan described his parents as typical conservative Muslim guest workers who conflated tradition and religion.[6] As a young boy, he had attended a Diyanet Isleri Turk Islam Birligi (Turkish Islamic Union for Religious Affairs, or DITIB) mosque affiliated with the Turkish Religious Affairs Ministry—the only mosque in his hometown—on weekends, where he learned how to pray and memorize the Qur'an. In his teenage years, he and his family moved to a larger town, which offered four different mosques. There, he liked the Görüş mosque better than the DITIB one, because "at the DITIB mosque there was no discussion, no relating Islam to real life. You could only perform your prayers and recite the Qur'an." Hasan told me that this was fine when he was really young, but as he grew older, he came to feel that a mosque should play a larger role:

> I started thinking that Islam should have an answer to social issues and should not only be about prayer. So the Görüş mosque was more attractive to me, because they were talking about political issues, even though it was mostly about Turkey and [Islamist Prime Minister Necmettin] Erbakan at that time. I cannot say that I really liked this community or found their issues very relevant to my questions, but nevertheless it was much more interesting than the DITIB mosque. Eventually, I also got tired of all the talk about Turkey and how magnificent the Ottomans were [laughs]. I was more interested about life here in Germany.

When he was eighteen and also not totally satisfied with any of the mosque communities in his town, Hasan heard about the HDI:

> Someone told me about an organization that had Islamic activities in the German language. I called them up right away, and because of my youth, they told me to go to an MJD meeting. So in 1998, totally on my own initiative, I attended the first yearly meeting of [the] MJD. It was their third meeting. There were about 250 young people in attendance. I was immediately taken with this group. You know how enthusiastic people are in their youth [laughs]. I immediately wanted to be a member. I loved that they talked in German. People had such different ethnic backgrounds and still all cared about Islam. Another really important aspect for me was that so many of them were doing their Abitur.[7] In my town I was the only Muslim I knew who wanted to attend college and felt quite lonely in this desire.

Hasan explained to me that even though he immediately became a member, his active participation in the MJD took several years. After the first big meeting he attended, he continued volunteering in a Turkish DITIB mosque, helping younger students with homework—the most meaningful thing he could do in and for the Muslim community in his town. Later, he decided to organize activities in his town, not for the MJD, but in the spirit of the MJD. He organized monthly German-language events, to which he invited young people from Turkish and Arab mosques. He chose topics that he thought they would find interesting, such as Islam and democracy. Hasan held the events in schools rather than mosques, so that the space would be neutral and go beyond established ideas about certain mosques. He knew that Turks would be reluctant to go to an event at an Arab mosque and vice versa, and that some of the young people would not want to go to a mosque at all.

When I asked him what made an event reflect the MJD spirit, Hasan replied that it should be in German and reflect the spirit of the Ummah instead of being based on a national group. It was also crucial that it should be an event that would capture the youths' attention. He invited people such as Murad Hofmann to talk about democracy and Islam, and Nadeem Ilays to speak about Muslims' place in German society. Once Hasan invited a Muslim rapper, not to sing—which many Muslims would then have considered inappropriate at an Islamically oriented event—but rather to explore his journey to Islam.

Over time, Hasan increasingly became more active with the MJD. He started attending its events three to four times a year. At one of these gatherings, he was asked to organize an MJD trip to Turkey, as one of its yearly travel abroad events. Here Hasan reminded me that this was how most events are organized at the MJD: "It entirely depends on the ability and the initiative of its members. If there is someone capable and willing, then that person will organize something. There is no professional staff at [the] MJD. It is a voluntary activity, and quite an expensive commitment too," especially for young people who come almost entirely from working-class families.

For Hasan, the MJD's most significant contribution to his life was that it enabled him to peacefully negotiate his being a Turkish Muslim born and living in Germany. "Frankly, it is not an always-easy way of being," he said. "At home your parents talk about Germans as 'infidels,' but you also somehow belong to here and want to be part of this society." Hasan thinks that the MJD is one of the few organizations that help youths bring these different parts of their lives together in a peaceful manner. "Most other Muslim organizations do not try to resolve these conflicts in a constructive manner. Some tell them that they should stick to their Turkish roots, no matter what. Others tell them if they want to be good Muslims, they should minimize contact with the rest of the society. I find these strategies neither satisfactory nor peaceful."

Between 2004 and 2006, Hasan did a training course with the MJD to deepen his Islamic knowledge. These meetings took place every four to six weeks, each time in a different town in Germany.[8] Hasan told me that it was important to him to meet young Muslims from all over Germany. He learned what all of them had in common and what made a German Muslim youth. In addition, Hasan learned what was specific to being a German Turk, and how German Arabs and Bosnians differed from both German Turks and one another. He learned for the first time, for example, that there are variations in the way Muslims pray, and all of them are legitimate.

The MJD allowed Hasan to feel connected not only to other Muslims in Germany but also to many other Muslims in Europe. Through the MJD, he became part of the Europewide Muslim Student Organization and went to Brussels representing the MJD. He became active in interreligious dialogue as well. Hasan thinks that meeting religious youths from other religions was a truly transformative experience for him. "Growing up in Germany as a believing Muslim," he observed, "it is easy to get the sense that only you and your Muslim friends care about religion. Through [the] MJD I met Christian and Jewish youth, and had remarkable conversations with them about religion and being religious in Germany."

The "MJD really expanded my world as someone born in a small town in western Germany to poorly educated, working-class Turkish parents," Hasan told me. "It allowed me to be part of the larger society, and provided me an excellent platform to engage in dialogues in matters that relate to society, religion, and politics." Hasan admits that he did not always agree with everything that the MJD argued for. He found its interpretation of Islam a little bit too conservative for his taste, for instance, but "any organization will have something you do not totally agree [with]. Overall, being a member of [the] MJD has been a wonderful experience." Through his connections in the MJD, Hasan was able to secure a job in Berlin with a US organization that wanted to organize events on Muslim minorities. Moreover, it was through his MJD connections that he built in the German-speaking Muslim scene that he secured a part-time job as a tour guide in the Jewish Museum in Berlin while writing his PhD thesis about Islamophobia in Germany. The MJD permitted Hasan to transcend the Turkish Muslim community in his little town, and connect to Muslims throughout Germany and Europe as well as to other religious groups.

NOT FEELING PART OF A MINORITY

Another Turkish-background MJD member, a friend I got to know well over a decade, told me that the MJD had helped her get over her feeling of being part of a minority in Germany. Ceyda took a somewhat-parallel but nonetheless-different path to the MJD. Unlike Hasan's parents, who were traditional Anatolian Muslims, Ceyda's parents were slightly better

educated than the average Turkish guest worker, and came from more af-
fluent and less religious western Turkey. This gave them a sense of slight
superiority to other Turkish guest workers as well as toward their practice
of Islam. When Ceyda's parents found Islam for themselves after their children were born in Germany, they felt that the company at typical Turkish
mosques was not satisfactory to them. They were thus happy when they
discovered the HDI, an organization of better-educated Muslims that promoted an understanding of Islam unconnected to Anatolian traditions.

The MJD was founded when Ceyda was a teenager, and her parents
encouraged her to take an active part in it. She told me that her parents had
been worried that she would be bored in the Turkish mosques, where the
teachers were often strict and most of the education was based on memo-
rization. Ceyda remembers that her parents worked hard to make sure that
she and her brother experienced the mosque as a fun place to hang out.
When she and her brother were little, her father would always make time
to play with them at the mosque. He would frequently take them to the
courtyard to play with a ball. When they heard about the MJD, a conservative Muslim organization geared to youths growing up in Germany, Ceyda's
parents must have been pleased.

Ceyda believes that the MJD played a crucial role for her having turned
out a devoted practicing Muslim today, not only because it was geared to
the needs of youths, but also because it used the German language. Even
though both her German and Turkish (along with her English and Arabic)
are impeccable, and she could easily go back and forth between all-German
and all-Turkish communities, Ceyda vividly recalls never liking the feeling
of being part of a minority. She mentioned that since her childhood, she
had wanted to be part of the majority society—someone who simply and
unquestionably belongs to Germany. But at the same time, she did not want
to leave her background behind; she wanted to make it a legitimate part of
mainstream life in Germany. During a long evening of deep conversation,
as Ceyda was telling me about these complicated emotions that she had
experienced since her childhood, she suddenly remembered how in her
early teens, she used to stay up at night to listen to Turkish pop music and
try to translate the lyrics into German. After a pause, Ceyda said that she
had felt as though she had a responsibility to translate these songs into
German. Surprised at her feeling so burdened by pop music lyrics, I asked
her to further elaborate about what she meant. Ceyda said contemplatively,
"I felt like only then these songs I liked so much could be real, legitimate,
and worthy—only when they are expressed in German." Then she giggled
and recollected how she had translated in the other direction as well. When
she was twelve, Ceyda had a crush on a Christian German boy in her class.
But in her diaries she wrote imaginary interactions with him as a Muslim
called Bilal—a common convert name. As she grew older, Ceyda fulfilled

her childhood dream of translating between her Muslim world and German ways. She became an active member of an organization that was devoted to translating Islamic knowledge and practice into German, and more important, making it part and parcel of German society. And just as she had fantasized doing when she was twelve, she married a German convert to Islam.

When she was only sixteen, Ceyda went to Turkish mosques in her hometown, and requested permission to explain the life of Muhammad to Turkish girls and young women in the mosque in German. Based on her own experiences and the tips she got from the MJD, she was convinced that she could help young women who had grown up in Germany to understand and embrace their religion better in German. Although this sounds like a simple request, it was not been easy to start or keep at it. "We got chased away from so many mosques," Ceyda told me, laughing. In one Turkish mosque, they said to her, "Listen, we bring all these Turkish teachers [*hocas*] from Turkey so that they can tell the younger generation about religion. Are you saying that makes no sense?" They wanted Ceyda to translate what the female hocas were talking about into German if she thought some in the mosque did not understand Turkish well enough to follow. For Ceyda, this was not a solution, because she contended that it was not only a matter of language but also the style of teaching and topics covered. Hocas brought from Turkey had no idea about the life experiences of Turks growing up in Germany. She remembers having the worst luck with mosques funded by the Turkish Nationalist Action Party. She had felt that these would be a good option, since they were really big mosques and often remained unused. When she asked to use one of the rooms for Islamic education in German, she was told of the danger of her becoming German as a result of teaching Islam in the German language. Finally, she had better luck with the Görüş mosques, whose imams believed that Islam is universal and not limited to Turks, even though most of their constituency consisted of Turks. There they wanted to first look at the books she was using to prepare her lectures, however. They eventually approved and let her use their mosques. Ceyda continued organizing weekly gatherings for many years, until she moved out of her hometown.

Ceyda's eyes lit up as she described the young women's group that she led. Knowing how engaging and entertaining she is, I can imagine what a great change it must have been for these young women to have chanced on one of Ceyda's lectures. In these weekly gatherings, they did not talk only about strictly religious matters. "We also talked a lot about social issues," Ceyda said, because she thinks that the mere practice of speaking about Islam in German introduces the topic of living in Germany as Muslims naturally into their conversation. According to Ceyda, the language in which religious issues are discussed in Turkish mosques is so archaic that

German Turkish youths do not understand it and cannot relate it to their life experiences. "For example, when they learn about the theory of evolution at school, they cannot give an answer to it from what they learn in the mosque. First, they do not understand well what they are told in the mosque, and, second, what they learn here does not translate to their outside experiences." She continued:

> At our first meeting, I sat down with the girls in front of the room on the floor. Older Turkish women were sitting at the back and looking at us suspiciously, not understanding what we were talking about. I told the girls to look discreetly behind them at the long faces of the older women, and tell me about what they thought about the relationship between Islam and happiness. The girls were thrilled to be talking in German in the mosque in a language their mothers did not understand and immediately distancing themselves from them. I told them that if they really tried to understand the message of Islam, rather than only memorizing passages from the Qur'an, it would put a smile on their faces. Then I talked about the meaning of the Fatiha, the first passage all Muslims memorize, whose meaning few Turks understand. The girls immediately loved it. We kept meeting once a week for years.

For Ceyda, the biggest problem of having Turkish as the language of Islam is that it turned religion into a separate sphere of knowledge that cannot be integrated into everyday issues in Germany: "What happens inside the mosque becomes very difficult to integrate into what happens outside of it." As a result, she told me, many women she knew ended up segregating themselves from the larger society and living entirely within their Turkish-speaking circles. Others became part of German society and left their religion behind.

Ceyda wanted to do something else too. Early on, her goal in life had been to live an Islamic life yet be part and parcel of German society at the same time. Today, she is proud to be the main accountant in a small firm owned by a Christian German. She thinks that perhaps because the owner of the company is a religious man, a member of an independent Protestant group, he is not troubled by Ceyda's headscarf. During her first interview, the man commented that integration is about working together and not about people's clothes. Ceyda feels proud that her life is how she wanted it to be. She noted that her best friend in her hometown is a Christian German woman who she has known since high school. Their children are also good friends. She told me that she wants it to be normal practice for her son to step aside briefly to perform his prayers in the middle of a play date. At that point, Ceyda's ten-year-old son, who was listening to us quietly, said, "But of course it's normal mom. Why shouldn't it be?" Ceyda looked visibly happy and pleased.

HALAL ENTERTAINMENT

One uncontroversial area where the MJD transformed Muslim culture in Germany is in how it paved the way for what one MJD member called "halal entertainment" in Germany. The MJD, which was in tune with emergent Muslim youths, was the first group in Germany consciously to build bridges between German youth culture and an Islamic lifestyle. "Fun and Islam?" is a question that the MJD provocatively asks on its Web site. It supplies the answer right away: "Yes please! It is possible to have fun in the Islamic way, without setting boundaries between the two."[9] Islamically proper fun, or fun Islam, involves going to concerts with Muslim rappers, joining workshops on how to rap, celebrating New Year's Eve, organizing paint wars, and taking field trips within and outside Germany. In one MJD gathering, I watched video-recorded funny skits of annoying little things some people do in mosques—such as taking too long during group prayer, not showering before coming to the mosque, moving around too much during lectures, and so on. The skit that made the audience of MJD members laugh their heads off started with the slogan "Because it is halal to laugh!" Such an approach that aims to bring fun and Islam together is genuinely unique to the MJD, or was until ten years ago. Before that, Muslim communities in Germany were not especially welcoming to youths, and Islam was not associated with having fun.

The past few decades of the Islamic scene across the globe have simultaneously witnessed increasing strictness and avoidance of "fun" alongside an increasingly widespread global culture of Islamic consumerism and fun. In his article "Islamism and the Politics of Fun," Asaf Bayat asks why puritanical Islamic movements such as the Taliban in Afghanistan, Wahabis in Saudi Arabia, and mullahs in Iran have been so vehemently against Muslims, especially the youths, having fun. He argues that what he calls "anti-fun-damentalism" has to do with preserving power: "At stake is not necessarily the disruption of the moral order, as often claimed, but rather undermining of the hegemony, the regime of power on which certain strands of moral and political authority rest" (Bayat 2007, 435). Perhaps it is no coincidence that especially in the West, global Muslim youth culture, which both stands in opposition to mainstream Islamic society and wants to be an integral part of it, has embraced fun, which Bayat (ibid., 434) defines as "a metaphor for the expression of individuality, spontaneity, and lightness, in which joy is the central element." Unlike the cases that Bayat discusses, Muslim youth culture in Germany is not hegemonic in its orientation. Fun-approving Muslim youth cultures such as the MJD aim to challenge the moral and political authority of both German mainstream society and the traditional authority structures of their Muslim communities.

Scholars have often focused on the consumerist aspect of the new global Islamic culture that manifests itself in Islamic cafes and restaurants (Houston 2001; Deeb and Harb 2013), the Islamic fashion industry (Gökarıksel and Secor 2009), Islamic comedy (Bilici 2010), Islamically dressed Barbies (Kupinger 2009), and Islamic music (Abdel-alim 2006). This culture is frequently connected to the rise of pious middle-class Muslims in the age of neoliberalism (Deeb and Harb 2013). In what he calls "Muslim consumerist society," Patrick Haenni (2009) sees a productive tension between the hedonism of market-related individualism and a reinvigorated religiosity that prioritizes outward expression. He suggests that this tension is resolved through being able to choose among different Islamic commodities, which makes it possible to represent different Islamic lifestyles.

The MJD took a leading role in localizing this kind of consumerist global Islamic culture in Germany. In local MJD offices, one can find Islamically dressed Barbies (Razanne), Gummi Bears produced without animal gelatin, CDs by global Muslim celebrities such as Sami Yusuf and Amir Khaled, and T-shirts, handbags, and key chains produced by the German company Style Islam with slogans in English like "I love my Prophet," "Keep Smiling: It is Sunnah," "Ummah Girl," and "Hijab: My Right, My Choice, My Life." A MJD member told me that along with his friends, he follows the global Muslim youth culture through comedians such as the US stand-up troupe Allah Made Me Funny, Muslim graffiti sprayers, successful Muslim athletes, Muslim intellectuals like Native Dean, and the Danish music group Outlandish. The MJD is part of this loosely connected worldwide youth movement that shows that Islam is hip and cool.

As in the Muslim-majority world, the Islamic youth culture spearheaded by the MJD in Germany is consumerist. Unlike examples in the Middle East, however, I see the main tension around the Islamic youth culture in Germany as not between modesty and consumerism but more so between Islamic piety and German/European identity and lifestyle. What is a new for many young Muslims in Germany, especially MJD members, is not increasing affluence, such as their sisters and brothers enjoy in Turkey, say, but rather their commitment to belonging in Germany. As Salih put it, MJD members want simultaneously to be pious Muslims and "model citizens" of Germany.[10]

GERMANY'S FIRST HALAL RAPPER

The life story and art of Ammar114, who produced "Muslim rap" for the first time in Germany within the MJD milieus, best exemplify the efforts that the MJD expends in bringing aspects of German youth experience into the realm of Islam, and how this combination poses a challenge to both mainstream German society and existing Muslim communities. Ammar was born in 1979 to Christian parents in Ethiopia. He came to Germany in 1983, at the age of four.[11] Ammar met Muslims when he began making rap and hip-hop music in Frankfurt in 1995. The first Muslim he met, at the age of fifteen, was a Croatian man who had converted to Islam and was also part of the hip-hop scene. He kept meeting other Muslims, but the one Muslim who influenced him the most in general and in his decision to convert in particular was his producer, Sayfoudin, the son of an Italian mother and Moroccan father, who had come to Islam after much wrongdoing.[12] Ammar was impressed by the fact that this man was a sincere believer, but also active in this worldly life and the hip-hop scene. After many conversations with him, Ammar converted to Islam when he was twenty, in 1999.

Following his conversion, Ammar adopted the name Ammar114, referring to the Qur'an's 114 suras, or chapters. On his Web site he explains that shortly after his conversion, he spontaneously wrote his first Islamic rap song, "Allah vergib mir" (Allah forgive me). Later he produced an album with additional songs and was surprised by the great attention it received. Soon after his conversion, too, Ammar met Siddiq, the founder of the MJD, a fellow convert who was deeply moved by his songs, and Siddiq invited him to participate in the MJD's meetings.

Apart from having been personally moved by Ammar's first song, Siddiq must be aware of the power of hip-hop in bringing youths to Islam.[13] One of Ammar's most significant contributions was that he took the leading role in establishing halal entertainment in Germany, thereby allowing practicing Muslim youths in Germany to enjoy rap and hip-hop in an Islamically acceptable way. An MJD member, Huseyin, who is also familiar with the Turkish Muslim scene in Germany, told me about the part Ammar played in creating an Islamic entertainment scene in Germany. He vividly remembered the first time Ammar took the stage as a Muslim singer at an MJD event: "All two hundred of us were sitting down during [the] MJD's annual meeting. Someone came onstage and announced that 'a brother will come to the stage. He will rap. Please sit quietly in your seats.'" Huseyin was laughing out loud as he portrayed this scene. "Can you imagine? This was like torture for us! He will rap, but hundreds of teenagers have to remain quiet! Of course, we started to move in our seats a little bit to the rhythm of the songs. Someone again took the microphone and said, 'Please do not exploit this situation. Stay quiet!'"

Huseyin recalls finding this situation funny at the time, yet looking back at how things changed since then, he told me, it seems absurd and unthinkable today. "But," he continued, this story really tells how things were different then. Ten years ago, having a singer at an Islamic event was unheard of. Especially having a guitar was really unthinkable. Nowadays there is a singer at almost every major Muslim gathering. Songs are very lively, and they have dance rhythms. The only thing people do not do is to get up and start dancing. I can say that [the] MJD made it possible for music to be considered halal in Germany. The rules [the] MJD established at the time for halal entertainment included no alcohol, no dancing, no cursing, and of course, a gender-segregated audience. Then it was considered halal.

It was no coincidence that the MJD found Ammar and that Ammar found the MJD. At the time he converted, there were no other Muslim youth groups that used German and were ethnically mixed. All other Muslim groups used either Turkish or Arabic, and would scarcely have approved of a converted Ethiopian German Muslim rapper. Ammar and the MJD spoke the same language, literally and figuratively. Ammar became associated with the MJD, wrote the semiofficial MJD anthem "Ich bin dabei" (I'm with it), and put out many more albums.

"The ethnically marginalized of the West—historically, mostly black, but nowadays also Latino, native American, Arab, [and] South Asian minorities, [are] attracted by the purported universalism and colorblindness of Islamic history and theology, are asserting membership in a transnational Islamic community of the umma, thereby challenging or 'exiting' the white West," Hishaam Aidi (2003, n.p.) writes. It is obvious that there is an antiracist, conversion-oriented Islamic hip-hop trend in the United States (Aidi 2002, 2003, 2011), France (Swedenburg 2001, 2002), and the United Kingdom.[14] In Germany, there is a similar but not as widespread trend. Most hip-hop artists and rappers in Germany are of Muslim origin, and beside Ammar, there are a few other African German rappers who converted to Islam.[15] Social discontent with German society is a theme for many Muslim rappers, although most rap music reproduces racist stereotypes about blacks and Muslims, depicting them as violent, criminal, and sexist (Güngör 2007). A few of the German rappers put their Islamic belief at the center of their art and use music to spread their belief, and among them a small handful are converts with non-German backgrounds. Ammar114, in particular, is a great example of how a nonwhite German convert to Islam can find a new voice and new perspective on German society, rather than exiting it.

On his Web site, Ammar114 defines his aim as building bridges between Muslims and the majority society through music in Germany. Ammar114's songs contain simple invitations to Islam: "When you want to know what Islam is all about, open the Qur'an and read. There you will find more than Hell and Paradise." He sings about peace and justice, and likens Islam to all other religions: "You call him God, I say Allah." In other songs, he speaks to born Muslims about violence, honor crimes, and terrorism. Most important, he takes a critical stance toward German nationalism in his songs, such as "In namen den Demokratie" (In the name of democracy). In "Wir sind Deutschland," the song that made him famous outside Muslim circles, he says, "We are Germany" and talks about racism in Germany.[16]

You are, he is, she is, we are Germany
You are, he is, she is, we are Germany
I don't have German parents, I was born abroad
But I grew up in this land
I froze, sweated, and endured with everyone
Yes, this land marked me
I am one of many who feel at home here
One of those who feel at home like a blond child
We are German even when we look different
. . . We are Germany
We live together, shape things together, move together
We are Germany
We are part of it
It is time for us finally to receive our full rights
. . .
It is time that you guys understood us as citizens and not merely guests
We are Germans
Our children are born here
. . . We have German friends and German colleagues
German brothers and sisters pray next to us
We pay German taxes and invest in German banks
In the German state that now attacks us
Disrespects us and takes away our rights
We should integrate, they say, even though we are Germans
When we fast for thirty days and go to the mosque
Eat no pork and pray five times a day
Every Friday hear the imam's sermon
Need black tea instead of beer in order to party
We are Germany, yes, we are a part of it
It is time for us finally to receive our rights

What is most interesting about these lyrics is that even though Ammar114 could be making these critical statements against German nationalism as an Ethiopian immigrant or African German, he is making them specifically as a German Muslim. The "we" in the song "We Are Germany" is not just any immigrant, not just any nonwhite German, but instead a Muslim German. The lyrics reference the racialization of immigrants by talking about their not being blond, but then quickly brings the issue back to Islam.

Ammar makes a similar move in another song, "Liebe Schwester" (Dear sister), where he encourages Muslim women to keep their headscarves on, no matter how hard it is in the German context. His lyrics also refer to the history of German racism, and declare that Muslims are the newest racialized group following Jews and blacks:

Don't they see how unfair they are?
They judge only the outer appearance with their prejudices.
Before there was the Jew with the crooked nose or the Black man with N . . .
    face
Now their aim is us, Muslims.
Sometimes I ask myself, Why do we keep turning around the same spot?
Is it really so important how you looked like, what you wore?
Whether you are Jewish, Muslim, or Christian?

Ammar114's case is in line with Aidi's (2002, n.p.) contention that "by embracing Islam, previously invisible, inaudible and disaffected individuals gain a sense of identity and belonging to what they perceive as an organized, militant, and glorious civilization that the West takes very seriously." But unlike the hip-hop artists and antiracist converts that Ted Swedenburg and Aidi talk about, Ammar114 and other German converts to Islam are harsher toward immigrant-background Muslim society than they are toward the mainstream society. In 2008, Ammar released a song titled "5:32" that is a direct critique of delinquent Muslim youths in Germany. In his words,

"Five 32" stands for a verse in the Koran that states the following: "If someone kills a person it is as if he killed all mankind and if someone saves someone's life it is as if he saved the life of all mankind." This is a clear statement that every devout Muslim should take to heart. The first verse of my song deals with juvenile delinquency. I comment about the young men who beat up an old man in the Munich underground and about the problem of juvenile delinquency in general. The second verse deals with honour killings. I start the verse with a true story that happened in Garching near Munich. The third verse deals with the issue of terrorism. These are three terms that the public often associates with Islam. With this song, I want to make it clear that it is not Islam that calls on people to do dreadful things like committing crime, honour killings, and terrorist acts. On the contrary, Islam expressly rejects and forbids such appalling acts as these. I hope that this song will help dispel prejudice and correct wrong impressions. I want it to reach anyone who has the wrong impression about Islam, regardless of whether they are Muslim or not.[17]

According to Ammar and many other converts discussed earlier in this book as well as MJD members, Muslim immigrants in Germany do not live up to the standards of Islam. While Ammar appreciates Islam, and acknowledges the marginalization of Muslims and the racism they face in Germany, he is also critical of their wrongdoing and eager to disassociate them from what he sees as true Islam. Even though something like conversion to Islam cannot be reduced to a political statement and vice versa, it is crucial to realize that global discourses about a bifurcation between Islam and the West do influence the way that individuals locate themselves in this divide. Hip-hop and rap, a realm of expression for the marginalized youths in urban metropoles, became a place of contact for these young individuals to meet Islam and convert to a religion with a universalist message, which offers the promise of going beyond racism, even if in reality it does not always deliver on that promise. Ammar114's lyrics underscore that having converted to Islam allows him to feel part of a critical mass that can stand in opposition to mainstream German society. At the same time, embracing the philosophy of an organization like the MJD that aims to overcome ethnic identities and national traditions allows its members to speak as Muslims from within the German nation, and thus expand its boundaries. This sometimes comes at the expense of leaving "traditional" Muslims outside this new definition of national values, though.

POLITICAL CONTROVERSY

No discussion of the MJD would be complete without referring to the political controversy about the organization. Despite or perhaps because of the way that the MJD defined itself as a decidedly German organization, it presented itself as an enigma to German authorities and generated conflicted reactions, oscillating between celebrating and punishing the organization.[18] In 2002, the MJD received funding from the Deutsches Bundesministerium für Familie, Senioren, Frauen und Jugend (German Ministry for Family, Seniors, Women, and Youth) to run a project with the title Ta'ruf/Kennenlernen (Introduction), in which young Muslims would speak to young Berliners with immigration backgrounds directly in schools in order to counter racism. This project was attacked in the press as "Muslim organization evangelizing in Berlin schools."[19] This brought the MJD to the public's attention. Another journalist spotted anti-Semitic and anti-US statements on the MJD's Web page. The MJD representatives quickly apologized and explained that parts of their Web site were open to their members, who could post text without being moderated. They deleted these texts and limited their members' access to their Web site. At this point, though, the ministry withdrew its support and the project was terminated. Worse, the MJD was implicated in having connections with the Muslim Brotherhood and came under investigation by the Bundesamt für Verfassungschutz (Federal Office for the Protection of the Constitution, or BfV).[20] "One of the shura [board] members for 2004 was the brother of Ibrahim el-Zayat, the president of the Islamic Community [in] Germany (Islamische Gemeinschaft in Deutschland), who the Federal Office for the Protection of the Constitution suspected of representing the Muslim Brotherhood in Germany" (Bendixsen 2013, 44).

The BfV is an intelligence-gathering agency with special political and symbolic power. Its function is to make sure that no one endangers the legitimacy or acts contrary to the German Constitution promulgated in 1949, when Germany was occupied by the Allied powers. The original targets of the BfV were neo-Nazis and the GDR. The BfV's aim is currently defined as follows:

> The Federal German Constitution grants its citizens a variety of civil rights and liberties. These basic rights are granted even to those who reject our free democratic order. A clear boundary is drawn, however, when those rights are abused to undermine the democratic order and eliminate the foundation of these liberties. Painful experiences during the end of the Weimer Republic have led to bracing the principles of militant or disputational democracy. (Ministerium des Innens 2012, 16)

Today the BfV follows right-wing, left-wing, and Islamist activists as well as extremist foreigners and the Church of Scientology, and writes yearly reports on them all. In 2012, its annual budget was €209 million, and it employed 2,757 people (ibid., 12). The BfV uses surveillance and infiltration to gather information, but it has no policing function such as arresting or interrogation (ibid., 18). According to Ewing (2008, 203), "Protection of the constitution operates as the idiom of a collective conscience that is dedicated to monitoring unruly impulses of violence and undemocratic tendencies in whatever form it appears." Given that it symbolically represents the collective German conscience, when the BfV puts an organization under surveillance, there are serious consequences, even if it does not find any concrete evidence against it, as the case of the MJD demonstrates. In addition to losing the status of being a registered association, the organization is marked as suspect, and other groups become unwilling to cooperate with it. This change of status not only had political but also economic consequences. Once under BfV surveillance, the MJD could not receive public funding for projects, and because it lost its status as a registered association, it also had to pay higher taxes. Moreover, members of groups and organizations under surveillance by the BfV have difficulty obtaining German citizenship; they may be interrogated by the police; and they are not considered legitimate interlocutors in public discussions of social issues with government or private organizations.

The BfV has been criticized for its failure to recognize the cells responsible for the 9/11 attacks as well as its inability to uncover the far-right National Socialist Underground, which murdered nine immigrants between 2000 and 2006. Muslims and scholars have criticized the sloppy, unjustified way in which the BfV makes accusations against Islamic groups. Werner Schiffauer (2008), who followed the so far unfounded charges against the Turkish diaspora organization Millî Görüş (National vision) over the years, describes the way that the BfV organizes its accusations as "guilt by association" or "practice of infection." He shows that any group that was in contact with a person considered suspect by the BfV was seen as infected by Islamism.

When I met one of the former leaders of the MJD, he had recently learned that yet another project it had planned, this time providing psychological counseling to Muslim prisoners, had been defined as unqualified for support after a long process of planning and negotiation. Looking frustrated, he told me,

> I think the German Constitution is great, and I totally agree with it. But I do not understand the logic of the Federal Office for Protection of Constitution. Because we are under their observation, we cannot get support for any project. When we are faced with this, how can I tell young Muslims that we really are part of this society and that they should do their best to contribute to it?

It is indeed ironic that in a country where Muslims are routinely accused of not being willing to integrate, not participating in the larger society, and not speaking German well, one of the few organizations that is committed to all these values is declared suspect based on shady evidence. Schiffauer's observations about Millî Görüş can be extended to the MJD. Conservative Muslim organizations that actually promote the idea that a Muslim life is compatible with German identity are regarded as security risks.

CONCLUSION

Germany's minority-majority politics parallel those that Viswanathan (1998, 5) has described in the cases of India and Britain in the late twentieth century. Religious minority groups can neither fully embrace their minority position nor entirely abandon it, nor completely disappear (Mufti 1995). As I discussed in the introduction to this book, contemporary German politicians insist that Muslims can live in Germany as citizens, but their religion or Islamic identity is not accepted. MJD members try to respond to this challenge by showing that one can be a conservative Muslim and model German citizen at the same time. They willingly let their ethnic identities as Arabs, Turks, Bosnians, or Indians slip into the background, emphatically underlining their German identity, while trying to prove that a conservative Muslim lifestyle is compatible with it.

MJD members came to embrace their German identity fully as they learned to define Islam universally, as something that can be detached from its Turkish and Arab roots. The MJD preaches and practices a German Islam, a youthful Islam, a fun Islam. Its chosen language is German, and it seeks to find halal alternatives or modifications of activities that mainstream German youths enjoy, pulling diverse Muslims out of their ethnic enclaves and bringing them together simply as German Muslims. It is through such practices that born Muslims became part of the larger German Muslim society in the first place and then German society in general. Through the MJD, Turkish or Arab Muslims as well as converted Muslims with different backgrounds find ways to be part of, and express themselves as part of, German society while defining themselves as German Muslims too.

This newfound German Muslim identity, however, comes at a cost. Like the indigenous German Muslims discussed in earlier chapters, MJD members also define the practices of their Turkish, Arab, or Bosnian parents as traditional, backward, and not necessarily Islamic, and hence a poor fit with German values. As Islamic identity is incorporated into the fold of German-ness, ethnic identities or practices that get defined as traditional are considered of no value and left behind.

Most likely, the MJD is identified by the BfV as a threat to the order of things in Germany precisely because it has been so successful in conflating the categories of German and Muslim. One might go so far as to venture that like German converts to Islam, MJD members are guilty in the state's eyes of confusing the categories of insider and outsider. Perceived as internal enemies who might potentially disrupt German society, they must thus be kept under constant observation.

Chapter 5

SALAFISM AS THE FUTURE OF EUROPEAN ISLAM?

To get to the notorious Salafi al-Nur mosque in Neukölln, allegedly the most radical in Berlin, I need to change trains twice. The first time I got off at the Neukölln stop, I encountered a wall of police officers with German shepherds trained to find drugs glaring at dark-haired, olive-skinned youths. I walked past them and waited too long for the S46 train to come. This less frequent line takes me to Königs Wusterhausen, an old industrial area in the eastern part of the city. By the time the train approaches my stop on a Sunday afternoon, it has filled up with groups of young men and women in their late teens and early twenties that seem to be heading in the same direction: to a lecture by the charismatic Abdul Adhim Kamouss. Colorful, glittery headscarves dot the train car. But there are also a number of women wearing long black dresses and oversize black headscarves. A few wear gloves and face covers. I notice big blue eyes shining from the thin slit of the black niqab leaves between the part that goes over the head and face. Men look sporty, wearing jeans and sneakers. A few wear skullcaps, fine mustaches, and full, long shiny beards treated with perfumed essential oils. Beards come in all colors: black, blond, and even red.

As we walk toward the mosque through the depressed, empty streets lined with defunct factories, suddenly the scene changes. Near the mosque, men loiter, greeting each other, while young ones steal looks at women. Groups of young women walk briskly, arm in arm, toward the entrance, trying—not always successfully—not to look back at the men and giggle. The small mosque store is busy with women buying halal gummi bears—made from beef gelatin from animals slaughtered in Turkey according to Islamic law—for their children as well as young men looking for energy drinks.

Like other buildings around it, the al-Nur mosque is an old factory with a bland cement facade. The only sign of its being a mosque is the green-on-white board on the outside that says Al-Nur Islamic Society in German and Arabic. I follow the trail of women into our entrance. We climb to the second floor, reserved for women only and completely cut off from the men's section by a separate entrance. There are more than a hundred women inside. They sit on the wall-to-wall carpet that features a pattern designating individual prayer spaces lined up in rows and pointing in the direction of Mecca. Long loose white skirts and oversize white headscarves line the walls. Young women in headscarves who come in with relatively tight clothes change into these before praying.

Volunteers work hard to keep the children contained in the playroom, but the kids end up running all over the hall, while babies roll around on the cushy floor. A couple of women patrol the space, reminding women not to feed their children or eat, not to talk on the phone, and to keep quiet, and also to welcome newcomers to the mosque. Heidi, a Slovenian convert to Islam, asks if I have come here to convert. "No," I answer. "I am already a Muslim. I came here to do research." Heidi's smile freezes. She tells me that I must get permission from the administration. I nod and say "of course," but the call to prayer is already being announced and women begin walking toward the front of the room to take their place for the group prayer. Some are hurrying to finish up their earlier devotions and prayers required to greet the mosque on arrival. Heidi makes sure everyone is lined up properly on the lines imprinted on the carpet. She gives instructions in German: "Foot to foot, shoulder to shoulder. Do not allow Satan to get between you." Then she takes her place. When the imam's call of "Allahu Akbar" (God is great) is piped in from men's section, the room becomes quiet, other than the yelping kids, who can now go wild, running around as their mothers' attention is directed elsewhere. We all raise our hands to our ears in unison and set our intention for the afternoon *'Asir* (prayer).

The large, flat television screen flickers on, and everyone finds a comfortable spot for themselves where they can sit together with friends. We'll be watching the lecture delivered downstairs in the men's section. Sunday lectures are given by a young preacher of Moroccan origin, Abdul Adhim, who is also a student of electric engineering at the Technical University in Berlin and married to a converted German woman. The talks are video recorded in order to be transmitted to the women's section, and are also posted on the mosque's Web site.[1]

I am not the only observer in the mosque. Abdul Adhim announces with a charming smile that a CNN crew is there to document German converts to Islam. The television network had missed ten people converting together the previous week. This week, there are four men and two women who will publicly proclaim that there is one God, and Muhammad is God's messenger.

Abdul Adhim was slightly more riled up than usual that day. After reciting from the Qur'an, he launched directly into his subject: "I invite all of you who are not Muslims here today to Islam, before it is too late. There are only two paths to take in this world. A person either believes or does not believe. Do you want to be the slave of human ideas or do you want to be the slave of God?"

As an experienced proselytizer in Germany, Abdul Adhim first takes into account the potential atheist tendencies among his listeners and tries to show how a belief in God can be rationally explained:

> I can see you, but I cannot see what is behind this wall. I can smell what is next to me. But I cannot smell what is beyond this wall. My senses and understanding is limited. If you accept this, you can believe in a God that you cannot see or feel with your five senses. This is called belief. And this is the path that goes to God. Come to Islam.

Then he moves to target the potential Christians in the crowd, preaching about how Islam is inclusive of Christianity, at least in a rhetorical way. "Dear Brothers," he says,

> Islam is the final religion. With its arrival, all religions were invalidated. The concept of the Trinity is wrong according to Islam. This is a concept invented four centuries after Jesus's death. It is a human invention. The Muslim perspective on Jesus is the correct one. We love and honor him as a prophet. But he is not God's son. Many verses in the Qur'an warn us against making an error, mistaking beings other than Allah as God. There can be no mediators between humankind and God. We Muslims honor him as a prophet, but do not exaggerate and call him son of God.

After making his basic points loud and clear, Abdul Adhim speaks directly to the topic of the spread of Islam in Europe, since that is what the CNN crew is most interested in. While explaining this, he draws parallels between the spread of Islam in Arabia and Europe, taking care to show that there is nothing different between Arabs and Europeans other than their belief:

> The Prophet Muhammad had visions that Islam will spread worldwide. Nobody would imagine that a religion that came first to the wild barbarian Arabs, who were so poor, so stupid, would spread so far. Within thirty years, Islam educated and civilized them. Now can we say Islam is in Europe? The answer is yes! That is why they are writing about us all the time in the newspapers. That is why our guests from the CNN are here today. They are here because they recognize that we are here! Allah is present. Whether they like it or not, people recognize the light of Islam despite the lies about Islam being a religion of terrorism, a religion of violence. This is all propaganda because they are afraid of the powers of Islam

to recruit so many people. Dear brothers and sisters, it was the same way in the seventh century. In those days too the youth and the poor quickly adopted Islam. The older and richer people rejected a change of their habits. It is exactly the same today. So do not listen to the unbelievers who want to misguide you. We have a simple answer to give to them. Islam is a living and vibrant religion, it is part of everyday life. In Islam there is no difference among human beings, except in their piety.

Following Abdul Adhim's sermon that day, six people declare the *sha-hada* publicly and convert to Islam. After finishing up with the conversion of men downstairs, Abdul Adhim comes to the women's section and assists women converts. He tells them that they should feel lucky because not everyone is lucky enough to find this path. He recommends that they go home and take a shower, so that they are cleansed of all their sins, and that they should pray *salat*, the Islamic prayer. If they do not know how to, they should just talk to God openly and tell him that they have come to him. He says, "Now you are like a clean slate, like newborns without any sins," adding," "Today is your birthday. You should remember this day, not your real day of birth." After that the women repeat Abdul Adhim's words, first in German and then in Arabic, that there is only one God and Muhammad is his messenger. Unlike the men, who greeted their new brothers in faith with hearty screams of "Allahu Akbar," the women quietly clap with the backs of their hands, according to proper Salafi conduct, and give the converts a round of teary hugs.

Almost every week that I attended the popular Sunday sermons at the al-Nur mosque, two to six people responded to Abdul Adhim's simple and direct invitation to convert to Islam. These new converts were indigenous Germans, immigrants from Russia, eastern Europe, Africa, and Latin America, or people of mixed background of every imaginable combination. They were often quite young—from their late teens to late twenties—and had been initiated to Islam by Muslim friends or lovers.

Why do so many German speakers find the allegedly most conservative and most radical mosque in Berlin so attractive? Why are Salafis, purportedly the most isolationist Muslim group, so successful in attracting non-Muslims? What accounts for their ability to manage diversity in their mosques, in a society where ethnic Germans and Germans with immigrant backgrounds do not normally mix well? More important, what effect does this have on the practice of Islam in Germany?

An increasingly growing literature attempts to explain the rise of Salafism in Europe over the past decade. In the face of the difficulty of conducting ethnographic research with isolationist Salafi groups, especially militant ones (Hemmingsen 2011), most of the scholarship favors a functionalist logic that reduces adherence to Salafism to an outlet for individuals who do not have strong ties of belonging to society. As Frazer Egerton (2010) convincingly demonstrates, the literature on contemporary Salafism relies heavily on the idea of alienation to account for adherence to Salafism. Scholars argue that the contemporary generation of European Muslims feels alienated because it is economically deprived and racially discriminated against (Kepel 1997; Sayyid 2003). As a result, these young people supposedly turn to Salafism, or other Islamist movements, that "deliberately play on their sense of being victims of racism, exclusion, and loneliness in the West" (Roy 2004, 309). In turn, scholars contend, Salafism provides youths with an outlet to rebel against the mainstream society that rejects them (Cesari 2007; Roy 2004; Coolsaet 2011). In the words of a French Muslim scholar, Salafism is "an exit strategy developed by young Muslims who are unable or unwilling to adjust to French society" (Adraoui 2009, 374). Other scholars maintain that the turn to Salafism offers a solution to the identity crisis that the current young European Muslims are assumed to experience, torn between the identities of their ethnic affiliation and country of residence. As Salafis, this reasoning goes, young European Muslims are able to bridge the divide they experience between being, say, Moroccan and Dutch (Koning 2009), Turkish and German, Algerian and French, or Pakistani and British. They feel themselves to be part of something bigger (Hamid 2009), and hence less marginal as adherents of the Ummah.

This is surely part of the explanation, especially for Muslims with immigrant backgrounds who turn to Salafism. Many of the born Muslims who do so are school dropouts, former criminals, or drug addicts, and I observed that after they joined Salafism, or turned to any interpretation of Islam for that matter, many were able to pull their lives together, get over their addictions, quit crime, and often go back to school, get degrees, establish families, and find jobs. In other words, Salafism not only gives one a sense of superiority in relation to non-Muslims as well as non-Salafi Muslims but also at times helps its members—at least men—improve their status in society. Still, I contend that this kind of functionalist thinking ends up pathologizing Salafis in that it depicts them as people who lack something that other members of the society have, and reduces engaging with Salafi morality to a simplistic instrumentalism. In that sense, these explanations are similar to earlier theories of religious conversion that pathologize individual converts. Scholars that focus on Salafism in Europe tend to expand the psychologism of conversion studies to an entire generation. The main problem with this kind of instrumentalist logic is that it "does not posit militant [and non-militant] Salafism as a coherent philosophical and political alternative" (Egerton 2010, 460).

More important, for our purposes here, the generational Muslim alienation thesis fails to grasp why converts choose this movement. Indigenous German or German-speaking converts, I estimate, make up at least

30 percent of the al-Nur mosque's congregation. Regardless of their German, Russian, or African backgrounds, these people were formerly Christians, and they did not have that much to gain sociologically, and in fact had much to lose, by converting to Islam. So why is Salafism, the form of Islam most suspected of radicalization and terrorism by the German authorities, and whose members are most isolated from mainstream society, the most attractive to newcomers to Islam in Germany?

In this chapter, I offer an alternative to the generation-specific alienation and deprivation thesis by concentrating on the theological aspects of Salafism that attract non-Muslims in postunification Germany. I argue that certain characteristics of Salafism, particularly its conversionism, literalism, and anticulturalist, antinationalist stance, make it appealing to many Germans of diverse backgrounds. In these respects, it works in quite similar ways to Evangelism and Pentecostalism in fulfilling people spiritually and psychologically—aspects greatly ignored by most scholars of contemporary Islam and especially Salafism. I contend that it is these characteristics of Salafism, which introduces itself as free of human interpretation and independent of national tradition, that works well in the anti-Muslim context of Germany. Converts to Salafism learn that they are much better Muslims than all those who follow national traditions, and Salafis do not need to associate with traditional Muslims in order to embrace their new spiritual path.

SALAFISM IN GERMANY

Those labeled Salafis by outsiders do not call themselves Salafis but rather followers of the Qur'an and Sunnah (Ahlu Sunnah). One can trace contemporary Salafism back to the eighteenth-century Islamic puritanism of Ibn Abd al-Wahhab (1703–92), which became the official ideology of the Saudi monarchy in the early twentieth century. Modern Salafis are also influenced by thinkers such as the Egyptian Muhammad 'Abduh (1849–1905) and Iranian Jamal al-Din al-Afghani (1839–97) as well as the Muslim Brotherhood.[2] As Salafism moves to newer contexts and grows by including many converts, it takes on new and sometimes-contradictory qualities. The attacks of 9/11 led to further divisions within the group, with a great majority of followers positioning themselves against such violence. Today, this global movement is only loosely connected. It has different branches and interpretations, such as apolitical quietism or jihadism, and more recently the Salafi political party al-Nur in Egypt.[3]

Despite its popularity among new Muslims, Salafism is quite a small movement in Germany. It is estimated that 30 out of 2,500 mosques and prayer houses in Germany are Salafi oriented. They represent from 2,000 to 5,000 Salafi-oriented Muslims.⁴ I contend that an overwhelming majority of the individuals who attend these mosques have an orientation that is not jihadist. Some jihadis also attend some of the mosques, such as the small group caught collecting explosives in order to plan a terrorist attack in the Sauerland in 2007 (Özyürek 2009). The most radical jihadi Salafis find one another on the Internet and meet in private homes. Al-Nur's leaders, notably Abdul Adhim, make their antiviolence position clear. But al-Nur, the oldest Salafi mosque in Berlin, which once had an imam accused of being a radical, is easily the Berlin mosque most mentioned in the press. As with all other mosques in Germany, one does not need to be a formal member of the al-Nur mosque to attend. Both members of congregations and imams engage in "mosque hopping" among German-speaking mosques. Even though the most devoted Salafis only attend Salafi mosques, I observed quite a high degree of flexibility.

In reaching out to its new members, Salafism is not that different from other fundamentalist movements spreading around the globe, and especially Evangelical and Pentecostal Christianity. First and foremost, like all other globally spreading religions, Salafism benefits from "missions and migrations" (Beyer 2006). Non-Muslim Germans encounter Islam first through a meaningful relationship with a born Muslim and then learn about Salafi mosques while doing research on the Internet. All the converts I met at Salafi mosques discovered the al-Nur mosque and Salafism after they had become Muslim or developed an interest in becoming Muslim. After proselytizing for years, a German convert to Islam told me that in the past fifteen years of her life as a Muslim, she had never met a single person who converted to Islam as a result of Salafi proselytizing. Salafis are known for setting up information stands in areas of heavy foot traffic, and distributing free Qur'ans or giving passersby pamphlets that explain the religion. My research shows that they owe their success not to random missionizing such as this but rather to their investment in creating accessible Web sites in the German language and providing German-language activities in their mosques—still a rarity. Salafism does not necessarily succeed in recruiting ethnic Germans to Islam in the first place; instead, it meets their needs as German Muslims after they convert.

SALAFISM IN THE CONTEXT OF GLOBAL FUNDAMENTALISMS

Over the past few decades, a number of scholars have attempted to define the central aspects of different fundamentalisms growing across the globe (Lawrence 1989; Keddie 1998; Lehmann 1998; Riesebrodt 1998; Nagata 2001). Several have pointed out structural similarities between Christian fundamentalist and Salafi discourses (Zeidan 2003; Henson and Wasserman

2011). There are a number of possible ways to make this comparison. For the purpose of explaining the attraction of non-Muslim Germans to Salafism, the following four aspects that Salafism shares with Christian fundamentalisms are most powerfully operative: conversionism; a rejection of tradition; literalism; and the breaking of traditional religious hierarchies. All these aspects, I argue, make Salafism welcoming to new Muslims, especially in a country where Islam is increasingly racialized. In particular, the emphasis in Salafi theology on an antitraditionalist understanding of Islamic teachings makes it easier for nontraditional individuals to embrace Islam and allows them to feel themselves to be better Muslims than born Muslims.

Conversionism

Salafis follow the example of the first Muslims in calling people to Islam. Even though this is a position shared by all other Muslims, Salafis seem to be the ones who take it as the central message. Almost all other Sunni mosques in Germany represent a national Muslim group. Even if they are in theory open to Muslims from other nationalities, mosques based on nationality exclude other groups in everyday practice, especially when they use a national language such as Turkish. Salafis, on the other hand, reach out to new Muslims in Germany in the German language. In 2012, Salafis kicked off a campaign to distribute free Qur'ans in German translation on busy street corners—not a practice other Muslim groups had ever engaged in, but one that evangelical Christians commonly use around the world by distributing free Bibles. Salafis keep their message simple and inviting at Web sites such as Die wahre Religion (True religion) and Facebook groups such as Einladung zum Paradies (Invitation to paradise).[5] These sites host German-language sermons by preachers of both Arab and German origin. The most important part of these Web sites are the numerous videos of Germans converting to Islam in Salafi mosques.

Rejection of Tradition

Salafis' success in attracting new Muslims is not only an issue of language. Their rejection of tradition and especially nationalism is also crucial in making new Muslims from nontraditional groups feel at home. Other groups discussed in this book are antitraditionalist too, but Salafism is the most extreme in this approach and also negates the idea of an Islam fitting the realities of life in Germany. Salafis promote an understanding of Islam that they believe is purified of any *bid'a*, or innovation, which is to say, a cultural or traditional change introduced after the first three generations of Muslims. Salafism shares a specific approach to time with other fundamentalisms, which Susan Harding (2001) defines as paying attention only to what happened at the beginning of time, the present, and the end of time. Everything that happened between the beginning and now is unimportant. For Salafis, most of what Muslims have done since the idealized time of the first three generations of Muslims is not only irrelevant but also bad, or at least not preferable. In that sense, according to Salafis, Muslim communities since that third generation have actually harmed Islam, and their practices are problematic from the perspective of a pure Islam.

A result of this principle is that Salafis reject blind imitation (*taqlid*) of the four legal schools (*madhab*) developed after the first three generations of Muslims. In the contemporary Muslim world, each of these legal schools is dominant in certain regions, and hence associated with nationalities. For example, the Hanafi school is commonly followed in Turkey, the Turkic republics of Central Asia, and the Balkans; the Maliki school is common in most of North Africa; the Hanbali school is the dominant one in Saudi Arabia; and the Shafi'i school is observed in East Africa, Indonesia, and Kurdistan. Ethnic or national mosques operating in Germany also follow these legal schools accepted in their respective countries of origin. They even have imams come from these countries who are trained only in one of these legal schools.

Salafis argue that rather than blindly following the four legal schools, Muslims should rely only on the Qur'an and Hadith, and apply their individual interpretations, *ijtihad*—of course, only within the strict and literalist Salafi methodology called *manhaj*. In their rejection of the madhabs, Salafis break the connection between ethnic or national groups and legal schools. It does not matter, then, if one is a Turk, an Arab, Japanese, or German to be a good Salafi. On the contrary, having been a good Turkish Muslim can impede being a good Muslim, since people who grow up with traditions established by the legal schools have to unlearn much of what they know.

Literalism

The literalism that is embraced fully by Salafism is one crucial aspect of fundamentalism that makes it possible to break the link between culture and religion in bringing nontraditional people to the religion. All Sunnis would agree that what is written in the Qur'an and Hadith constitute the basics of their religion, and that these texts have the highest level of authority over anything else. Salafis differ from other Sunnis in that they believe that everything is explicitly stated in the Qur'an and Hadith, and should be taken literally. Scholars such as Roel Meijer contend that the real power of Salafism lies in this strict focus on doctrinal purity rather than politics. This focus, Meijer (2009, 13) asserts, "has been able to empower individuals by providing a universal alternative model of truth and social action even in its passive form of rejecting existing religious, cultural, and political systems."

Literalism and doctrinal purity promise that questions asked at any time, any place, and by any Muslim will be answered from an Islamic perspective with absolute certainty. Bernard Heykel (2009, 36) maintains that "Salafism's claims to religious certainty . . . explain a good deal of its appeal and its seemingly limitless ability to cite scripture to back these up. A typical Salafi argument is that Salafis, unlike other Muslims, rely exclusively on sound proof texts from revelation as the basis for their views, and they adduce the relevant verses or traditions every time they issue a judgment or opinion."

Such certainty seems to be especially valuable to many newcomers to Islam in Germany. Most new Muslims report the experience of a deeply felt inner peace following their conversion. Spending time with new converts, I observed that they also experience much anxiety in their daily lives in trying to fulfill their newly learned religious obligations in a society not organized around them. The many rules and rituals to learn, numerous prayers to memorize in Arabic, and desire to quickly master the Arabic language, at least well enough to recite the Qur'an, is often overwhelming for many new Muslims. They frequently say that the worst part of being a new convert in Germany is the sensation of being bombarded with competing sources of information and a simultaneous scarcity of systematic information in the German language.

Most of the older converts to Islam recalled the intensity of their belief and overwhelming experience of being faced with so much information. A woman who had converted eight years earlier said with a nostalgic smile, "I forced so much into my head that I could not remember a single thing when I went to bed." Right after conversion, converts often desire to completely transform their lives and purify themselves of all non-Islamic elements. Many, but clearly not all, new converts adopt a new Islamic name, change their clothes, abandon old friends, and erase all or inappropriate music from their iPods. I observed that Salafism is most attractive to new Muslims exactly at this early phase of conversion. Many friends who converted in the 1990s told me that when they first did so, they Salafism appealed to them because of the clear-cut worldview it presented and way it accommodated new Muslims. Some of them later moved on to less strict interpretations of Islam. A number of converted men and women mentioned that after several years of being Muslim, they relaxed and realized not everything had to be so rigid. Iman, for example, reflected on how she would never shake a man's hand when she first converted. "Now, after years of being a Muslim," she explained to me, "when I cannot avoid shaking a man's hand without being rude, I do not lose sleep over it. Now I have a better sense of the things I cannot compromise and the things I can compromise when I have to. Knowing that my intention is in the right place is the most important thing."

Aamal gave me a window on to the anxieties of new Muslims. I met her only a few months after she had converted, just before she married her Afghani husband. Previously, she had been married to a Thai man and was a practicing Buddhist. We met at the Saturday lecture of the DMK, which she had found on the Internet. Aamal looked a little confused and stressed, and had a long list of questions. She had been going to many mosques in her neighborhood, asking for German-language activities and materials. Her purse was full of pamphlets in different languages and scripts she had collected from different mosques.

The first break for the Saturday lecture was timed according to the noon Dhuhr prayer. As we lined up for the prayer, Aamal kept looking at women on either side of her. Afterward, she walked up to the prayer leader and asked her the right place to put her hands during *ruku* (bending down). She had been told to put her hands on her upper leg, but had noticed that here and in some other mosques, women put their hands on their knees. The prayer leader, an older convert to Islam, smiled understandingly. She tried to calm Aamal by assuring her that she should not be anxious about such details, that her intention was the most significant thing. "But," she added, "on top of your knees is the right place for your hands during ruku." Aamal nodded seriously. Then she asked how to place her feet during the sitting between the two *sujuds* (prostrations). The prayer leader responded, "There are different traditions on this issue, and God willing, they are all acceptable." Aamal listened to her carefully, but the anxious look remained on her face.

After the lecture, Selda, who had converted to Islam as a young girl more than fifteen years earlier, invited Aamal and me to her home for tea. Just as we settled down in Selda's small but tidy living room, Aamal said she had almost died when she heard today that one cannot pray with food in their mouth. The other day, she had put a piece of chocolate in her mouth right before she began her prayer. After a brief second of tense silence, she added daringly, "And you know what, I did not die!"

Aamal informed us that she was not going to just believe in everything anybody told her. "I need to see something in writing before I can believe in it." She pulled out her pamphlet stash from her bag, went through them quickly, and found the one she was looking for. It was a sheet from a Pakistani mosque, with Urdu writing on one page and German on the corresponding page, along with Arabic scattered in between. It announced that it is haram (forbidden) for women to put henna on their hands. She said, "This woman who gave the lecture to us today had henna in her hands. And you tell me to believe in everything she says?" Selda said she heard that it is OK to apply henna but not nail polish, even though she could not show it to Aamal in writing. She said, "I believe it is because you can still take ablutions with henna on, since the water touches the skin. But you cannot do it with the nail polish. But you can put nail polish on if you are willing to take it off before you take each ablution. But you cannot wear acrylic fingernails because you cannot take them off." After sharing her knowledge on matters regarding hand decorations, Selda continued,

> But we cannot always know the reasoning behind everything we are told. It might be the case that some things are more important for us converts. Take the chocolate thing. Maybe people who grew up praying five times a day find it easy to concentrate on their prayer, and maybe as converts we need to be extra careful so that we are not distracted. I personally sometimes find it difficult to concentrate.

Even fifteen years after her conversion, Selda said, she still does not know which information is more critical.

> Some people will tell you that it is haram to watch TV, haram to sit on a sofa, haram to wear a dress that you like, haram to buy something for yourself. They will tell you so many things are haram that you will not be able to do anything! I personally try to go with [the] iman's advice. What she says makes sense to me and stays in my mind.

Aamal and Selda agreed that one should not take born Muslims, especially Turks, too seriously. "As a Muslim for only a few months, I already know so much more than my Turkish friends," Aamal noted. "They do not read anything. All they know is hearsay." To congratulate her on her conversion, a Turkish friend had given Aamal a pendant with the word Allah on it in Arabic. Aamal was furious. "Why doesn't a Muslim know that you are not supposed to wear anything that has God's name on your body?" Selda agreed enthusiastically, telling us about many Turkish friends who knew nothing or, worse, clung to wrong information. She told us about a Turkish friend who did not know how to pray despite the fact that she was wearing a headscarf. Selda claimed she is the one who had taught her how to pray. Selma said, "Yes, most of the time you cannot rely on Turks for Islamic knowledge."

Seeing how stressed out she looked, I felt an urge to comfort Aamal. I told her that I was not the best person to give advice—for one thing, I was one of those ignorant Turks, and raised in a nonpracticing Muslim family, I had never been formally trained in Islamic practices—but it made sense to me to go slowly, without worrying herself too much. I told her that I had heard about new Muslims who were so overwhelmed that they quit

Islam altogether. Aamal disagreed with me. She said she wanted to learn about all the rules right away and follow them precisely. "Because," she said, "the Satan in me is very strong." She told us that she used to wear sexy, skimpy clothes and heavy makeup, and went out to nightclubs. Her body still bore the residues of her pre-Islamic life. She had a nose ring and rhinestone implanted in one of her front teeth as well as permanent makeup on her eyebrows, around her lip line, and on her eyelash line. She rubbed her hand on her face and then showed us her clean palms to demonstrate that she wasn't wearing any makeup. She said she was easily tempted. About a month ago, her brother had come to visit her. All day long he told her that there is no God and that she was being ridiculous. He kept drinking beer after beer. Aamal, who had once enjoyed drinking beer herself, decided that if she drank only half a bottle without getting drunk, it would not be a big deal. So she did. But then all night she had horrible nightmares and saw herself going to hell.

When I met Aamal, she was attending activities at the DMK and was not going to a Salafi mosque. Salafi mosques, however, offer satisfactory answers along with welcoming contexts for converts like Aamal who feel overwhelmed by contradictory information and doubt that lower-class, undereducated born Muslims in Germany are reliable sources of information. Because Salafi mosques take a literalist stance, they answer all questions with reference to the Qur'an and Hadith. The newer and older converts I met at Salafi mosques, or who had gone through a Salafi phase, told me that they found such emphasis on sources satisfying. Salafi literalism and clarity as well as its tendency to cut followers off from everything seen as unacceptable to Islamic lifestyle seem to ease some of the anxiety that many new Muslims such as Aamal experience.

Breaking Traditional Religious Hierarchies

A related attraction of the Salafi movement for converts is its relatively democratic approach to religious learning. Traditional Islamic learning is deeply hierarchical, and access to authority positions is practically inaccessible to newcomers to Islam. In Germany, it is not even possible to receive formal training to be an imam, and most imams come from countries such as Turkey, Bosnia, and Morocco. These imams are usually trained at a relatively young age and are often state officials, whose salaries are paid by their governments. Salafis, on the other hand, provide an easy path to anyone who wants to study Islam and become an authority. Their practice is in line with their understanding that any Muslim should be able to study the scriptures and come to a level of learning where they can perform ijtihad (individual interpretation). Because it is based on a narrowly defined textual frame and organized around a set of binary opposites—the oneness of God (*tawhid*) versus divine associations (*shirk*), and loyalty to the prophetic example (*Sunna*) as opposed to adherence to one school of Islamic law (taqlid)—the Salafi perspective is powerful in minimizing human agency and intellect in interpreting issues from an Islamic perspective (Wiktorowicz 2006). Heykel (2009, 36) observes that "it is striking how relatively easy it is to become an authority figure among the Salafis. In fact, as an interpretive community Salafis are, in contrast to other Muslim traditions of learning, relatively open, even democratic."

Pierre Vogel's quick rise in Salafi circles from being a new convert to Islam to the public face of the movement in Germany attests to the nonhierarchical and democratic character of Salafi learning structures. A former boxing champion, Vogel converted to Islam in 2001 at the age of twenty-three. In autobiographical video recordings, Vogel describes how he was impressed by some of the Muslims, particularly an American and then a Turk, who he met through his boxing career. Shortly after his conversion, Vogel went to Mecca to study Arabic and Islam. When he returned in 2006, he was fluent in Arabic, and had studied the Qur'an and Hadith according to the Salafi manhaj. He was able to quote long passages in Arabic and translate them into German on the spot when he had to address the proper Islamic stance on practically any topic. He also adopted what is believed to be the look of the early Muslims: he shaved his head, grew a beard without a mustache, and donned a jalabiyya and skullcap.

Shortly after he returned from Mecca, Vogel began preaching in German at the Salafi al-Nur mosque. From that time on, the al-Nur mosque became the main point of attraction for a new generation of young male converts to Islam. Vogel soon launched his own Web site, where he posted dozens of videos of himself preaching in the Salafi tradition.[6] He calls on unbelievers to embrace Islam and born Muslims to be better Muslims. Vogel also teaches how to proselytize for Islam (*da'wa*) in the German context. In interviews, he emphasizes that he is the perfect person to give advice to young people and summon them to Islam, because as someone who used to live like them, he can tell them that living a pious life and being married is much better than going to nightclubs, drinking, doing drugs, and fooling around with women. Hundreds of videos of young German men converting to Islam are the main focus of his Web site.[7]

Salafism as a Path to Radicalization

Although the great majority of Salafis in Germany are not involved in politics and are against the use of violence to attain religious goals, in the larger group of Muslims who adhere to some of the basic Salafi principles, there are small radical jihadi groups. It is quite difficult to study these subgroups, because of the obvious reasons that they are tiny in numbers and secretive, and also because individuals who end up being radicalized by ascribing to extreme ideologies and then get connected to violent jihadi cells do so by way of the Internet rather than in the mosques. Hence, during my study I did not meet a single person who defined themselves as jihadi. Instead, I only met individuals who despised the actions of jihadis. Yet since jihadi terrorism is a small subsection of the Salafi movement and converted Muslims are part of this scene too, I discuss it briefly here.

Although research shows that people generally acquire extreme ideas on the Internet as isolated individuals, and not in mosques, Salafi mosques have been under the German government's scrutiny over the past ten years. Marc Sageman (2011), one of the most insightful experts on Islamic violence, notes that in Belgium, his area of expertise, not a single foreign recruiter came to the country to attract individuals to terror groups. Rather, individuals frequently join the jihadi cause totally voluntarily and on their own. Arid Uka, a twenty-one-year-old Albanian German who committed the first Islamically motivated terror act in Germany in 2011 by killing two US airmen and injuring two others on their way to Afghanistan, struck out totally on his own after watching a propaganda film purporting to show US soldiers raping Muslim women that was posted by a friend on Facebook. The video clip had been made by using scenes from Brian De Palma's 2007 film *Redacted*, a work of fiction.[8]

Guido Steinberg (2013, 5) writes in his book *German Jihad* that Uka learned about the jihadi ideology and politics on his own, without the guidance of any authorities or masterminds: "After only a few months, Uka was ready to join the battle in Iraq or Afghanistan, but he later told his interrogators—to their surprise—that he didn't have the necessary contacts. Thus, after having watched the rape video, he decided to act alone and kill Americans on their way to Afghanistan." Based on Uka's interrogation reports, Steinberg notes, he did not intend to kill soldiers on their way back from Afghanistan but only on their way to that country. Hence, he killed the US airmen after asking if they were on their way to Afghanistan.

Even though jihadis based in the West seem to join these groups totally on their own initiative, it would be wrong to overlook the internationally determined reasons for the development of the jihadi groups and their choice of targets. Steinberg observes that jihadis based in Germany came into being only after Germany's intervention in Afghanistan and targeted Germany in order to put pressure on Germany to withdraw its troops. Individual jihadis follow the international scene and also get their ideas about potential targets as a result of being informed about this scene through radical sources on the Internet, such as the propaganda video seen by Uka. "Many [jihadis] stated that the suffering of Afghan Muslims at the hands of Western forces was one of their prime motives for joining the jihadist caravan" (ibid., 29). Between 2007 and 2010, several dozen young men and women from different parts of Germany joined the jihad in Afghanistan as a result. In 2009, they even founded the first exclusively German jihadist group, the German Taliban Mujahideen (ibid., 30–31).

Some scholars and security experts point to the high number of converts among those who join jihadi groups. Robert Leiken (2011, 236), for example, argues that "if a German Muslim is a convert he is eighty times more likely to become a jihadi than is a born Muslim," making the obvious mistake of assuming that all born Muslims are practicing Muslims—whereas most converts are. He also puts converts in a suspect position, notwithstanding that only a handful of converts are jihadis—perhaps a few dozen out of tens of thousands of converts.

Here it is important to underscore that individuals who joined these jihadi groups had different motivations, "including a lust for adventure, the wish to leave their allegedly corrupted home society, the prospect of imitating the life of the first Muslims in Mecca and Medina in the seventh century, and hatred of the US, Germany, and their allies. . . . In all cases in which the course of their radicalization has been established, however, non-Muslim interventions in Muslim countries played an important role" (Steinberg 2013, 31).

The story of an African German convert to Islam who became a Salafi jihadi sheds light on some of the dynamics discussed above. Denis Mamadou Cuspert was born to a German mother and Ghanian father in Kreuzberg, Berlin. His father left the family when he was a baby, and he grew up with an African American stepfather who had formerly been a US army officer. Cuspert had many conflicts with this man, who was strict and used brutal disciplining methods.[9] After tough years with his stepfather, Cuspert was sent to a facility for difficult children.[10] On leaving the facility in 1995, he found a way to channel his energies into rap music and became well known in the German rap scene as Deso Dogg. His music depicted "ghetto" life in Kreuzberg with images of street violence, criminality, and racialized confrontation with the police borrowed from African American rap. In his videos, Deso Dogg portrayed gangs in Kreuzberg consisting of blacks, Turks, and Arabs.[11] Deso Dogg's music also had a political dimension that criticized this racism, and in interviews he has said that he is rapping about the racist German society he was raised in: "I grew up with racism. Though my mother is German, some teachers would call me 'Negro' and treat all Muslim kids bad."[12]

Following a car accident in 2010, at a time when his music career had plummeted, Deso Dogg announced that he had converted to Islam and changed his name first to Abou Maleeq and then to Abu Talha al-Almani.[13] He quickly became part of the Salafi scene and was affiliated with the converted Salafi preacher Vogel. During that period, he gave many proselytizing lectures in Salafi mosques, and those talks have been posted online. After his conversion, he seemed less interested in the realities of Germany and showed signs of wanting to leave the country. In an interview he gave in November 2010, the ex-rapper describes Berlin as a "Kuffar" (infidel) metropole, and declares his desire to join Muslim mujahideen in Afghanistan, Chechnya, or Somalia. In 2012, he met an Austrian Al-Qaeda member named Mohamed Mahmoud, who had recently been released from prison. Through this connection, it seems, the ex-rapper joined the most radical Salafi faction. The tone of his Islamic speeches changed during this time. In his early videos, he talks about his self-transformation in an emotional tone. In this narrative of redemption, he details the kind of "bad life" he led from his adolescence on, and subsequent feelings of dissatisfaction and emptiness, despite his success and money. He is frequently overwhelmed and tears roll down his cheeks. Soon afterward, his tone changed in his videos, and he started singing German-language Islamic chants (*nasheeda*), celebrating Osama bin Laden and calling on Muslims to join the jihad.[14] He also made a video that threatened Germany with further attacks, and since then has been under the observation of German authorities.[15] While under surveillance, he left Germany, first going to Egypt along with dozens of German Salafis, including Mahmoud, and then to Syria in order to fight on the side of the Salafi Al-Nusra front.[16] As this book was being written, he was still in Syria, and had uploaded a video that showed him in a warrior outfit and with a gun in the mountains of Syria. In the short video, he calls on Muslims to join the jihad, while he gleefully plays with water in a small pond and fires his gun in the air. German officials have expressed concern about these activists further radicalizing and learning military techniques that they can use to terrorize people back in Germany.

It should be kept in mind that Deso Dogg converted to Salafism at a time when German troops were increasingly active in Afghanistan and jihadi Web sites were seeking to recruit German jihadis online to put pressure on Germany. The Austrian Al-Qaeda member Mahmoud, who had just been released from prison, was behind most of the open German-language Internet calls to jihad.[17]

Breaking with Traditional Muslims

Since Salafis seek to emulate the lifestyle of the first three generations of Muslims and follow Islamic scripture to the letter, they distance themselves from Muslims who they see as having diverged from that path. They do so on the basis of the principle of loyalty and disavowal (*wala' wa-l-bara'*), which calls on Muslims to distance themselves from Muslims who are insufficiently devout. Salafis feel that a true believer must demonstrate their enmity toward Muslim "idolaters." The distinctive appearance of Salafi men—full beards, skullcaps, jalabiyyas, and pants three or four inches above the ankle—and women, often with their faces covered, is among the most effective ways in which they display their difference from other Muslims groups in Germany. Salafis also often shun events that aim to bring different Muslim groups together, such as the annual Muslim Cup sporting event and Islam Day in Berlin, which strives to explain Islam to non-Muslims. Men and women sitting together as well as women playing sports, even when fully covered, do not fit their view of proper Muslim behavior. Instead, Salafis create distinct, close-knit communities and keep their distance from other Muslim groups.

Newcomers to Islam or older Muslims who newly affiliate with Salafism similarly need to learn how to disassociate themselves from situations that might be unacceptable or unfavorable from the perspective of their new creed. In my observations at the Salafi mosque in Berlin, even though newcomers were never explicitly told to stay away from their non-Salafi family and friends, and they were always encouraged to be respectful of their parents, the practical advice given for everyday matters leads to Salafis' isolation from their previous communities, including family and friends. New Muslims frequently want to know if it is acceptable for them to take part in Christmas, Easter, or birthday celebrations with their families; if they can go to baptism ceremonies or funerals; or if they can be present at a dinner table where there is alcohol. Imams or other counselors in mosques often advise that although there is nothing wrong in theory with, say, taking part in Christmas dinner, in reality it would be unadvisable, because the family would be practicing idolatry or would drink alcohol. Or when they ask if it would be acceptable to continue sending their child to a church-based preschool, which are widespread in Germany, the typical answer I heard was that it would be acceptable if they did not teach them about the Trinity there, but since they do, it is not advisable.

Similar rules of distancing oneself from people who do not adhere to the correct path, according to the Salafi perspective, apply not only to non-Muslims but also to other Muslims who are under the influence of national traditions. Thus, regardless of their ethnic background, those who become Salafis often end up shedding connections with their families and friends in exchange for the close-knit community they find among like-minded Salafis. In the end, even though the new community is quite strict in the way it organizes daily life, it is wildly diverse and welcoming to newcomers of any background. Born and converted Muslims in Salafi circles enjoy a feeling of superiority in relation not only to non-Muslims but to traditional Muslims as well. Salafis make frequent reference to a Hadith in which the Prophet Muhammad says, "My people will split into seventy-three sects. All of them are damned to hellfire except one." Looking at the world from the perspective of this Hadith, there is not much difference between the majority of the Muslims who do not purify themselves and non-Muslims. None of them will be saved in the end.

ETHNIC MUSLIMS IN SALAFI MOSQUES

Like other Salafi mosques in Europe, the al-Nur mosque also is heavily attended by born Muslims of Arab, Turkish, or African background. I focused on converts to Islam during my research, but I met many born Muslims in the al-Nur mosque too. I found that most of the born Muslims there shared common experiences with converts. They also came from nonpracticing families and had found Islam for themselves. They were young individuals alienated from ethnic mosques, either because they were not fluent in the languages spoken there or did not feel part of these communities. They told me that they appreciated that German was spoken in the Salafi mosque and they felt welcome there. Narratives of the experiences of three born Muslims from nonpracticing families who regularly attended the al-Nur mosque with quite different expectations will illustrate their perspective.

Canan is a seventeen-year-old Turkish German high school student with an imposing personality for her tiny frame. When I met her, it was clear that at least one of the imams saw her as the perfect person to be responsible for new young Muslim women members in the near future. This imam would make sure that Canan came to classes and understood all the arguments. He would always joke with her. When I asked Canan why she found this mosque appealing, she replied that she really liked the ease of relationships in this mosque. She said that when she went to Turkish mosques, she felt oppressed by older Turkish women, who seemed too serious to her. She liked the fact that everyone in this mosque was young and always ready to joke. Furthermore, what she had learned about the details of religious practice in this mosque put Canan in conflict with the women in Turkish mosques. Canan said that she kept going to Turkish mosques for a while, carrying printouts from German-language Salafi Web sites to try to prove to the Turks that their practices were inventions, *bid'a*, and therefore not valid in Islam. Yet she got frustrated when Turkish women there did not take her seriously. "I'd take them information that is supported with references to the Qur'an and the Hadith, and they would say, 'This is information from your mosque. That is not how we do things here!'"

Canan came from a nonpracticing family. She told me that until a year earlier, she had only been interested in boys. Everything changed when she fell in love with a young Arab man in her class who attended the al-Nur mosque. Even though the nature of their involvement was ambiguous, and he never promised to get married, he always made sure to keep Canan under his control. He made sure that she never went home late and never talked to other men. It was apparent that one reason for the ambiguity of the relationship lay in the fact that the young man was Arab and Canan was Turkish. Intermarriage between Germans and Arabs is common, but not between Turks and Arabs. And when it does happen, it is not devoid of conflict.

This Arab man told Canan to take off her nose ring and come to the al-Nur mosque. The al-Nur mosque ended up being a spiritual and social home for Canan. She started going there almost every day. She began praying regularly, and wearing a headscarf and conservative clothing. Canan took off her nose ring. One of the imams in the mosque, who Canan really respected and adored, told her that having this kind of relationship with a man was not acceptable, even if it mainly consisted of exchanging texts. "You should either should get married or end this relationship," he advised Canan. The imam was of Lebanese background, like the young man; he even volunteered to act as an intermediary and talk to the young man's father. Following this intervention, the relationship came to a halt.

I met Canan during my first year of fieldwork. A year later, when I returned to continue my research, I did not see her there. Acquaintances told me that she no longer attended the mosque. I could not find out why; she may have married another man and moved elsewhere, or simply stopped attending the mosque after things did not work out with the Arab man. Perhaps she became alienated from the mosque because the imam's actions had led to her losing that relationship. It is also possible that she married someone else from the Salafi community and moved to another city.

Esin is a thirty-year-old Turkish woman who came to Germany several years ago to continue her studies in art. She painted abstract figures expressing pain. Religion had played almost no role in her life when she was in Istanbul or during her first few years in Berlin. She told me that her life followed a typical pattern for art students in Istanbul and Berlin—alcohol, drugs, and ill-defined relationships with men. During this time, she began having intense nightmares, which she interpreted as calls to Islam. She frequently dreamed that she was in a small boat in the middle of a rough sea at night. She had to hold on tight to the boat's mast, and fire rained on her. In her dream, she recited the Shahadah, and then things would calm down. She began saying the Shahadah when she was awake and withdrew from her art circles.

At the time, she was romantically involved with a German student, Manfred, in the same program. Manfred had grown up without religion in the former East Germany. But he had a great interest in it, and they spent a lot of them talking about different religions, reading the Bible and Qur'an together. As a result of her being called through dreams, Esin started practicing Islam. Eventually, Manfred also converted and they married. After his conversion, Manfred stopped painting and changed his major to Arabic literature, so that he could read and understand the Qur'an in its original language.

Esin told me that she felt at home in Islam, but did not feel at home in Turkish mosques. When she went to the Turkish mosques, she felt as though everyone was scrutinizing and judging her. On her first day at a Turkish mosque, one woman found her headscarf not conservative enough and tried to put another scarf over her head. That offended Esin. Turkish mosques also did not work for her husband, who did not speak any Turkish. Then they heard about the al-Nur mosque and started going there. Esin did not have any special opinions about this mosque, yet she felt like she was not being judged by how she looked, which was especially gratifying given the African-style headscarf she wore.

Hamza is a sweet-mannered seventeen-year-old Arab German with a big smile that never seems to fade. He was born to a Palestinian father and Lebanese mother in Berlin. When we first met, he mentioned that I looked just like his mother. He later explained that I reminded him of his mother not because of my physical features but instead because I was not wearing a headscarf, and my clothes were neither too revealing nor too conservative. According to Hamza, his mother would have nothing to do with religion. She fasted during Ramadan, but that clearly was not enough to impress Hamza. His father sometimes went to Arab mosques, yet Hamza did not go with him since he did not understand Arabic. Hamza's siblings shared his passion for religion. His brother was a mosque-going Muslim who took his religion seriously. His sister had become a Christian active in an evangelical church group. Hamza told me that his friends would get angry when they saw his sister wearing a big cross. "When that happens," Hamza said, "I repeat the verse from the Qur'an, 'There is no compulsion in religion. We all do what we want!'"

Hamza told me that he liked going to mosques, especially because it was so easy to find friends there. "You go to a mosque," he commented, "and immediately people say, 'Welcome, brother,' and start talking to you. How else can I meet people? After lectures we go and drink tea together, [and] we talk." He explained that he likes the al-Nur mosque because it is the most fun. "It is full of young people, and Abdul Adhim is so funny," he said with a big smile on his face. We exchanged some of Abdul Adhim's jokes from his lectures and laughed together. We both found it especially hilarious when Abdul Adhim waved at the camera in front of himself enthusiastically and said, "Hello sisters!" to the women watching him on the big flat-screen television in the women's section. But al-Nur was only one of the many mosques that Hamza attended. He went to several Turkish and Arab mosques, all with German-speaking activities. He pretty much listed all the mosques in which I did my research: the Bilal mosque, where the DMK is housed, and the Mevlana, a Turkish mosque open to other ethnicities with German-speaking activities. Hamza told me that he had recently begun attending another mosque affiliated with the Fethullah Gülen movement, and really liked it.[18] He noted that they read works by Said Nursi, which he found extremely deep.[19] Hamza shared something he had learned there that impressed him: "When you look at a beautiful picture, you know that someone made it even if you do not see the painter. And the painter of the world is Allah. You can know him in the beauty you see here. At the al-Nur mosque, they tell us not to read anything other than the Qur'an and the Hadith. But why shouldn't I read such meaningful things?" Hamza viewed this as limiting.

He confided to me that there were some things that he did not like about the al-Nur mosque, such as being told not to go to other mosques. Moreover, "most brothers there had really difficult lives," he said. "They were drug addicts, alcoholics; they were in prison. But in the Gülen mosque, everyone is a student. I really like that too."

What these born Muslims have in common is that they were all new to Islam or Islamic practice in one way or another. They all went to the al-Nur mosque to learn about Islam in a context outside their families and national traditions. They attended the mosque to learn about Islam in German and a diverse context welcoming to people like themselves who knew little about Islam. And they did not feel burdened by their previous lives and backgrounds there. The al-Nur mosque felt welcoming without making them feel judged, at least for a newcomer. Unlike national mosques, which they said often felt as though they were exclusively for Turks, Bosnians, Indonesians, or Pakistanis, it seemed to them that the al-Nur mosque did not belonged to any specific group, and thus belonged to anyone in Germany who could speak and understand German. These born Muslims represent a new generation of new Germans who are less invested in their ethnic backgrounds, and more interested in finding spiritual and social meaning in the context in which they live.

CONCLUSION

Despite the negative publicity that Salafi mosques such as the al-Nur receive in the media, they continue to attract newcomers to Islam. Salafi da'wa may not always be, and generally is not, the reason that Germans convert to Islam.[20] But it is the reason why they remain Muslims, or at least why they practice their religion while feeling perfectly acceptable members of the Ummah. Salafi puritanism—that is, a conversionist, literalist, anticulturalist, and antihistorical version of Islam—is attractive to both converts and born Muslims who did not necessarily grow up as practicing Muslims, since it places them on equal footing with—or even better, makes them feel superior to—all other Muslims. This is especially powerful in a context where immigrant Muslims are routinely accused of being misogynistic, violent, uneducated, and simply stupid. Salafism allows new converts to fully embrace their religion without having to deal with the anti-Muslim sentiment with which they find themselves surrounded. It even permits them to feel superior to Muslims with immigrant backgrounds and invite them to true Islam, which is not Turkish, Arab, or Pakistani. Salafi mosques are the only Muslim spaces in Germany where piety matters more than ethnic or national background.

In that sense, Salafi Islam is the only Sunni Islamic practice in contemporary Germany that totally bypasses the question of national tradition along with the difficult issue of double consciousness for both converted German Muslims and Muslims with immigrant backgrounds. In their unique ability to bring together people of all possible backgrounds, Salafis show that they are able to present Islam as a fitting spiritual home to utterly diverse people. They truly queer ethnicity and create a totally new community consisting of people of diverse backgrounds united by their new identity as Muslims. Salafi Islam is thus a model of postethnic sociability that fits the realities of the contemporary postindustrial, postsocialist, postunification, and ethnically mixed Germany, where people are not preoccupied with the unitary consciousness favored by both middle-class ethnic German converts to Islam and DuBois, educated in the tradition of German idealism as a graduate student in late nineteenth-century Berlin. Given Salafis' nostalgia for early Islam, in which Meccans and Medinans of different tribes came together to form the first Ummah, their practice allows for a space where no ethnic background is relevant.

Chapter 6

CONCLUSION

Every day a small but steady number of Germans engage in a seemingly simple act. In the presence of two people, they say one phrase out loud. Most often they say it first in Arabic, "la 'ilha 'illa l-Lah Muhammadur rasulu l-Lah," and then in German: "Es gibt keinen Gott außer Gott und Muhammad ist sein Gesandter" (There is only one God, and Muhammad is His messenger). By engaging in this simple act of shahada (witnessing), converts first transform themselves into Muslims, then they transform Muslim communities in Germany into places where indigenous Germans are members, and finally they transform German society in general into a place where mainstream Germans are also of the Islamic creed. By seemingly so easily and simply becoming Muslim, converts show the fragility of post–Cold War dichotomies between European and Muslim identities. The difficulties and marginalization from the mainstream society they face, sometimes-xenophobic arguments they defend, and efforts they engage in separating Islam from Turkish and Arab traditions, however, attest to the power of these same dichotomies.

In his essay "Muslims and European Identity: Can Europe Represent Islam?" Talal Asad (2002, 209) formulates the paradox of the Muslim question in Europe in the most succinct way: "[Muslims] are included within and excluded from Europe at one and the same time in a special way." In this study I have sought to show how indigenous Germans who embrace Islam at once deal with this paradox and contribute to it. Their efforts at putting a German face on Islam and maintaining an ambivalent relationship with immigrant Muslims can be understood only in relation to this contradictory way in which "'Europe' is conceptualized by Europeans" (ibid.). Prevalent ideas of secularism that define religion as a sphere separate from all other social realities combined with the increased racialization of Muslims prompt converts along some other European-born Muslims to promote an Islam that can be rescued from its association from the despised aspects of Middle Eastern values and practices, and shown to be fit for European and German minds and lives. Hence an understanding of a European Islam, unsurprisingly, is often part and parcel of how Europe is conceptualized by Europeans. In the stories of many converted Germans who I followed in this book, an inclusion of Islam into Europe comes at the expense of a simultaneous exclusion of racialized Muslims from it. Despite or more precisely because of their efforts of inclusion, converts end up receiving the brunt of Islamophobic anxieties, though.

German converts to Islam apply different and at times conflicting strategies in order to demonstrate how Islam is a perfect—and indeed better—fit for German/European society. A few converts reach out to liberal traditions that emphasize the primacy of individual choice, and others talk about Enlightenment traditions that embraced religious diversity and promoted curiosity. They trace genealogies back to celebrated German figures such as Lessing and Goethe, whose openness toward diversity was later suppressed by the anti-Semitic ideology of National Socialism. Such converts promote the understanding that conversion to Islam is not only compatible with German culture but also actually in line with the best parts of the German intellectual tradition, which have been silenced and pushed aside since the romantic movement.

The flip side of a stress on an Islam compatible with Germanness sometimes involves the disqualification of immigrants as good Muslims. In order to claim Islam as German, converted Muslims and some born Muslims emphasize that Muslims and Islam are two different things. Like non-Muslim German intellectuals, many converts believe that second-, third-, and fourth-generation Muslims of immigrant ancestry need to be educated, integrated, and transformed. Yet for them, this transformation should happen not through leaving Islamic practices behind or reforming Islam but on the contrary, by making immigrant Muslims abandon their Turkish and other cultures as well as traditions, and persuading them to apply fundamental Islamic teachings to their everyday lives. In other words, they suggest, it is the immigrant Muslims in Germany who need to change and not Islam.

It is not only converts who search for an Islam that fits the best of German values and lifestyle. Throughout Europe, there are a number of born Muslims—the best example being the Swiss-born Ramadan—who promote the idea that a conservative interpretation of Islam can be perfectly European. Such an approach advances the notion of a true and tradition-free Islam, and is in line with reformist Islamic traditions throughout the world. In the European context, however, this approach ends up being Europeanist, defining only European practices and mentalities as tradition free. It brands the ways of ethnic Muslims as not properly Islamic, and hence not fitting for life in Germany and Europe.

Despite the great emphasis many converts place on the question of European identity, the newest and youngest converts as well as born Muslims attracted to Salafi Islam seem less concerned with this. Despite their small numbers, Salafi communities are significant inasmuch as they are now the main attraction for converts, and easily accommodate new eastern European, Russian, and African Muslims in addition to born Muslims of Middle Eastern origin who have found Islam on their own, independent of their families. Salafism, which introduces itself as completely free of human interpretation and any tradition, turns out to best welcome nontraditional newcomers to Islam. In doing so, Salafis generate the deepest fears among Islamophobes.

CONVERTS AS A THREAT TO THE NEW GERMANY

I want to end this book by talking about a moral panic over converts to Islam that swept Germany in the 2000s, which suddenly moved German converts from their previously invisible position to center stage in the media.[1] The details are especially important, since they highlight the most novel aspects of Islamophobia. The reason for the panic was the fear of a potential terrorist attack. The then federal minister of the interior, Schäuble, repeatedly warned the nation against the danger posed by German converts to Islam (see, e.g., Schmid 2007). After two German Muslims were caught collecting chemicals used to make explosives (Lander 2007), the CDU's leader, Bosbach, and its Bavarian interior minister, Günther Beckstein, suggested that the government register and follow everyone who had converted to Islam. "A convert registry only makes sense given that we know some of them may be radicalized after converting," Bosbach said (Ringel 2007).

Another public fear in 2000s' Germany parallel to that of Germans converting to Islam was the worry that Islamic culture was taking over Germany. An older alarmist strategy spotlighted the high birthrates of immigrants; the new alarmism underscored the spread of Islamic ways of thinking and living among mainstream Europeans and Germans. The idea behind this new anxiety was that Muslim values had already begun to dominate European public culture, because liberal Europeans were too permissive to stand up for their values and protect them. This understanding was best represented by a 2006 issue of *Der Spiegel* titled "Mecca Germany: The Silent Islamization" (Mekka Deutschland: Die stille Islamisierung). The cover of the issue dramatically displayed a crescent shining over the Brandenburg Gate in Berlin, the symbol of the city.

The harsh Muslim critic Henryk M. Broder (2006, 2007) has been prominent in promoting a similar fear of Muslims taking over Europe, especially in his best-selling book *Hurra, Wir Kapitulieren* (Hurray! We are capitulating). As the son of two Jewish Polish Holocaust survivors, and a sharp-tongued critic of German society, Broder has a key position in German public discourse. Most of his writings focus on anti-Semitism and the liberal tolerance of Islam in Germany. In his book he writes: "The prevailing feeling among Muslims is that they are being abused by the West. What should we do about it? We might as well surrender. After all, we're already on our way" (Broder 2007). Believing that Europe has almost turned Muslim already, Broder once even suggested that young Europeans who love their freedom should emigrate to Australia or New Zealand. Because he is sixty years old, he said, he would stay in Berlin (quoted in Belien 2006). Broder and his conservative European supporters, such as Paul Belien in Belgium, suggest that Islam literally means submission, and that liberal secular Europeans who submit to Islam's upsurge in Europe have already submitted. "Many Europeans have already become Muslims, though they do not realize it or do not want to admit it" (Belien 2006).

In a context dominated by fears of Islamic religion and culture taking over Europe, worries about individual converts to Islam come to the surface. Ethnically European and, more specifically, German Muslims become the most visible manifestations of Islam taking over the European mind, lifestyle, and culture, which do not have an agreed-on, positive self-definition. Critics of Islam often accuse converts of embracing politically wrong positions that they associate with Islamic culture. For example, in its July–August 2002 issue, *Emma*, the most popular mainstream feminist journal in Germany, published an article titled "Die KonvertitInnen . . . und wer dahinter steckt" (The converts . . . and who is hiding behind them?) (Filter 2002). The article discusses numerous well-known German Muslims, and argues that they are anti-Semites, Holocaust deniers, Nazis, supporters of Islamic terrorism, and deniers of women's rights. These accusations are not well founded and definitely not generalizable to the large convert populations. But what they clearly indicate is a desire to put converts on the wrong side of the distribution of political values in Germany. At the same time, converts seem to generate fears not about "totally foreign" values and lifestyles but rather about German values that prevailed only a few decades ago and today are considered embarrassing. In that sense, because Muslim converts are so indistinguishably German, both in their ethnicity and beliefs, they challenge the new united German identity in the making all the more.

As Islam and Muslims became increasingly integrated into German society, popular and stately angst about this ostensibly non-European but well-established element is directed at the small number of ethnic Germans who have embraced Islam. Converts provoke so much anxiety not because they may turn Germany into a Muslim-majority country or terrorize the entire nation but instead because simply through their most often politically unmotivated personal choice of another religion, they defy the newly established boundaries between political alliances, cultures, and civilizations. Converts to Islam break ground for genuinely new ways of being and becoming Muslim, German, German Muslim, and Muslim German. At the same time, they provoke new anxieties about the changing realities of being European.

Notes

INTRODUCTION
GERMANIZING ISLAM AND RACIALIZING MUSLIMS

1. Similar sentiments have been recorded among Swedish (Roald 2004, 264) and Spanish converts (Rogozen-Soltar 2012).

2. For the complete speech, see http://www.bundespraesident.de/Shared Docs/Reden/EN/ChristianWulff/Reden/2010/101003-Deutsche-Einheit-englisch .html.

3. *Die Stern* 42, no. 10 (December 10, 2010): cover.

4. Quoted in "The World from Berlin: 'Should Muslims Be Treated on an Equal Footing?'" *Der Spiegel Online International*, October 8, 2010, http:// www.spiegel.de/international/germany/the-world-from-berlin-should-muslims -be-treated-on-an-equal-footing-a-722065.html.

5. Quoted in Madeline Chambers, "Merkel Ally Says Islam Not Part of Germany," Reuters, April 19, 2012, http://www.reuters.com/article/2012/04/19 /us-germany-islam-idUSBRE83I0DN20120419.

6. Since tracking converts to Islam is not possible, their exact numbers are not known. Estimates regarding German converts vary between twenty and one hundred thousand (Blashke 2004). In a 2007 interview, the director of the Islam Archive of Germany estimated that there were eighteen thousand converts (Ackermann 2007). The same person also estimated that in 2005, four thousand Germans converted to Islam—four times more than the previous year. The archive does not, however, have a reliable way of counting the converts. Similar wide-ranging estimates are also made for Muslim converts in comparable European countries, such as Britain (Zebiri 2008) and France (De La Baume 2013). The safest approximation for any one of these countries would be in the lower tens of thousands. The trend of conversion I discuss here is widespread throughout Europe. Other scholars speak of increasing European conversion to Islam in France (Allievi 1996), Britain (Köse 1996; Zebiri 2008), Sweden (Roald 2004;

Sultan 1999), Denmark (Jensen 2006), the Netherlands (van Nieuwkerk 2004; Badran 2006), Spain (Rogozen-Soltar 2012), and Germany (Hofmann 1997; Wohlrab-Sahr 1999).

7. Local Danish (Jensen 2006), Dutch (van Nieuwkerk 2006), and British (Zebiri 2008) converts are all reportedly viewed with similar suspicion. Leon Moosavi (2012) notes that in the United Kingdom, white British converts are accused of being traitors, whereas black British converts are not.

8. Deeb (2006) explains that her notion of authenticating Islam is somewhat like that of "objectification," used by Dale Eickelman and James Piscatori (1996, 39) to define similar dynamics of Islamic revivalism with "a heightened self-consciousness" along with "the systematization and explicitness of religious tradition."

9. For the persistence of Enlightenment ideas about religion in contemporary thought, see Asad 1993.

10. The earliest studies of conversion focused on the psychology of the convert and saw the conversion process as a sudden, emotional change (Hall 1904; James 1902). Even though at the middle of the century greater numbers of sociologists studied conversion, the attention on individual psychology remained central. These scholars concentrated on conversion as a factor of problems experienced in late adolescence and early adulthood (Buckser and Glazier 2003). Today, more scholars, especially anthropologists, focus on the social, cultural, and political context in which the conversion takes place, and how conversion is shaped by and shapes this social context (Kravel-Tovi 2012).

11. In a study of conversion to Pentecostalism and violent anticonversion movements in India, Roberts (2012) argues that looking at conversion as colonization of consciousness—a prevalent idea among anthropologists—is based on a secular liberal model that ignores how the production of so-called universal secular knowledge also entails a power relationship. In the German context, this line of thinking about the naturalization of secular liberal knowledge and belief can easily be extended from conversion to a discussion of Islam in general.

12. Writing of Danish converts to Islam, Tina Jensen states (2006, ix) that "conversion to Islam has a political dimension, whether intended by the convert or not."

13. One of the most well-known ex-converts to Islam is the former Muhammad Sven Kalisch. Kalisch converted to Islam at age fifteen and was the first person to hold a chair in Islamic theology at Munster University established in 2004 to train teachers who would teach Islam in public schools. In 2008 he declared that through his studies, he came to the conclusion that "Muhammad probably never existed" and eventually in 2010 announced that he was no longer a Muslim (*Der Spiegel Online* 2013). Kalisch continues to teach at Munster University, but no longer holds the chair in Islamic theology.

14. Over the past few decades, scholars have focused on the multiple and intersecting ways in which different forms of discrimination and marginalization

interact. This approach was first formulated by the feminist sociologist Kimberle Crenshaw (1989), and became more prominent through the work of Patricia Hill Collins (2000), who uses the concept in her discussion of black feminism.

15. After two decades of legal struggle, the Berlin Islamic Federation was granted the right to teach Islamic courses in public schools when parents demand them (Yükleyen 2012, 161).

16. Survey by the Pew Research Center's Global Attitudes Project, spring 2008, http://www.pewglobal.org/category/datasets/2008/.

17. Findings from the At Home in Europe Project, http://www.soros.org /initiatives/home/articles_publications/publications/berlin-muslims-report -20100427/berlin-english-20100427.pdf.

18. Surveys by the European Monitoring Center on Racism and Xenophobia (2006) demonstrate significant differences in employment, and between native and immigrant Germans. Unemployment is twice as high among Germans with Muslim backgrounds (44), and these same people have a harder time in apprentic- ing (ibid.). Migrant Germans and those with Muslim backgrounds tend to live in overcrowded areas, pay relatively high rents, and have less security in their rental contracts (56). The center's reports also show that children with migrant back- grounds face greater difficulty attending elite high schools and universities (Lu- ciak 2004).

19. For a critical discussion of these reports, see Allen 2010; Bunzl 2005.

20. For an astute discussion of the history of the racialization of immigrants in Europe where they have been turned from being conceptualized as nomads to Muslims, see Silverstein 2005.

21. Liz Fekete (2009) also contends that Islamophobia is another name for xe- nophobic racism.

22. More recently, Habermas (2010) has sought to account for the vitality of global religiosity, calling for translating religious ideas into a post-secular stance opposing global capitalism.

23. In his discussion of the role of religion in the public sphere, Craig Cal- houn (2011, 77) writes: "This use of the public/private distinction to enforce a kind of secularism is embarrassingly reminiscent of the use of the same distinc- tion to minimize not only women's political participation but also opportunities to put certain issues associated with gendered private sphere on the ostensibly gender neutral public agenda." For an examination of the queer way of being as a counterpublic that challenges the straight public sphere, see Warner 2002.

24. For the racialization of immigrants in post–World War II Europe, see Sil- verstein 2005. He shows the multiple processes through which immigrants are ra- cialized and put into the new savage slot. As part of this process, they are then problematized as objects are national integration.

25. Millî Görüş, an organization established to spread the ideas of the Islamist politician Necmettin Erbakan among indigenous workers in Turkey, has played the most important role here. It came to Germany in 1970, and since the 2000s,

Millî Görüş has advocated that Muslims be seen as residents of Germany rather than as guest workers. The Federal Office for the Protection of the Constitution treats the organization as a potential threat to national security (Schiffauer 2000; Yükleyen 2012).

26. In 1982, Kohl privately told Margaret Thatcher that half of the Turks in Germany should leave the country within four years (Hecking 2013).

27. Not only Germany, but also all other Western European countries "outsourced the management of Islam" to Turkey, Algeria, Morocco, Pakistan, and Saudi Arabia, which supported Islamic associations, trained and paid for imams, and provided education to children in their parents' language (Laurence 2012, 14).

28. Schäuble's statement was contradicted by his successor, Hans-Peter Friedrich, on March 3, 2011, when he said, "It is one thing to say Islam belongs to Germany but it never belonged here historically" (*Independent* 2011).

29. For an excellent and innovative look at how Muslims make the United States their home, see Bilici 2012.

30. Studies of the pre–World War II Muslim presence in modern Germany have emphasized the "foreignness" of Islam, while paying little attention to conversion and the way that German converts made Islam local (Abdullah 1981; Höpp 1997, 2001; Bauknecht 2001; Clayer and Germain 2008; Cwiklinski 2008; Germain 2008; Backhausen 2008). For an exception to this body of literature, discussing the role that bourgeois immigrant and converted Muslims played in articulating Islam in Germany, see Motadel 2009.

31. For an extensive look at multiple aspects of Weimar Germany, see Weitz 2013; Gay (1968) 2001.

32. For a history of this group in India and in Europe, see Backhausen 2008.

33. Weiss was born in 1990 to a well-off secular Jewish family in Vienna. He was introduced to Islam during a visit to Jerusalem. Following his conversion, Asad joined a Bedouin tribe for decades. During the later stages of his life, he moved to Spain. Asad has been hugely influential among both European Muslims and reformist movements in the Middle East. See Asad 1954. Nussimbaum was born in 1905 to a well-off Jewish family and grew up in Georgia. He converted to Islam in 1922 in Berlin, although he never was an orthodox Muslim. His conversion enabled him to pass as a non-Jew in Germany and his anti-Bolshevik stance made him popular among Nazis for a while. See Reiss 1999. Marcus was born to a middle-class family in Poznań (Posen) in 1880. He studied philosophy and encountered Islam while tutoring Arab students. See Backhausen 2008.

34. Damani Partridge (2012) talks about similar relationships between African refugee men who are in need of papers to stay in Germany and German women.

35. George Paul Meiu (2011) describes the tourism industry along with its literary representations of European and especially German women traveling to East Africa in the hope of romance with local men.

36. Kate Zebiri (2008), Ali Köse (1996), and Anne Sofie Roald (2006) discuss the rise of all-white communities of converted Muslims in other parts of Europe. In my observations, I noted that these groups were not all indigenous Germans but included other immigrant converts as well.

37. Karin van Nieuwkerk (2006, 1) confirms that women converts are frequently treated with greater hostility, "because traditions have often constrained women as symbols of ethnic and religious boundaries."

38. Zebiri (2008) notes a similar change of demography among British converts to Islam in the last hundred years from upper to middle to lower classes.

39. Here I embrace Lewis Rambo's (1995, 20) definition of the context of conversion: "Context is more than a first stage that is passed through; rather it is the total environment in which conversion transpires."

40. For comparative purposes, I also conducted six semistructured interviews with German converts to Judaism. Even though these interviews were crucial to understanding the specificities of conversion to Islam, they are not systematically analyzed in this book.

41. Even though Sufism is popular among German converts to Islam, I decided to leave Sufi Muslims—other than the Weimar group—out of this study. During my research, I found that most Sufi groups are isolated from all other Muslim communities, and as a result, their attitudes to religious and national identities tend to be significantly different from those I focus on here. For a discussion of Sufi groups, see Schlessmann 2003.

CHAPTER 1
GIVING ISLAM A GERMAN FACE

1. All the names used in this book are pseudonyms, unless referencing public figures. While choosing pseudonyms, I made sure that the names reflected the choice of individuals in using German, Arabic, or Turkish names. Some German converts use their original German names, and other adopted Arabic or Turkish names.

2. It is important to note that a number of Muslims in Europe with second- or third-generation immigrant backgrounds also embrace a similar stance (Bowen 2010). This spirit is best expressed in the work of the Swiss Muslim Tariq Ramadan (2004).

3. Mikaela Rogozen-Soltar (2012, 612) refers to a similar sentiment expressed by Spanish converts to Islam: "Converts often claim to practice a 'culture-free' Islam, which they contrast to Moroccans' 'traditions,' using a discourse that cloaks convert religiosity within an unmarked category of 'European' and marks migrant Muslims as outsiders."

4. See www.dmk-berlin.de.

5. Schroeder said this in an interview with the weekly *Bild am Sonntag* on December 21, 2003. For the full statement, see Bundeszentrale fur Politische Bildunge, http://www.bpb.de/politik/innenpolitik/konfliktstoff-kopftuch/63251/gerhard-schroeder.

6. Horsch recalled Goethe's (2010, 78) observation in *West-östlicher Diwan* (East-West divan) that "if Islam means submitting to God, we all live and die in Islam." Katherina Mommsen (forthcoming), the most important Goethe scholar of our time, remarks that this has frequently been misinterpreted as suggesting that Goethe was a confessing Muslim. She argues that it is rather connected to his overall critique of dogmatism and intolerance. Goethe actually endorsed acceptance of human subservience to fate and the concept of a God for all people, regardless of creed. He believed that religious zeal and intolerance are pointless, and having no creed is superior.

7. See http://www.al-sakina.de/inhalt/artikel/lessing_islam/lessing_islam.html.

8. In 1754, Lessing (2003) published an essay titled "Der Rettung des Hieronymus Cardanus." Cardanus was a Renaissance figure who in 1550 published an imaginary conversation between an unbeliever, a Jew, a Christian, and a Muslim, in which Christianity appears as the best religion. In Lessing's rewriting of this conversation some two hundred years later, Islam appears as the most rational religion.

9. The original in German is "Toleranz sollte eigentlich nur eine voruebergehende Gesinnung sein: Sie muss zu Annerkennung fuhren. Dulden heist beleiden."

10. See http://www.dmk-berlin.de/download/diverses/Islam_und_Aufklaerung.pdf.

11. See http://www.abd-al-hadi-publications.com/20040603.pdf.

12. It is important to note that Ramadan's view would not be approved of in some other settings frequented by converted German Muslims, such as Sufi lodges or Salafi-oriented Sunni mosques. Sufis would find him too politically oriented, and Salafis would argue that he is making new and hence undesirable innovations.

13. For more on the organization, see http://www.muslimische-akademie.de.

14. See http://www.ekd.de/statistik/mitglieder.html.

15. See http://www.inssan-ev.de.

16. See https://www.narrabila-verlag.de.

17. See http://www.allaha.de.

18. Many converts I met acquired a Muslim name on conversion. Yet they did not change their legal names because this involved a cumbersome legal process. In chapter 5, I discuss a recent trend of keeping the original name among converts.

19. In the end, the German Federal Administrative court heard the case, and the student was denied the right to pray anywhere and anytime at school, with the court ruling that it could damage the smooth functioning of the school. The

court also decided that granting the student a prayer room was beyond the school's capacity. "No Religion in School: Berlin Court Decides against Muslim Student Prayers," *Der Spiegel Online*, 2011, http://www.spiegel.de/international /germany/0,1518,697182,00.html.

20. Rachel Woodlock (2010) makes a similar observation. She discusses how female converts to Islam in Australia demand easier access to mosques, especially because they need to go there to learn about Islam.

21. The idea of natural religion first developed in England, and spread to continental Europe and the United States. The deism that developed out of this thinking has different ideas about creation, God's involvement, afterlife, miracles, and so on. It is mainly the basic ideas regarding the rational individual and simple religion that are relevant to the above discussion. For the history of natural religion and deism, see Gay 1968.

CHAPTER 2
ESTABLISHING DISTANCE FROM IMMIGRANT MUSLIMS

1. After World War II, East Germany received immigrants from other socialist countries such as Vietnam and Angola. Yet these immigrants were far fewer in number than the Turks who migrated to West Germany.

2. Jeffrey Jurgens (2005) notes that Berliners and especially immigrants rarely travel outside their neighborhoods. He describes how members of the Turkish German soccer team he was playing with became uncomfortable when they had to travel to other parts of the city and country for tournaments.

3. I observed that there are other Sufi groups, such as the Mevlevis, who choose to locate their communities consisting of all converts in immigrant-Muslim free zones of eastern Germany, too.

4. The Hanafi school is one of the four legal schools in Sunni Islam. It follows the teachings of Abu Hanafi an-Numan (699–767). This school has the most adherents in the Muslim world, and Turks in Turkey traditionally subscribe to it.

5. Another common reaction that I received following the recognition of my profession was a statement that it must be really easy to become a professor in the United States—since even a Turk could do it.

6. For a discussion of the intrinsically racist nature of the Enlightenment, see Eze 1997.

CHAPTER 3
EAST GERMAN CONVERTS

1. Other research such as the German Social Survey suggests that young east Germans are more open to religious ideas if those notions are presented outside

the church, especially topics such as the afterlife, magic, spiritualism, and the oc-
cult (Frank 2007, 148). In interviews conducted with the younger generation,
those East Germans who came of age after the fall of the Berlin Wall, researchers
found that this group "broke with the strict atheistic position" commonly held
by their parents and/or grandparents (ibid., 156).

2. It is interesting to note that even in atheistic East Germany, Christmas services were held and proved popular.

3. Karl May (1842–1912) is a popular German author who wrote fiction
about Native Americans, the Middle East, and the Orient in general.

CHAPTER 4
BEING MUSLIM AS A WAY OF BECOMING GERMAN

1. In contemporary Germany, there is a widespread belief that Muslims are
not interested in the history of the Holocaust and are more anti-Semitic than
mainstream Germans, despite the fact that neither statement is supported by research. For the meaning and ramifications of this discourse, see Özyürek 2013.

2. Quoted in "Wir brauchen muslimische Lehrerinnnen," *Der Tagesspiegel*,
January 22, 1999, 32.

3. See www.muslimische-jugend.de.

4. The interview can be watched on the newspaper's Web site, www
.islamische-zeitung.de/iztv.cgi?id=12293.

5. When I interviewed him, he was in his mid-thirties and was no longer an
active member of the MJD, which as a youth organization permits active engagement only until the age of thirty.

6. As with the DMK (discussed in chapter 1), one of the MJD's central aims is
for young German Muslims to learn to differentiate between religion and
tradition.

7. The Abitur is the exam that German students take at the end of their sec-
ondary education. Alongside conferring personal prestige, the successful comple-
tion of this exam gives students the right to attend the university.

8. Another MJD member, who had been active in the organization from the
beginning, informed me that all this traveling was not done for its own sake.
They simply had to do it this way, because there were so few of them. Regardless,
constant travel through Germany allowed members such as Hasan to have a
larger sense of being German Muslims.

9. See http://www.muslimische-jugend.de/freizeit.

10. Interview with the author, October 2013.

11. This narrative on Ammar114 is based on the biography that he provides
on his Web site. See http://www.ammar114.de/index.php?article_id=30.

12. "Gutes über die Texte Vermitteln," *Islamiche Zeitung*, 2004, http://www
.ammar114.de/index.php?article_id=24.

13. Scholars of hip-hop argue that this music brings youths living on the margins of the first world together, and that Islam plays a central role in this culture. "In the 1990s Islamic hip-hop emerged as the language of the disaffected" (Aidi 2002, n.p.).

14. Islamic hip-hop as an antiracist solidarity movement among people of color is most visible in France (Swedenburg 2001, 2002); the most prominent example is Akhenaton (Philippe Fragiona, born in 1968) or Diam's (Veiel 2010). Even though these two artists have different genres and styles, they are both children of immigrants and converted to Islam following their engagement hip-hop.

15. There are three other famous German rappers whose conversion to Islam is publicly known. M.Bilal, formerly Manuellsen, is a German rapper of Ghanian origin who converted to Islam in 2010. Kollegah is a German Canadian rapper who converted to Islam more than ten years ago. Both rappers have continued their stage career following their conversion and do not seem to be part of a conversionist Islamic scene. The third well-known converted rapper, with a Ghanian German background, is the former Desso Dog, who adopted the name Abou Maleeq and joined the radical Islamist scene (see chapter 5).

16. This song received great circulation. Recently, it was included in the gymnasium ethics textbook for years five and six in the state of Saxony (Abenteuer Ethik, CC Buchner).

17. See http://www.babelmed.net/Countries/Mediterranean/EU_Project /rapper_ammar114.php?c=3582&m=146&l=en.

18. For a detailed description of the political scandal around the MJD, see Bendixsen 2013, 42–54.

19. "Muslimischer Verein missioniert in Schulen," *Der Tagesspiegel*, November 6, 2003. Bendixsen (2013, 43) states that one participant in the project told her that the journalist was approached by a teacher in one of the schools.

20. Bendixsen (2013, 44) notes that the official recordings of the discussion about the relationship between the MJD and Muslim Brotherhood in the German Parliament shows that there was no clear information regarding such a relationship.

CHAPTER 5
SALAFISM AS THE FUTURE OF EUROPEAN ISLAM?

1. See http://www.al-nur-moschee.de/.

2. For a history and the contemporary condition of Salafism, see Meijer 2009.

3. Quintan Wiktorowicz (2006) argues that there are three kinds of Salafis: quietists, politicos, and jihadis.

4. These numbers appear in the 2011 BfV report; see Bartsch, Popp, and Scheuermann 2012.

5. See www.diewahrereligion.de; www.einladungzumparadies.de.

6. See https://www.facebook.com/PierreVogelOffiziell.

7. Vogel is under observation by the German Interior Ministry, suspected of being a hate preacher and having ties to jihadists groups. He denies both accusations and offers to give a thousand euros to anyone who can find hate speech in the thousands of videos he has posted.

8. *Redacted* is written and directed by Brian De Palma. It is a fictional dramatization of killings in 2006 by the US Army in Mahmudiyah, Iraq. The film received a Silver Lion best director award at the 2007 Venice Film Festival.

9. During a mosque lecture that he gave after his conversion, Cuspert talks about how his stepfather used to punish him physically and shows one of the big scars remaining from these beatings. See www.youtube.com/watch?v=9QIM 5Wtju.

10. Schmitt 2011.

11. See, for example, the 2009 video *Wilkommen in meiner Welt*.

12. Quoted in Schmitt 2011.

13. Deso Dogg's conversion does not look like a sudden decision, since Muslim themes, such as people taking ablutions or images of Ali's sword as tattoos, were present in his videos in the mid-2000s. See, for example, the 2006 video *Das ist die Realitat*, www.youtube.com/watch?v=xIEV5XyKJI4.

14. See, for example, "Mujahid lauf, Mujahid kämpf! Guck' wie der Kafir stirbt und brennt! . . . Allah hat versprochen, der Sieg wird kommen. . . . Unser Ziel ist die Scharia, bis der Tod zu uns kommt! (Mujahid go, Mujahid fight! Look how the Kafir dies and burns. Allah has promised that the victory will come. . . . Our goal is Sharia, until death comes to us!)." Florian Flade, "Islamistische Kampflieder auf den Index gesetzt," *Die Welt*, March 16, 2012, www.welt.de/politik /deutschland/article13924439/Islamistische-Kampflieder-auf-den-Index-gesetzt .html.

15. Schmitt 2011.

16. Jansen 2013.

17. "In Search of 'True Islam': Salafists Abandon Germany for Egypt," *Der Spiegel Online*, August 13, 2012, www.spiegel.de/international/world/german -islamists-travel-to-egypt-a-849802.html.

18. The movement taking the name of Fethullah Gülen (born 1941) is a transnational Islamic one based in Turkey. For a discussion of the movement, see Turam 2006; Ebaugh 2009.

19. Said Nursi (1878–1960) was a Muslim scholar who wrote extensively while Turkey was going through rapid secularization. The faith movement that he started played an important role in the revitalization of Islam in Turkey. For a discussion of Said Nursi, see Mardin 1989.

20. Sadek Hamid (2009) also notes that all the Salafis he met in Britain came to Salafi mosques not owing to Salafi missionizing but rather following their dissatisfaction with other mosques, including the Tablighi Jemaat.

CHAPTER 6
CONCLUSION

Portions of this Conclusion were originally published in "Convert Alert: Turkish Christians and German Muslims as Threats to National Security in the New Europe." *Comparative Studies in Society and History* 51(1): 91–116, copyright © 2009 by the Society for the Comparative Study of Society and History; permission for their use is courtesy of Cambridge University Press.

1. For a more detailed look at this panic, see Özyürek 2009.

References

Abdel-Alim, Hesham Samy. 2006. "Reinventing Islam with Modern Unique Tones: Muslim Hip-Hop Artists at Verbal Mujahidin." *Souls* 8 (4): 45–58.

Abdullah, Muhammad Salim. 1981. *Geschichte des Islams in Deutschland.* Cologne: Styria.

Ackermann, Lutz. 2007. "Muslim Converts in Germany: Angst Ridden Germans Look for Answers and Find Them in the Quran." *Der Spiegel Online*, January 18, http://www.spiegel.de/international/spiegel/muslim-converts-in -germany-angst-ridden-germans-look-for-answers-and-find-them-in-the -koran-a-460364.html.

Adelson, Leslie. 2005. *The Turkish Turn in Contemporary German Literature: Toward a New Critical Grammar of Migration.* New York: Palgrave.

Adraoui, Mohamed-Ali. 2009. "Salafism in France: Ideology, Practices, and Contradictions." In *Global Salafism: Islam's New Religious Movement*, edited by Roel Meijer, 364–83. New York: Columbia University Press.

Aidi, Hishaam. 2002. "Jihadis in the Hood: Race, Urban Islam, and the War on Terror." *Middle East Report* 224, http://www.merip.org/mer/mer224/jihadis -hood.

———. 2003. "Let Us Be Moors: Islam, Race, and 'Connected Histories.'" *Middle East Report* 229, http://www.merip.org/mer/mer229/let-us-be -moors.

———. 2011. "The Grand (Hip-Hop) Chessboard: Race, Rap, and Raison d'Etat." *Middle East Report* 26:25–40.

Allen, Christopher. 2010. *Islamophobia.* Burlington, VT: Ashgate.

Allievi, Stefano. 1996. *Les convertis à l'islam: Les nouveaux musulmans d'Europe.* Paris: L'Harmattan.

Amir-Moazami, Schirin. 2013. "Islam and Gender under Liberal-Secular Governance: The German Islam Conference." In *Religion, Identity, and Politics*, edited by Haldun Gülalp and Günter Seufert, 72–86. London: Routledge.

Asad, Muhammad. 1954. *The Road to Mecca.* London: M. Reinhardt.

Asad, Talal. 1993. *Genealogies of Religion: Discipline and Reasons of Power in Christianity and Islam.* Baltimore: Johns Hopkins University Press.

———. 2002. "Muslims and European Identity: Can Europe Represent Islam?" In *The Idea of Europe: From Antiquity to the European Union*, edited by Anthony Pagden, 209–27. Cambridge: Cambridge University Press.

———. 2003. *Formations of the Secular: Christianity, Islam, and Modernity*. Stanford, CA: Stanford University Press.

Backhausen, Manfred. 2008. *Die Lahore-Ahmadiyya-Bewegung in Europa: Geschichte, Gegenwart und Zukunft der als "Lahore-Ahmadiyya-Bewegung zur Verbreitung islamischen Wissens" bekannten internationalen islamischen Gemeinschaft*. Wembley, UK: Ahmadiyya Anjuman Lahore Publications.

Badran, Margot. 2006. "Feminism and Conversion: Comparing British, Dutch, and South African Life Stories." In *Women Embracing Islam: Gender and Conversion in the West*, edited by Karin van Nieuwkerk. Austin: University of Texas Press.

Balibar, Etienne. 1991. "Is There a 'Neo-Racism'?" In *Race, Nation, Class: Ambiguous Identities*, edited by Etienne Balibar and Immanuel Wallerstein, 17–28. London: Verso.

Balibar, Etienne, and Immanuel Wallerstein, eds. 1991. *Race, Nation, Class: Ambiguous Identities*. London: Verso.

Barker, Martin. 1981. *New Racism: Conservatives and the Ideology of the Tribe*. London: Junction Books.

Bartsch, Matthias, Maximilian Popp, and Christoph Scheuermann. 2012. "A Growing Following in Germany: The Dangerous Success of Radical Young Clerics." *Der Spiegel Online*, http://www.spiegel.de/international/germany /a-growing-following-in-germany-the-dangerous-success-of-radical-young -clerics-a-816642.html.

Bauknecht, Bernd. 2001. *Muslime in Deutschland von 1920 bis 1945*. Cologne: Teiresias Verlag.

Bayet, Atef. 2007. "Islamism and the Politics of Fun." *Public Culture* 19 (3): 433–59.

Belien, Paul. 2006. "The Rape of Europe." *Brussels Journal: The Voice of Conservatism in Europe*, October 25, http://www.brusselsjournal.com/node /1609.

Bendixsen, Synnøve K. N. 2013. *The Religious Identity of Young Muslim Women in Berlin: An Ethnographic Study*. Leiden: Brill.

Berdahl, Daphne. 1999. *Where the World Ended: Re-unification and Identity in the German Borderland*. Berkeley: University of California Press.

Bernstein, Richard. 2004. The Continent Watching Anxiously Over the Melting Pot. New York Times, 15 Dec., http://newyorktimes.com/2004/12/15 /international/15letter.htm.

Beyer, Peter. 2006. *Religions in a Global Society*. New York: Routledge.

Bilici, Mücahit. 2010. "Muslim Ethnic Comedy: Inversions of Islamophobia." In *Islamophobia/Islamophilia: Beyond the Politics of Enemy and Friend*, edited by Andrew Shryock, 195–208. Bloomington: Indiana University Press.

———. 2012. *Finding Mecca in America: How Islam Is Becoming an American Religion*. Chicago: University of Chicago Press.

Blaschke, Jochen. 2004. "Tolerated but Marginalized: Muslims in Germany." In *State Policies towards Muslim Minorities, Sweden, Great Britain, and Germany*, edited by Muhammad Anwar, Jochen Blaschke, and Ake Sander, 41–197. Berlin: Parabolis.

Bloul, Rachel A. D. 2008. "Anti-Discrimination Laws, Islamophobia, and Ethnicization of Muslim Identity in Europe and Australia." *Journal of Muslim Minority Affairs* 28 (1): 7–25.

Borneman, John. 1991. *After the Wall: East Meets West in the New Berlin*. New York: Basic Books.

Bowen, John R. 2007. *Why the French Don't Like Headscarves: Islam, the State, and Public Space*. Princeton, NJ: Princeton University Press.

———. 2010. *Can Islam Be French? Pluralism and Pragmatism in a Secularist State*. Princeton, NJ: Princeton University Press.

Broder, Henryk. 2006. *Hurra, Wir Kapitulieren*. Berlin: Wolf Jobst Siedler Verlag.

———. 2007. "Hurray! We Are Capitulating." *Der Spiegel Online*, January 25, http://www.spiegel.de/international/spiegel/0,1518,462149,00.html.

Buckser, Andrew, and Stephen D. Glazier. 2003. Preface to *The Anthropology of Religious Conversion*, xi–xviii. Lanham, MD: Rowman and Littlefield.

Bundesministerium des Innern. 2013. Verfassungschutzbericht 2012. Berlin: Bundesministerium des Innern.

Bunzl, Matti. 2005. "Between Anti-Semitism and Islamophobia: Some Thoughts on the New Europe." *American Ethnologist* 32 (4): 499–508.

Calhoun, Craig. 2011. "Secularism, Citizenship, and the Public Sphere." In *Rethinking Secularism*, edited by Craig Calhoun, Mark Juergenmeyer, and Jonathan Vanantwerpen. New York: Oxford University Press.

Cesari, Jocelyne. 2002. "Islam in France: The Shaping of a Religious Minority." In *Muslims in the West: From Sojourners to Citizens*, edited by Yvonned Haddad, 36–51. New York: Oxford University Press.

———. 2007. "Muslim Identities in Europe: The Snare of Exceptionalism." In *Islam in Europe: Diversity, Identity, and Influence*, edited by Aziz Al-Azmeh, 49–67. Cambridge: Cambridge University Press.

Chin, Rita. 2009. *The Guestworker Question in Postwar Germany*. Cambridge: Cambridge University Press.

Chin, Rita, Heide Fehrenbach, Geoff Eley, and Atina Grossman. 2009. Introduction to *After the Nazi Racial State: Difference and Democracy in German and Europe*. Ann Arbor: University of Michigan Press.

Chow, Rey. 2002. *The Ethnic Protestant and the Spirit of Capitalism*. New York: Columbia University Press.

Clayer, Nathaie, and Eric Germain, eds. 2008. *Islam in Inter-War Europe*. New York: Columbia University Press.

Collins, Patricia Hill. 2000. "Gender, Black Feminism, and Black Political Economy." *Annals of the American Academy of Political Science* 568:41–53.

Coolsaet, Rik. 2011. *Jihadi Terrorism and the Radicalisation Challenge in Europe*. Aldershot, UK: Ashgate.

Comaroff, Jean, and John Comaroff. 1991. *Of Revelation and Revolution: Christianity, Colonialism, and Consciousness in South Africa*. Vol. 1. Chicago: University of Chicago Press.

Crenshaw, Kimberle. 1989. "Mapping the Margins: Intersectionality, Identity, Politics, and Violence against the Women of Color." *Stanford Law Review* 43 (6): 1241–99.

Cwiklinski, Sebastian. 2008. "Between National and Religious Solidarities: The Tatars in Germany and Poland in the Inter-War Period." In *Islam in Inter-War Europe*, edited by Nathalie Clayer and Eric Germain, 64–88. New York: Columbia University Press.

De la Baume, Maïa. 2013. "More in France Are Turning to Islam, Challenging a Nation's Idea of Itself." *New York Times*, February 5, 2013, http://www.nytimes.com/2013/02/04/world/europe/rise-of-islamic-converts-challenges-france.html?pagewanted=1&_r=0.

Decker, Oliver, et al. 2010. *Die Mitte in der Krise: Rechtsextreme Einstellungen in Deutschland 2010*. Berlin: Friedrich-Ebert-Stiftung.

Deeb, Lara. 2006. *An Enchanted Modern: Gender and Public Piety in Shi'i Lebanon*. Princeton, NJ: Princeton University Press.

Deeb, Lara, and Mona Harb. 2013. *Leisurely Islam: Negotiating Geography and Morality in Shi'ite South Beirut*. Princeton, NJ: Princeton University Press.

DuBois, W.E.B. (1903) 2013. *The Souls of Black Folk*. Heart and Soul. Chapel Hill: University of North Carolina Press.

Ebaugh, Helen Rose Fuchs. 2009. *The Gülen Movement: Sociological Analysis of a Civic Movement Rooted in Moderate Islam*. Dordrecht: Springer.

Egerton, Frazer. 2010. "Alienation and Its Discontents." *European Journal of International Relations* 17 (3): 453–74.

Eickelman, Dale, and James Piscatori. 1996. *Muslim Politics*. Princeton, NJ: Princeton University Press.

El-Tayeb, Fatima. 2011. *European Others: Queering Ethnicity in Postnational Europe*. Minneapolis: University of Minnesota Press.

European Monitoring Center on Racism and Xenophobia. 2006. *Muslims in the European Union: Discrimination and Islamophobia*. Vienna: European Monitoring Center on Racism and Xenophobia.

Ewing, Katherine. 2008. *Stolen Honor: Stigmatizing Muslim Men in Berlin*. Stanford, CA: Stanford University Press.

Eze, Chukwudi. 1997. *Race and the Enlightenment: A Reader*. Oxford: Blackwell Publishers.

Fekete, Liz. 2009. *A Suitable Enemy: Racism, Migration, and Islamophobia in Europe*. London: Pluto Press.

Fetzer, Joel S., and J. Christopher Soper. 2005. *Muslims and the State in Britain, France, and Germany*. Cambridge: Cambridge University Press.

Filter, Cornelia. 2002. "Die KonvertitInnen . . . und wer dahinter steckt." *Emma*, July–August, http://emma.de/632065091485469.html.

Frank, Anja. 2007. "Young Eastern Germans and the Religious and Ideological Heritage of Their Parents and Grandparents." In *Religion and the Secular in Eastern Germany, 1945 to the Present*, edited by Esther Peperkamp and Małgorzata Rajtar, 147–66. Leiden: Brill.

Gay, Peter. 1968. *Deism: An Anthology*. Princeton, NJ: D. Van Nostrand.

———. (1968) 2001. *Weimar Culture: The Outsider as Insider*. New York: W. W. Norton.

Gerlach, Julia. 2006. *Zwischen Pop und Dschihad: Muslimische Jugendliche in Deutschland*. Berlin: Ch. Links Verlag.

Germain, Eric. 2008. "The First Muslim Missions on a European Scale: Ahmadi-Lahori Networks in the Inter-War Period." In *Islam in Inter-War Europe*, edited by Nathalie Clayer and Eric Germain, 89–118. New York: Columbia University Press.

German Ministry of Interior Affairs. 2006. Deutsche Islam Konferenz, http://www.bmi.bund.de/nn_211020/Internet/Navigation/EN/Topics/German__Islam__Conference/German__Islam__Conference__node.html__nnn¼true.

Goethe, Johann Wolfgang. 2013. *Maximen und Reflexionen*. Berlin: Holzinger.

———. 2010. *West-East Divan: Poems, with "Notes and Essays": Goethe's Intercultural Dialogues*, translated by Martin Bidney. New York: Global Academic Publishing.

Gökarıksel, Banu, and Anna Secor. 2009. "New Transnational Geographies of Islamism, Capitalism, and Subjectivity: The Veiling Fashion Industry in Turkey." In *Muslim Societies in the Age of Mass Consumption: Politics, Culture, and Identity between the Local and the Global*, edited by Johanna Pink, 23–52. Cambridge, UK: Cambridge Scholars Publishing.

Göle, Nilufer. 1997. *Forbidden Modern: Civilization and Veiling*. Ann Arbor: University of Michigan Press.

Guist, Erich. 2004. "Islam und Aufklärung." Http://www.dmk-berlin.de/download/diverses/Islam_und_Aufklaerung.pdf.

Güngör, Murat. 2007. "Ganz verliebt ins Ghetto-Klischee." Taz.de, www.taz.de/!2637.

Habermas, Jürgen et al. 2010. *An Awareness of What Is Missing: Faith and Reason in a Post-Secular Age*. Cambridge, UK: Polity Press.

Haenni, Patrick. 2009. "The Economic Politics of Muslim Consumption." In *Muslim Societies in the Age of Mass Consumption: Politics, Culture, and Identity between the Local and the Global*, edited by Johanna Pink, 327–42. Cambridge, UK: Cambridge Scholars Publishing.

Hall, Stanley G. 1904. *Adolescence: Its Psychology and Its Relation to Physiology, Anthropology, Sociology, Sex, Crime, Religion, and Education*. New York: Appleton.

Halliday, Fred. 1999. "Islamophobia Reconsidered." *Ethnic and Racial Studies* 22 (5): 892–902.

Hamid, Sadek. 2009. "The Attraction of 'Authentic Islam': Salafism and British Muslim Youth." In *Global Salafism: Islam's New Religious Movement*, edited by Roel Meijer, 384–403. New York: Columbia University Press.

Harding, Susan. 2001. *The Book of Jerry Falwell: Fundamentalist Language and Politics*. Princeton, NJ: Princeton University Press.

Haug, Sonya, Stephanie Mussig, and Anja Stichs. 2009. *Muslimisches Leben in Deutschland: Im Auftrag der Deutchen Islam Konferenz*. Nuremberg: Bundesamt für Migration und Flüchtlinge.

Hecking, Claus. 2013. "Secret Thatcher Notes: Kohl Wanted Half of Turks Out of Germany." *Der Spiegel Online*, http://www.spiegel.de/international /germany/secret-minutes-chancellor-kohl-wanted-half-of-turks-out-of -germany-a-914376.html.

Hefner, Robert W., ed. 1993. *Conversion to Christianity: Historical and Anthropological Perspectives on a Great Transformation*. Berkeley: University of California Press.

Hemmingsen, Ann-Sophie. 2011. "Salafi Jihadism: Relying on Fieldwork to Study Unorganized and Clandestine Phenomenon." *Ethnic and Racial Studies* 34 (7): 1201–15.

Henson, James Scott, and Jason Adam Wasserman. 2011. "Six in One Hand, Half a Dozen in the Other: An Ontological Content Analysis of Radical Islam and the Christian Right." *Culture and Religion* 12 (1): 39–58.

Heykel, Bernard. 2009. "On the Nature of Salafi Thought and Action." In *Global Salafism: Islam's New Religious Movement*, edited by Roel Meijer, 33–50. London: Hurst.

Hirschkind, Charles. 2009. *The Ethical Soundscape: Cassette Sermons and Islamic Counterpublics*. New York: Columbia University Press.

Hoffmann, Christian H. 1995. *Zwischen alle Stühlen: Ein Deutscher Wird Muslim*. Bonn: Bouvier.

Hofmann, Gabriele. 1997. *Muslimin werden: Frauen in Deutschland konvertieren zum Islam*. Frankfurt am Main: Institut für Kulturanthropologie und Europäische Ethnologie, Johann Wolfgang Goethe-Universität.Hofmann, Murad W. 1998. *Journey to Makkah*. Beltsville, MD: Amana Publications.

Höpp, Gerhard. 2001. "Islam in Berlin und Brandenburg: Steinerne Erinnerungen." In *Berlin für Orientalisten: Ein Stadtführer*, edited by Gerhard Höpp and Norbert Mattes, 1–25. Berlin: Das arabische Buch.

Horsch, Silvia. 2004a. "Lessing, Der Islam und Toleranz." Http://www.al-sakina .de/inhalt/artikel/lessing_islam/lessing_islam.html.

——. 2004b. *Rationalität und Toleranz: Lessings Auseinandersetzung mit dem Islam*. Würzburg: Ergon.

Houston, Christopher. 2001. "The Brewing of Islamist Modernity: Tea Gardens and Public Space in Istanbul." *Theory, Culture, and Society* 18 (6): 77–97.

——. 2008. "Der Islam—eine europaische tradition." Al-Sakina, February 6, http://www.al-sakina.de/inhalt/artikel/Islam_Europa/islam_europa.html.

Independent. 2011. "Minister Insists Islam 'Does Not Belong in Germany.'" *Independent*, www.independent.co.uk/news/world/europe/minister-insists-islam-does-not-belong-in-germany-2234260.html.

James, William. 1902. *The Varieties of Religious Experience: A Study in Human Nature*. New York: Longman, Green.

Jansen, Frank. 2013. "Europäische Islamisten zunehmend in Syrien." *Tagesspiegel*, February 22, 2013, www.tagesspiegel.de/politik/salafisten-europaeische-islamisten-zunehmend-in-syrien/7824314.html.

Jensen, Tina Gudrun. 2006. "Religious Authority and Autonomy Intertwined: The Case of Converts to Islam in Denmark." *Muslim World* 96:643–60.

Jonker, Gerdien. 2000. "What is other about other religions? The Islamic Communities in Berlin between Integration and Segregation" *Cultural Dynamics*. 12 (3): 311–329.

———. 2002. *Eine Wellenlänge zu Gott: Der "Verband der Islamischen Kulturzentren" in Europa*. Bielefeld: Transcript.

———. 2005. "The Mevlana Mosque in Berlin-Kreuzberg: An Unsolved Conflict." *Journal of Ethnic and Migration Studies* 31 (6): 1067–81.

Jurgens, Jeffrey. 2005. "Plotting Immigration: Diasporic Identity Formation among Immigrants from Turkey in Berlin." PhD diss., University of Michigan.

Keddie, Nikki. 1998. "The New Religious Politics: Where, When, and Why Do Fundamentalisms Appear?" *Comparative Studies in Society and History* 40 (4): 696–723.

Kepel, Gilles. 1997. *Allah in the West: Islamic Movements in Europe and America*. Stanford, CA: Stanford University Press.

Koning, Martijn de. 2008. *Searching for a "Pure" Islam: Religious Beliefs and Identity Construction among Moroccan-Dutch Youth*. Amsterdam: Bert Bakkar.

———. 2009. "Changing Worldviews and Friendship: An Exploration of the Life Stories of Two Female Salafies in the Netherlands." In *Global Salafism: Islam's New Religious Movement*, edited by Roel Meijer, 404–23. New York: Columbia University Press.

Köse, Ali. 1996. *Conversion to Islam: A Study of Native British Converts*. London: Kegan Paul International.

Kravel-Tovi, Michal. 2012. "Rite of Passing: Bureaucratic Encounters, Dramaturgy, and Jewish Conversion in Israel." *American Ethnologist* 39 (2): 371–88.

Kupinger, Petra. 2009. "Barbie, Razanne, Fulla: A Tale of Culture, Globalization, Consumerism, and Islam." In *Muslim Societies in the Age of Mass Consumption: Politics, Culture, and Identity between the Local and the Global*, edited by Johanna Pink, 187–224. Cambridge, UK: Cambridge Scholars Publishing.

Lander, Mark. 2007. German Police Arrest 3 in Terrorist Plot. *New York Times*, September, http://www.nytimes.com/2007/09/06/world/europe/06germany.html.

Laurence, Jonathan. 2012. *The Emancipation of Europe's Muslims*. Princeton, NJ: Princeton University Press.

Lawrence, Bruce. 1989. *Defenders of God: The Fundamentalist Revolt against the Modern Age*. Columbia: University of South Carolina Press.

Lehmann, David. 1998. "Fundamentalism and Globalism." *Third World Quarterly* 19 (4): 607–34.

Leiken, Robert. 2011. *Europe's Angry Muslims: The Revolt of the Second Generation*. Oxford: Oxford University Press.

Lessing, Gotthold Ephraim. 2003. *Werke und Briefe*, vol. 3, *1754–1757*. Berlin: Deutscher Klassiker Verlag.

Luciak, Mikael. 2004. *Documenting Discrimination and Integration in 15 Member States of the European Union*. Luxembourg: Office for Official Publications of the European Communities.

Mahmood, Saba. 2004. *Politics of Piety: Islamic Revival and the Feminist Subject*. New Jersey: Princeton University Press.

Mamdani, Mahmood. 2004. *Good Muslim, Bad Muslim: America, the Cold War, and the Roots of Terror*. New York: Harmony.

Mandel, Ruth. 2008. *Cosmopolitan Anxieties: Turkish Challenges to Citizenship and Belonging in Contemporary Germany*. Durham, NC: Duke University Press.

Mandeville, Peter. 2001. *Transnational Muslim Politics: Reimagining the Umma*. London: Routledge.

Mansson, Anna. 2002. *Becoming Muslim: Meanings of Conversion to Islam*. Lund: Akademisk Avhandling.

Mardin, Şerif. 1989. *Religion and Social Change in Modern Turkey: The Case of Bediüzzaman Said Nursi*. Albany: State University of New York Press.

Meer, Nasar. 2011. "Overcoming the Injuries of 'Double Consciousness.'" In *The Politics of Misrecognition*, edited by Simon Thompson and Majid Yar, 46–65. Surrey: Ashgate.

———. 2013. "Semantics, Scales, and Solidarities in the Study of Antisemitism and Islamophobia." *Ethnic and Racial Studies* 36 (3): 500–515.

Meer, Nasar, and Tariq Modood. 2010. "The Racialisation of Muslims." In *Thinking through Islamophobia: Global Perspectives*, edited by S Sayyid and AbdoolKarim Vakil, 69–83. New York: Columbia University Press.

Meijer, Roel, ed. 2009. *Global Salafism: Islam's New Religious Movement*. New York: Columbia University Press.

Meiu, George Paul. 2011. "On Difference, Desire, and the Unexpected: The White Masai in the Kenyan Tourism." In *Great Expectations: Imagination and Anticipation in Tourism*, edited by Jonathan Skinner and Dimitrios Theodossopoulos, 96–115. New York: Berghahn Books.

Meyer, Birgit. 1998. "Make a Complete Break with the Past: Memory and Post-Colonial Modernity in Ghanian Pentecostalist Discourse." *Journal of Religion in Africa* 28 (3): 316–49.

Miles, Robert, and Malcolm Brown. 2003. *Racism*. 2nd ed. London: Routledge.

Mommsen, Katherina. 2001. *Goethe und der Islam*. Frankfurt am Main: Insel.

———. Forthcoming. "Zu Goethe und der Islam—anlässlich der immer wieder aufgeworfenen Frage: War Goethe ein Muslim?" *Yearbook of the North American Goethe Society*.

Moosavi, Leon. 2012. "British Muslim Converts Performing 'Authentic Muslimness'?" *Performing Islam* 1 (1): 103–28.

Motadel, David. 2009. "Islamische Bürgerlichkeit: Das soziokulturelle Milieu der muslimischen Minderheit in Berlin, 1918–1939." In *Juden und Muslime in Deutschland: Recht, Religion, Identität*, edited by José Brunner und Shai Lavi, 103–21. Tel Aviver Jahrbuch für deutsche Geschichte 37. Göttingen: Wallstein.

Mufti, Aamir R. 1995. "Secularism and Minority: Elements of a Critique." *Social Text* 14 (4): 75–96.

Mühe, Nina. 2010. *Muslims in Berlin*. At Home in Europe Project. Budapest: Open Society Institute.

Nagata, Judith. 2001. "Beyond Theology: Towards an Anthropology of Fundamentalism." *American Anthropologist* 103 (2): 481–98.

Ong, Aihwa. 1999. *Flexible Citizenship: The Cultural Logics of Transnationality*. Durham, NC: Duke University Press.

Ostergaard-Nielsen, Eva. 2003. *Transnational Politics: Turks and Kurds in Germany*. London: Routledge.

Özyürek, Esra. 2007. "German Converts to Islam Are an Asset, not a Threat." *Der Spiegel Online*, September 13, 2007, http://www.spiegel.de/international /germany/0,1518,505586,00.html.

———. 2009. "Convert Alert: Turkish Christians and German Muslims as Threats to National Security in the New Europe." *Comparative Studies in Society and History* 51 (1): 91–116.

———. 2013. "Creating Parallel Communities of Perpetrators: Muslim-Only Holocaust Education and Anti-Semitism Prevention Programs in Germany." Talk at the Center for Jewish Studies, University of Illinois, March.

Partridge, Damani. 2012. *Hypersexuality and Headscarves: Race, Sex, and Citizenship in the New Germany*. Bloomington: Indiana University Press.

Pautz, Hartwig. 2005. "The Politics of Identity in Germany: The Leitkultur Debate." *Race and Class* 46 (4): 39–52.

Paley, Julia. 2001. *Marketing Democracy: Power and Social Movements in Post-Dictatorship Chile*. Berkeley: University of California Press.

Pelkmans, Mathijs. 2009. "Introduction: Post-Soviet Space and the Unexpected Turns of Religious Life." In *Conversion after Socialism: Disruptions, Modernisms, and Technologies of Faith in the Former Soviet Union*, edited by Mathijs Pelkmans, 1–16. New York: Berghahn Books.

Pence, Katherine, and Paul Betts. 2011. *Socialist Modern: East German Everyday Culture and Politics*. Ann Arbor: University of Michigan Press.

Peperkamp, Esther, and Małgorzata Rajtar. 2007. Introduction to *Religion and the Secular in Eastern Germany, 1945 to the Present*, edited by Esther Peperkamp, 1–18. Leiden: Brill.

Ramadan, Tariq. 1999. *To Be a European Muslim: A Study of Islamic Sources in the European Context*. Leicester, UK: Islamic Foundation.

———. 2004. *Western Muslims and the Future of Islam*. Oxford: Oxford University Press.

Rambo, Lewis. 1995. *Understanding Religious Conversion*. New Haven, CT: Yale University Press.

Reiss, Tom. 1999. "A Reporter at Large: The Man from the East." *New Yorker*, October 4, 68.

———. 2005. *The Orientalist: Solving the Mystery of a Strange and Dangerous Life*. New York: Random House.

Rex, John. 1973. *Race, Colonialism, and the City*. London: Routledge and Kegan Paul.

Riesebrodt, Martin. 1998. *Pious Passion: The Emergence of Modern Fundamentalism in the US and in Iran*. Berkeley: University of California Press.

Ringel, Michael. 2007. "Wolfgang Bosbach, schnatter, schnatter, schnatter." *Tageszeitung*, September 13, http://www.taz.de/1/archiv/digitaz/artikel/?ressort= wa&dig=2007%2F09%2F14%2Fa0220&cHash=f5fb4d842957033b67a2577f2 26e4696.

Roald, Anne Sofie. 2004. *New Muslims in the European Context: The Experience of Scandinavian Converts*. Leiden: Brill.

———. 2006. "The Shaping of Scandinavian 'Islam': Converts and Gender Equal Opportunity." In *Women Embracing Islam: Gender and Conversion in the West*, edited by Karin van Nieuwkerk, 48–70. Austin: University of Texas Press.

Robbins, Joel. 2007. "Continuity Thinking and the Problem of Christian Culture: Belief, Time, and the Anthropology of Christianity." *Current Anthropology* 48 (1): 5–38.

Roberts, Nathaniel. 2012. "Is Conversion a Colonization of Consciousness?" *Anthropological Theory* 12 (3): 272–94.

Rogozen-Soltar, Mikaela. 2012. "Managing Muslim Visibility: Conversion, Immigration, and Spanish Imaginaries of Islam." *American Anthropologist* 114 (4): 611–23.

Roy, Olivier. 2004. *Failure of Political Islam*. Translated by Carol Volk. Cambridge, MA: Harvard University Press.

———. 2010. *Holy Ignorance: When Religion and Culture Part Ways*. New York: Columbia University Press.

Runnymede Trust Commission. 1997. *Islamophobia: A Challenge for us All*. London: Runnymede Trust.

Sageman, Marc. 2011. "The Turn to Political Violence in the West." In *Jihadi Terrorism and the Radicalization Challenge*, edited by Rik Coolsaet, 117–30. Burlington, VT: Ashgate.

Sayyid, Bobby. 2003. *A Fundamental Fear: Eurocentrism and the Emergence of Islamism*. London: Zed Books.

Schiessl Michaele and Caroline Schmidt. 2004. Eyes Wide Shut. *Der Spiegel Online*, November 25, http://spiegel.de/international/spiegel/0,1518,329261,00 .html.

Schiffauer, Werner. 2000. *Die Gottesmänner: Türkische Islamisten in Deutschland*. Frankfurt am Main: Suhrkamp.

———. 2010. *Nach dem Islamismus: Eine Ethnographie der Islamischen Gemeinschaft Milli Görüş*. Frankfurt am Main: Suhrkamp.

Schlessmann, Ludwig. 2003. *Sufismus in Deutschland: Deutsche auf dem Weg des mystischen Islam*. Cologne: Böhlau.

Schmid, Thomas. 2007. "Schaüble: Vielleicht hatten wir bisher einfach Glück." *Die Welt Online*, February 4, http://www.welt.de/politik/article716643 /Schaeuble_Vielleicht_hatten_wir_bisher_einfach_Glueck.html.

Schmidt, Carolina. 2007. Haber wir schon die Scharia? *Der Spiegel* 13 (March 26): 22–35.

Schmitt, Eric. 2011. "German Officials Alarmed by Ex-Rapper's New Message: Jihadism." *New York Times*, August 31, 2011, www.nytimes.com/2011/09/01 /world/europe/01jihadi.htm.

Scott, Joan Wallach. 2007. *The Politics of the Veil*. Princeton, NJ: Princeton University Press.

Shooman, Yasemin. 2011. "Islamophobie, antimuslimischer Rassismus oder Muslimfeindlichkeit? Kommentar zu der Begriffsdebatte der Deutschen Islam Konferenz," http://www.migration-boell.de/web/integration/47_2956.asp.

Shryock, Andrew. 2010. "Introduction: Islam as an Object of Fear and Affection." In *Islamophobia/Islamophilia: Beyond the Politics of Enemy and Friend*, edited by Andrew Shryock, 1–28. Bloomington: Indiana University Press.

Silverstein, Paul. 2005. "Immigrant Racialization and the Savage Slot: Race, Migration, and Immigration in the New Europe." *Annual Review of Anthropology* 34:363–84.

Sökefeld, Martin. 2008. *Struggling for Recognition: The Alevi Movement in Germany and in Transnational Space*. New York: Berghahn Books.

Der Spiegel Online. 2013. "Streit um Islamgelehrten: Muslimische Verbände attackieren Theologen Khorchide." *Der Spiegel Online*, www.spiegel.de /unispiegel/islam-muslimische-verbaende-attackieren-theologen-khorchide -a-939864.html.

Spielhaus, Riem, and Alexia Farber. 2010. "Zur Topographie Berliner Moscheevereine Stadträumliche Voraussetzungen und urbane Kompetenzen der Sichtbarmachung." In *Stoffwechsel Berlin: Urbane Präsenzen und Repräsentationen*, edited by Alexia Farber, 96–111. Berliner Blätter 53. Berlin: Panama Verlag.

Steinberg, Guido. 2013. *German Jihad: On the Internationalization of Islamist Terrorism*. New York: Columbia University Press.

Stolcke, Verena. 1995. "Talking Culture: New Boundaries, New Rhetorics of Exclusion in Europe." *Current Anthropology* 36 (1): 1–24.

Sultan, Madeline. 1999. "Choosing Islam: A Study of Swedish Converts." *Social Compass* 46 (3): 325–35.

Swedenburg, Ted. 2001. "Islamic Hip-Hop vs. Islamophobia: Aki Nawaz, Natacha Atlas, Akhenaton." In *Global Noise: Rap and Hip-Hop Outside the USA*, edited by Tony Mitchell, 57–85. London: Taylor and Francis Ltd.

———. 2002. "Islamic Hip-Hop versus Islamophobia: Aki Nawaz, Natacha Atlas, Akhenaton." In *Global Noise: Rap and Hip-Hop Outside the USA*, edited by Tony Mitchell, 57–85. Middletown, CT: Wesleyan University Press.

Taguieff, Pierre-André. 1987. *La force du préjugé: Essai sur le racism et ses doubles*. Paris: Editions La Découverte.

Taylor, Charles. 2011. "Why We Need a Radical Redefinition of Secularism." In *The Power of Religion in the Public Sphere*, edited by Judith Butler, Jürgen Habermas, Charles Taylor, and Cornell West, 34–59. New York: Columbia University Press.

Tibi, Bassam. 1998. *Europa ohne Identität: Die Krise der multikulturullen Gesellschaft*. Munich: Bertelsmann.

Turam, Berna. 2006. *Between Islam and the State: The Politics of Engagement*. Stanford, CA: Stanford University Press.

Tyrier, David. 2010. "Flooding the Embankments: Race, Bio-Politics, and Sovereignty." In *Thinking Through Islamophobia: Global Perspectives*, ed. S. Sayyid and AbdoolKarim Vakil, 93–110. New York: Columbia University Press.

van Nieuwkerk, Karin. 2004. "Veils and Wooden Clogs Don't Go Together." *Ethnos* 69 (2): 229–46.

———, ed. 2006. *Women Embracing Islam: Gender and Conversion in the West*. Austin: University of Texas Press.

Veiel, Axel. 2010. "Diam's—France's Female Rapper: The Rebel Submits to Islam." Qantara.de, January 1, http://en.qantara.de/wcsite.php?wc_c=9138.

Viswanathan, Gauri. 1998. *Outside the Fold: Conversion, Modernity, and Belief*. Princeton, NJ: Princeton University Press.

Warner, Michael. 2002. *Publics and Counterpublics*. Brooklyn: Zone Books.

Weitz, Eric D. 2013. *Weimar Germany: Promise and Tragedy*. Princeton, NJ: Princeton University Press.Wieviorka, Michael. 2002. "Race, Culture, and Society: The French Experience with Muslims." In *Muslim Europe or Euro-Islam: Politics, Culture, and Citizenship in the Age of Globalization*, edited by Nezar AlSayyad and Manuel Castells, 131–46. Lanham, MD: Lexington Books.

Wiktorowicz, Quintan. 2006. "Anatomy of the Salafi Movement." *Studies in Conflict and Terrorism* 29:207–39.

Wohlrab-Sahr, Monika. 1999. "Conversion to Islam: Between Syncretism and Symbolic Battle." *Social Compass* 46 (3): 351–62.

————. 2002. "Säkularisierungprozesse und kulturelle Generationen: Ähnlich-keiten und Unterschiede zwischen Westdeutschland, Ostdeutschland und den Niederlanden." In *Lebenszeiten: Erkundungen zur Soziologie der Genera-tionen*, edited by Günter Burkart and Jürgen Wolf, 219–28. Opladen: Leske and Budrich.

Woodlock, Rachel. 2010. "Praying Where They Don't Belong: Female Muslim Converts and Mosques in Melbourne, Australia." *Journal of Muslim Minority Affairs* 30 (2): 268–78.

Yükleyen, Ahmet. 2012. *Localizing Islam in Europe: Turkish Islamic Communi-ties in Germany and the Netherlands*. Syracuse, NY: Syracuse University Press.

Yurdakul, Gökçe. 2009. *From Guest Workers into Muslims: The Transformation of Turkish Immigrant Associations in Germany*. Newcastle upon Tyne, UK: Cambridge Scholars.

Zebiri, Kate. 2008. *British Muslim Converts: Choosing Alternative Lives*. Oxford: One World Publications.

Zeidan, David. 2003. "A Comparative Study of Selected Themes in Christian and Islamic Fundamentalist Discourses." *British Journal of Middle Eastern Studies* 30 (1): 43–80.

Zick, Andreas, Beate Küpper, and Andreas Hövermann. 2011. *Die Abwertung der Anderen: Eine europäische Zustandsbeschreibung zu Intoleranz, Vorur-teilen und Diskriminierung*. Berlin: Friedrich-Ebert-Stiftung, Forum Berlin.

PRINCETON STUDIES IN MUSLIM POLITICS